Anonymous

Ladies' Manual of Art

Or, profit and pastime: a self teacher in all branches of decorative art, embracing

every variety of painting and drawing on china, glass, velvet, canvas, paper and

wood

Anonymous

Ladies' Manual of Art

*Or, profit and pastime: a self teacher in all branches of decorative art, embracing every
variety of painting and drawing on china, glass, velvet, canvas, paper and wood*

ISBN/EAN: 9783337164270

Printed in Europe, USA, Canada, Australia, Japan

Cover: Foto ©Thomas Meinert / pixelio.de

More available books at **www.hansebooks.com**

LADIES'

MANUAL OF ART

—OR—

PROFIT AND PASTIME.

A SELF TEACHER IN

All Branches of Decorative Art,

EMBRACING EVERY VARIETY OF

PAINTING AND DRAWING

On China, Glass, Velvet, Canvas, Paper and Wood.

THE SECRET OF ALL

GLASS TRANSPARENCIES, SKETCHING FROM NATURE,
PASTEL CRAYON DRAWING, TAXIDERMY, Etc.

CHICAGO:

DONOHUE, HENNEBERRY & CO.

407-425 DEARBORN STREET

1890

PREFACE

IN presenting to the public and our artistically inclined people our "Art Manual" we should do so with some trepidation had we not the assurance, in placing before them this work, that it would instantly win its way into their favor by its merits. Most books produced by the press of the present day are novels, compilations, scientific and theological ones, meeting as they do only certain classes, and are subjects which have been constantly before the people. We present you a "new book" in every sense of the word. We propose entering with our readers into the beautiful realms of Art, than which there is no more interesting subject; our object being its promotion and dissemination. We want to see the great majority of our refined, educated, but needy women embrace it as a source of profit as well as pleasure, many of whom with an intellect for greater things, but incapable of muscular labor or exposure, can, by applying themselves energetically to this occupation, earn a good livelihood and famous name, and assist in disseminating its beauties everywhere. Many homes are there in our land, which they can ornament, and embellish to their profit, and the pleasure of others. Those comfortably situated in life, whose home decorations they prefer to be the product of their own hands, will hail our "Manual" as "a friend indeed." To the child in whom is observed traits of genius it will be of invaluable assistance in developing those traits. Our aim is to combine in this work all the different methods of producing portraits, landscapes, painting on canvas, wood, china, etc., etc., to furnish to all lovers of the useful and beautiful in art a true teacher, making every instruction so plain and comprehensive, that a child can grasp the meaning. In thus combining all these arts in one volume, we save the learner the expense of purchasing a large number of books at a cost which effect-ually precludes the possibility of many engaging in this profitable and pleasant occupation. Then, to those whose tastes are artistically inclined, and who find it most incon-venient to obtain instructions in all the branches desired; to those in whom genius lies dormant and whom necessity com-pels to earn their own livelihood; to those who desire to combine pastime with pleasure, and to those who have the means, tastes and desire but not the necessary assistance at hand to ornament their homes, we respectfully dedicate our "Art Manual."

THE PUBLISHERS.

INTRODUCTORY REMARKS.

In learning the art of drawing or writing, like all other Arts and Sciences, there are certain first and fixed principles to be observed as a foundation upon which the whole is built. A right understanding of these is absolutely necessary that we may become masters of that art which we undertake to learn. A neglect of these first principles is the reason why so many who have spent time sufficient to become accomplished artists, are, after all their pains and loss of time, incapable of producing even fair work; and are often at a loss to know how to begin. Many commence by copying the work of others, and are surprised to find how little such ability avails them when attempting to make sketches from nature. The instruction for those who intend prosecuting this delightful study, is prepared with great care by the author, who has had very many years of experience in landscape drawing. 'Tis true that much of his ability has been attained by years' of patient industry and practice. Yet time might have been saved by little earlier attention to principles and study of works on the subject, prepared by experts. The best advice to those contemplating a study of the art—who possess any degree of skill in the use of the pencil, is to go out into the field, with the "instructor" in one hand and your sketch-book in the other, select some object of interest, and "take it in." If not satisfactory, try again—be not too easily discouraged. You will find the study of nature a source of pleasure, objects of interest will appear on every hand, in the valleys, on the mountains, the lakes, or by the river side, and as you become familiar with the scenes in nature, difficulties will disappear, and you are happy in the thought that sketching from nature is truly one of the most pure and refined of intellectual pleasures and professions, and the sketch-book with you, as with the writer, will ever be a chosen companion.

When this branch of the work has been completed, and the landscape transferred to paper and shaded up, the most difficult part of the task is accomplished. The next essential element in the advancement of the picture, and that which renders it more beautiful to the eye, is color. 'Tis well to turn aside from your unfinished landscape or portrait, and study the colors in nature, the mixing of tints, and how to apply them, as shown on a subsequent page of this book.

To become an artist requires only a love for the art, a good eye, and an abundance of continuity.

CONTENTS

SKETCHING

FROM

NATURE

"GOD HAS DIFFUSED BEAUTY, AND ART HAS COMBINED IT."
—*Houssaye.*

SKETCH is a graphic memorandum. "The field of labor is the wide world of nature—her beautiful truths the lessons to be learned by heart. Once fairly within her school, Art awakens to a life of sympathy with its teacher that lasts forever." A capacity for *drawing* means more than producing a linear representation. The sculptor *draws* when he models the plastic clay into imitative or ideal creations. The painter *draws* when he disposes his pigments with like impulse. The stalwart smith *draws* when he shapes the heated metal into form. He that cannot draw a crooked line, cannot draw a straight one, and he who cannot draw a straight line, the simplest, easiest, and most comprehensible, has certainly much to learn, and should begin **with it.**

In Making a Drawing from Nature, we start out with one of two things in view, a desire to make a perfect copy of the scene before **us, or a** wish to **make** a choice selection from the whole, and **arrange** it to suit our fancy. The first is historic, from the **fact** of its being a true and faithful copy. The second is called poetic, as **the** effort is for beauty of arrangement and general make up. In the latter, the artist is generally better satisfied with his effort when the picture **is** complete, than if he **followed** closely to the laborious work **of** perfectly copying that which is not altogether interesting. But at the same time the first, that of picturing **facts,** must form the basis of the art. **By** it we acquire a knowledge of detail, and store the mind with **true** nature, which is essential in good work. A true and faithful copy **is what is** sought after. In following our **own** fancy, we go out into the field and select from a combination of objects, and make up our picture. We find a log cabin standing beside a rocky stream of rippling water, which is spanned **by** an ancient log bridge; in another place we find cows grazing; and again a horseman is coming down the road. We combine the three. The cattle are driven into the stream, the horse and his rider are brought into and form a part of the picture, which is now complete.

In sketching from nature it is first essential that we should be trained to some extent in a course of perspective drawing.

Linear Perspective is the application of the principles of geometry **to** the accurate delineation of the principal lines of the picture. Drawing on a plain surface an object as it appears, **or** as it **would** appear on a pane of glass, held between you and the object.

Perspective is absolutely necessary in drawing from nature, not only in perfecting finished work, but in all circumstances. Theoretically, as well as practically, it bears more or less upon all the great requisites of perfection in art. We can by its aid, select our own point of observation, even though it be imaginary.

Materials. Of the variety of instruments and materials for drawing and sketching, there is the lead pencil of different degrees of hardness, and tint; then there is the French crayon, tinted crayons, etc.; French sketching boards, prepared of various tints, with skies, and suggestive effects ready laid in; "solid sketching blocks," bound as a portfolio, will be found convenient. Paper for "cartoons" can be obtained of most any size, up to six feet wide.

In a Picture we have Six Terms, the center of the picture, or center of view, the distance of the picture, the base line, the horizontal line, the perpendicular line, the point of view.

Lines in Nature. It is a remarkable fact that all the lines in nature are curve lines, the body of trees, the branches and their leaves, and the fruit that grows thereon; the blades of grass, and flowers in the field; the swells of the ocean, the hills and hollows, are all composed of curved lines. Nature is all loveliness and perfection, all her effects are true, and the desire of the student should be to realize them thoroughly, and let nature, and nature alone, be the teacher, following her faithfully, in the full assurance of the attainment of truth, whatever else he may fail to accomplish.

> Then let the pencil, the servant of thought,
> Copy the lessons which nature has taught;
> For the skillful hand of the artist entwines,
> No garland more fair than her beautiful lines.

A LESSON IN DRAWING.

BEFORE going into the field to make a sketch, it is essential you become familiar with the different lines used in drawing, the less difficulty you will have in sketching from nature.

The first effort will be to get control of the hand and pencil, or pen, which is the leading essential in learning to write or draw. Secondly, a right understanding of the straight and curve lines used cannot be dispensed with. A neglect of these first principles, and the want of a thorough drilling by an experienced teacher, in our educational institutions, is the leading difficulty in the advancement of students in these branches, and has often been a subject of comment.

There are three leading lines in drawing, the straight horizontal line, thus:

made by carrying the pencil from left to right, and vice versa, beginning and ending abruptly; then perpendicular ones, commencing at the top, draw the pencil down; then a straight oblique line, with 52 deg. slant, which is about the proper angle for writing.

The right and left curve is used as the beginning and ending of all the small letters.

Fig. 1.

The Line of Beauty, as it is called, is the two curves combined; commencing at the top, making first the left and then the right line, equal in length, forming a compound curve, the basis of two-thirds of all the capital letters. A combination of curves lying horizontally, as in fig. 2, gives the line which is formed by the meeting of the lips, from these different lines our sketches from nature are made up.

Fig. 2.
A *curved* line changes its direction at every point.

A circle is a figure comprehended by a single curve line, called its circumference, every part of which is equally distant from a

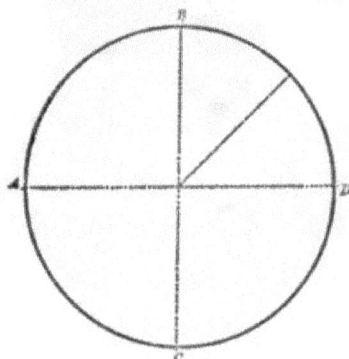

Fig. 3.

point called the center. From *a* to *b* will be found the left, or convex, and from *c* to *d* the right, or concave curve. The whole may be made by a quick movement of the hand, with crayon, on the black-board, thus: Turn your right side to the board, place the crayon at the bottom, *c*, and with the elbow as the radius, carry the crayon toward the left from *c* to *a*, and so on until you reach the starting point, *c*, again, moving the hand at as rapid a rate as is possible.

Now, if these lines can all be drawn correct, and with freedom, take the equilateral triangle and practice it without a ruler.

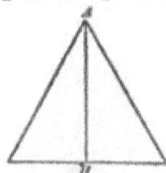

Fig. 4.
An *angle* is the space between two lines that start from the same point.

The perpendicular line, passing from the vanishing point *a*, to the base *b*. The whole of the fig. 4 forms what appears to us the gable of a house, *a* the point where the rafters meet, *b* the center of the plate. This gives the horizontal, vertical, and oblique lines.

I shall endeavor to make these lessons clear and concise for the beginner, touching only on those points which are indispensable in learning to draw. Although many of these principles you may have acquired, the elements of linear perspective is the very first thing to which your attention should be directed.

Landscapes. All objects which present themselves to the eye, such as buildings, forests, fields, mountains, water, &c., whether viewed from a hill or on a level, we will call a landscape. Now as it is impossible to make an exact copy of the subject before us, by means of any transfer process, it can only be effected by a distinct apprehension of the real form of the objects themselves, and of those apparent forms under which they are presented to the eye, in their different positions in the landscape. All these objects have their outlines, composed either of straight or curve lines, which may be irregular in their relation to each other. Now if we were placed on a flat, horizontal plain, the water or ground which we would have in view before us, would appear to rise from the spot on which we stood, the limit of that rise being determined by a clear and well defined straight line, called the horizontal line. It will appear in the lake; between this and the sky no object intervenes. This horizontal or boundary line lies directly opposite to the range of the eye, and the one to which every other line is referred, and by which the accuracy of the drawing is secured. The point where it crosses the perpendicular line will be the center of our picture.

In Placing a Landscape **on Paper,** first arises the question as to how much of the landscape we will introduce into our picture. Let us suppose it to be taken from the point of view, then that position of the scene which the eye can easily take in, without moving the head, will constitute the picture. The space included between the point where we are standing and a point where our picture commences, establishes the required distance of the eye from the proposed picture. Now, if through this point a straight line be supposed drawn, perpendicular to the horizon, this line will pass through, and determine the foremost objects of the picture—touching all the leading objects directly in front of us.

Position of the Horizontal Line will depend upon whether or not we make the sketch from the ground, or from an elevation. If the view be made from the level with it, the horizontal line may be drawn at about one-fifth of the space of the paper we intend for our picture. If we take the sketch from an elevated point, a little above the level of the ground, then the horizontal line may be placed at about one-third the height, and so on. If the view is to be made from a high hill, or top of the house, place the horizontal line at one-half the height.

Now, in holding up the pencil or ruler horizontally with the eye, and on a level with it, you will see what objects will appear on that horizontal line. In making a photograph of a building it is always best to have the camera a little elevated, and at a considerable distance from the object, as a better picture can be secured. All horizontal planes seem to ascend if they lie below the horizontal line, and to descend if they lie above it, vanish or merge into it, as shown in figures 5 and 6.

In making a sketch from an elevation, the distant part of the view seems higher than the foreground. This occurs when the point from where the view is taken is too much elevated. A better, and much more natural perspective, can be obtained by lowering the point of view, which also changes the horizontal line.

After knowing the position of the horizon of your subject, point of sight for the point of distance, you have to extend the line of horizon from the point of sight to the limits of such distance.

For illustration, fasten a thread with a pin to the table, at a

point corresponding to the line of the horizon of your picture;
a thread thus adjusted will, when drawn out over the picture, fall
exactly over all the lines seeking

The Vanishing Point. In this way you get the lines for
the cornice in a building, or row of buildings, upper and lower
lines of the windows and doors, base and sidewalk.

In making a sketch of a building, it is only necessary to get
the general outlines, and instead of working in all the doors and
windows, finishing up the cornice, etc., all that is necessary will
be to get the outline of one door or window, and the style of
cornice, and indicate the remainder by merely a mark showing
the position, and make a memorandum of the essential points
which is needed in completing the work. In figure 5, street view,

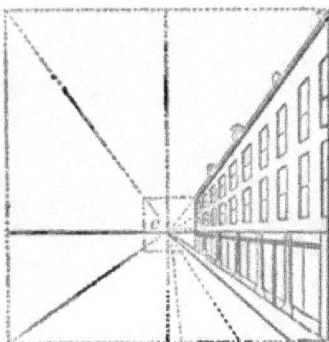

Fig. 5.

make a dot on the sketch board at a point where you wish the
first upper corner of the building to commence, draw a perpendicular line for the corner, do likewise at such a distance to the
left as you wish the building to extend on the sketch, and you
have the other corner. Holding the drawing book perpendicular
between you and the building, and on a level with the eye, place
the ruler on the sketch-book corresponding to the upper horizontal line of the building, and make a line for the cornice, the base
line is produced in the same manner. The point C, where the
two lines would meet, were they continued toward the left, will
be the vanishing point, from which run all the other horizontal
lines when you come to finish up the drawing.

THE HORIZONTAL LINE.

A HORIZONTAL right line has, with respect to the plane of the picture, one of three positions. It is either parallel to it, oblique to it, or perpendicular to it. We will sit with the back against one of the walls of a rectangular room. The wall opposite is parallel to that behind us, and consequently to the plane of our picture in that

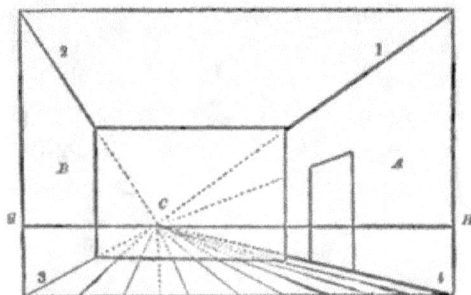

Fig. 6.

position. The two remaining walls being at right angles with that opposite, are evidently perpendicular to the plane of the drawing, and all horizontal right lines on those two walls, are also perpendicular to that plane, and will appear to tend towards a point immediately opposite to the eye. H. H. is the horizontal line or level of sight; C the point opposite the eye, and that point toward which all horizontal right lines on the walls, A & B, appear to slant, though in reality they are perpendicular to the wall C. The lines 1 & 2, where the ceiling and sidewalls meet, and 3 & 4, the lower limit of the walls, as well as the horizontal lines of the door, and its panels, are in that position, all perpendicular to the plane of the opposite wall, and therefore to the plane of the drawing. The effects of the drawing in different positions of the horizontal line, should be carefully studied; if it

be placed above the level of the eye, and removed to the right or
left, it will appear like this:

If below the level of the eye, it will assume a direction like this:

But placed to the right or left of the eye, on a perfect level, and
horizontal, it will appear thus:

If drawn from, and directly opposite to the eye, the end may
appear thus:

A *point* has position, but not magnitude.

If a book, or block of wood, having a square base, be represented at different distances, seen from a point in which its sides

Fig. 7.

are oblique to the plane of the picture, and seen from both points,
under the same circumstances in all respects, as regards surrounding objects, except that the distance of the artist from the
base line is much less in one than the other, then it will appear
as do figures 7 and 8.

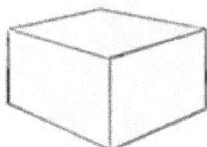

Fig. 8.

A *surface* has length and breadth only. A *solid* has length, breadth, and
thickness.

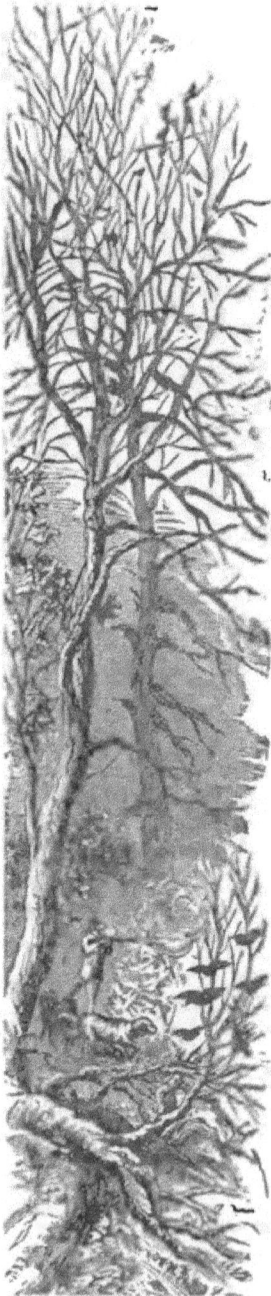

In figure 7 the distance from us is much greater than in figure 8, and the vanishing point farther away. We will find the first the most pleasing to the eye, although both are accurate. In these figures we make the two oblique lines of the base equal in length, and our position directly opposite the center perpendicular line. If we should change our position further to the right, the left oblique line at the base would apparently shorten, and *vice versa*.

In making a sketch from nature, the artist must choose a position that will command the best view of the scene about to be placed on paper, and from a standpoint that will secure the leading objects in the landscape before you. Begin by sketching those *objects nearest you first.* The reasons will be shown hereafter.

In attempting to make a "bird's eye" view of buildings, where an elevation cannot be obtained, it will be found somewhat difficult. We can only mark down on the sketch-book what can be seen from the position we occupy on the level with the objects before us, and imagine the remainder. At the same time three things should be kept in view, the perspective, the perpendicular lines, and proper elevation, in order to give to our picture the appearance it would have if others viewed it from the supposed point of observation as the sketcher.

The intention of the writer has been

to touch upon all the points and rules in drawing, and dwell upon each separately, and sufficient for a person of ordinary ability, and a good many grains of continuity, to make a sketch artist.

"It matters not what a man's vocation may be, if he has the taste to discern, and mind to esteem, the good and beautiful in nature and art, an expression of refinement will be manifest in all that he undertakes."

In this work I did not expect more than to take the first step toward teaching to sketch from nature. An easy, rapid, and decided manner of sketching is to be acquired only by practice. It is an acquisition essential to excellence in all the other artistic qualities, to which it serves as a basis. Having given you the necessary instruction, I will now assist you in

Selecting a Position. Choose a point that will command a good view of the scene, and prevent closer and more immediate objects from concealing any portion of the remote distance; and though the height of the horizontal line in this case may sometimes be more than half the height of the paper, according to the elevation attained by the artist to command the view. In this case the horizontal line is at about one-half the height of the paper. It frequently occurs in making a sketch, that the artist cannot place himself at the desired point for the best view. In such case we will imagine a point above the highest object in the foreground of the proposed sketch. That point may be on the land, or on the water. The artist, with a knowledge of perspective and elevation in view, may make a memorandum of the whole; but should he attempt to draw it from the point he is compelled to see it, no one would recognize it as a truthful representation. We regulate the whole by our knowledge of perspective, as accurately as if we stood upon the very spot from which we desired to be understood that the view was taken.

In Making a Bird's Eye View of a village or city, the first thing to be done is to get a plat, or outline, of the streets and blocks, and mark them on the sketch-book in squares, (or rather diamond shape), each line and cross line representing a street. Commence sketching *in* the buildings from the point chosen, which should be the one nearest the business center, and where the best houses stand, or from a point where you can secure the best material for a foreground, such as a stream of water and bridge, or a forest, etc. Transfer each block to paper, showing the fronts of one side and the rear of the buildings of the other side, and so on through the entire row of blocks, when you return to the place of starting, and go down the second row, always working toward the vanishing point.

After you have gone over the entire city, and taken every building, tree, and other objects of interest, and completed the sketch, you are ready for working it up. Lay out the blocks and streets on drawing paper, with pencil, in perspective, ruling from the vanishing point, the center of the picture, toward the point of view, which enlarges the objects of the foreground, and diminishes those in the distance.

In drawing *in* the buildings, begin with the first house in the foreground, drawing the roof lines, which should be parallel with the lines of the street; next the gables, after which the corner lines, which should be perpendicular to the drawing paper.

The drawing should be made first with pencil, and then in ink, with fine pointed steel pen; for shading, use small camel hair brush and India ink.

Lights and Shades. In a sketch it is found that mere outline is insufficient to the representation of an object in relief; it cannot give substance, nor define relative distances so as to maintain the objects in their proper places. The matter of fact representation of the breadth of a meridian light, and the same passage of landscape viewed under the shades of evening, affects the feeling very differently. In the latter, there is a charm which operates even upon minds least susceptible of impressions from the beauties of nature. The general principle acted upon by artists, is to dispose the lights and shades in the manner best suited to the treatment they propose for their work.

There are two extremes of light and shade, and between these lie all those half tints and reflected lights, and exquisite gradations of shade, which must be so carefully placed in the drawing as to clearly indicate the graceful curve of each individual petal, without in any way destroying the roundness and breadth of a flower. The gradations of shade are sometimes perplexing to the learner ; but in this respect the eye is a very safe guide. It requires no cultivated taste—not even any great amount of critical observation—to see when an object which should look perfectly round, appears flattened on the one side, or swell too much on the other. The theory of foreground and middle distances and background, has much to do with the principles of light and shade. It is not the line of perspective alone which makes one portion of a picture retreat, and another come forward.

In the drawing of a round object, apple or ball, the shades fall on the concave part, and incline toward the side opposite to light. All shades of objects in the same picture must fall the same way, or farthest from the light. That part lying nearest to the light must receive the least shade. This rule will be noticed in the face, folds of the drapery, etc. Landscapes show the heaviest shades nearest us, the greater the distance the lighter grows the picture. In clouds, the shades are the lightest that are nearest the horizon, it being the greatest distance from us, and those nearest the center of the picture the strongest,

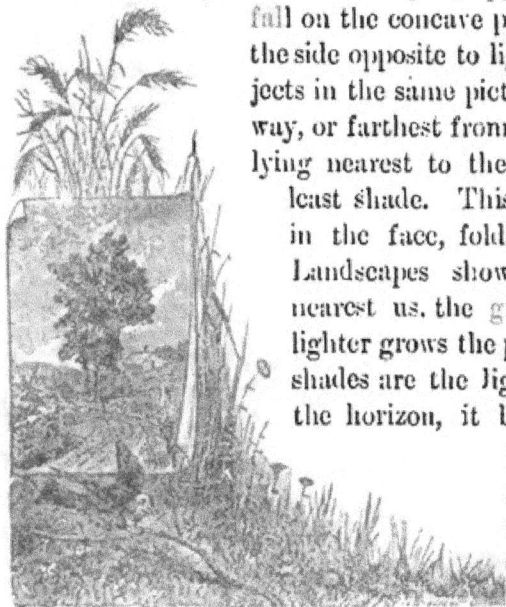

COLORS IN NATURE.

Colors are merely sensations produced by the action of light on the nervous tissue of the retina, which covers the back of the eye.

HERE ARE THREE PRIMARY COLORS IN NATURE, Blue, Red,-and Yellow. From these are formed all the other beautiful tints which well up from the bosom of the deep, glows in every flower, blossoms in the trees, and sparkles in the dew drop; softly stealing from the moon and stars, and written upon the blue arc of night. Red indicates anger, and sometimes guilt. Blue is said to be true, but denotes melancholy and gloom. Yellow indicates cautiousness and prudence, and reflects the most light of any, after white.

Yellow-green is the color nature assumes at the falling of the leaf, and this was worn in the days of chivalry, the emblem of despair. Green denotes tranquility. In heraldry it is used to express liberty, love, youth and beauty, and at one time all letters of grace were signed with green.

The color of all objects depend on the action of those bodies on the light which fall upon them, the different rays of which they reflect, either entirely, or only partially. The light of the sun, and the lights used for illumination, gas, etc., seem to consist of an infinite number of rays, of different color, and however widely they may be spread out by the prism in the spectrum, can never be entirely separated, but always form an even gradation of color, from red at one end of the spectrum, through orange, yellow, green, etc., to purple at the other end. Sir Isaac Newton divided the spectrum into seven parts, thinking he could distinguish seven different colors, red, yellow, blue, orange, green, indigo, and violet, which he called primary colors. Sir D. Brewster showed that those colors which Newton considered simple were, in reality, compound, and mixed up with a considerable proportion of white light. He concludes from his experiments that there were but three simple colors, red, yellow, and blue—by the mixing of which the other colors were produced.

The principal advantages attending the choice of red, blue, and yellow, as primary colors, are: That the choice seems to agree with the fact that whenever a ray of white light has one of these three colors removed by absorption, the remaining colors of the ray is that which would be found by an equal mixture of the other two colors. And when a ray has two of its primary colors removed, the remaining color of the ray is that of the third primary color. The color which opposes the strongest contrast to any primary color, is that secondary color, which is formed of a mixture of the remaining two primaries, in such proportion as would form with the first white light. This color is called its complimentary color—colors being called complimentary to each other when they together form white light. For instance, blue has for its complimentary color the neutral secondary orange, formed of a mixture of red and yellow, and this color gives the most vivid contrast that can be opposed to blue. Green is the complimentary, and strongest contrasting color to red, and red to green; and yellow the strongest contrast, and complimentary to purple, and purple to yellow.

When the colors of the spectrum in a circle, in a perfect gradation all around the circumference, and so that the three primaries, red, yellow and blue, are at points in the circumference equal distance from each other, the strongest contrast to any color will be found at a point on the other side of the circle diametrically opposite to it. Thus, blue will be found exactly opposite to orange, which will be intermediate between red and yellow; and, in the same way, yellow-green will be found exactly opposite purple-red, etc. Now, as red, blue and yellow are the three primaries, and that all other colors are composed of mixtures of these, let us decide which of the many different colors called reds, yellows, and blues we are to consider as pure, and true primaries. A pure *yellow* has been decided upon; *chrome-yellow* (No. 1), chromate of zinc (citron yellow), or light cadmium. A mixture of any two bright primaries will produce a bright secondary, and any admixture of the third primary will make the secondary color produced much duller or blacker. We consider that would be the purest blue which gave the brightest green with yellow, at the same time that it gave the brightest purple with a red, and it was decided that *cobalt blue* was the pure primary, which was blue with regard to the yellow chosen. It is obvious that if the blue were a greenish blue, although it might give a very bright green with yellow, it would give but a dull purple with the red. The yellow contained in the blue, and which made it greenish, would blacken or dirty the purple produced, but would not interfere with the brightness of the green. We choose *carmine* for the primary red as the color which gives the brightest purple with cobalt blue, at the same time that it gave the brightest orange with chrome yellow. Thus we have chrome (No. 1), for yellow, cobalt for blue, and madder carmine for red. These are the primaries.

Colored objects appear colored owing to their action on light. This action consists in absorbing one or more of the different colored rays which fall upon it, and reflecting the rest; and it is these reflected rays that give the color to the object. Bodies which emit light are called *luminous*, as the sun. Bodies which transmit light, and through which objects can be distinguished, are called *transparent*, as water, glass, etc. Bodies which transmit light, and not so as to permit objects to be seen through them, are called *translucent*, as ground glass, etc. Bodies which absorb **or** reflect all the rays **of light, or** transmit so few rays that the eye **does not** perceive them, are called *opaque*, as wood, metal, etc.

What we call a pure white object, **such** as chalk or white paper, appears white by reflecting all the light which falls upon it, and is therefore precisely the same color **as** the light which falls upon it. A pure black object is **one** which *absorbs* all the light which falls upon **it, and** reflects *none*. **Such** an object will always appear black, whatever may be the color of the light which falls upon **it.** Gray objects, (pale black), absorb the three primary rays equally, or in equivalent proportions, but not *entirely*, so that there is a certain portion of the white light reflected unchanged. **A pure** green absorbs *all* the red, and reflects *all* the yellow **and blue.** A pale but pure **green** absorbs only *part* of the red, and reflects the remainder **of the red,** together with all the yellow **and blue.** A dull and blackish **green is formed by the** absorption of **all the red,** and also part **of the blue and yellow,** and **the** reflection of the remainder of the **blue** and yellow. The **same** rule will apply **in all** cases of all other colored objects, **except** transparent ones. **Silks** and satins of either color reflect **light.**

When three colored rays are mixed **together** in neutralizing proportions, white light is produced. The easiest way **of** finding what are the equivalent proportions of the primary colors **is** this: divide a circle of paper into three equal parts, by lines drawn from the center **to** the circumference. Paint one of these spaces with pure yellow, such **as** lemon yellow, or the palest chrome yellow, and paint one of the remaining spaces pure but weak blue, with cobalt, and the other **space** pure but **weak red,** with madder carmine. Then try, by spinning the **card rapidly on** a pivot, whether these colors neutralize each other, and **if not, darken** that color that is deficient until the gray produced **is neutral—** that **is, of** the **color of** lampblack mixed with **white; and when** this **is** the case, **the** colors **on** the three spaces will be of the proper neutralizing strength **for equal spaces.**

PEN AND PENCIL DRAWING,

BY AID OF THE TRANSFER PROCESS.

THE art of transferring pictures from one paper to another is what few understand. Many have drawings or engravings which they hold as valuable keepsakes, and wish to preserve copies. The plan of duplicating almost exactly a picture by the method given here, is original with the author of this book, who has many a time found it valuable in getting perfect the outlines of engravings, prints, and pictures of various kinds for pen or crayon drawings. Penmen produce very fine specimens of pen drawing, aided by the above process of copying; and although many a novice in the art of pen drawing exhibits equally as good designs as older professionals, they are, nevertheless, borrowed.

The paper used for transferring purposes is light tea paper, generally found in a tea store, or on sale at paper stores.

We Prepare it as follows : Procure a piece of soft pine or cedar, and burn to a coal, paste one side of the tea paper with it until quite black, and you have a neat transfer sheet. (In choosing the wood be sure and get soft white pine). Lay this black paper upon the white, where you wish the drawing to be made, the dark side down; upon this lay the copy, face up, and fasten the whole to the table with thumb tacks, to prevent its moving around and changing the outlines. This done, go over the whole with a tracer made of wood or ivory, with sufficient pressure to carry the lines through to the paper underneath, following every outline of the picture until the whole has been gone over. Lift the tracing paper, and you have upon the sheet below the desired drawing, which you now go over with pen or pencil. After this is done, rub the crayon from off the picture with your handkerchief, and complete the shading with a fine pointed steel pen or pencil, keeping the copy before you. Use Spencerian Artistic Pen, Crow-quill, or Gillott's No. 170.

THE USE OF THE PENTAGRAPH.

THIS is an instrument in four sections, so arranged that you can enlarge or diminish in size, and copy a photograph, engraving, or any kind of picture. It contains a screw to fasten it to the table, a small steel needle to guide in the outlining, and a lead pencil to do the drawing.

How to Use it. Screw the Pentagraph to the table, with the needle point to your left, upon the photograph, (which is fastened to the table also), holding the end containing the pencil with the fingers, to the right. With your eye on the photo, move the hand so that the needle follows the outlines of the copy, and the pencil is producing the same on your drawing paper at the right. In this way go over the entire picture until you have a complete copy of the same. You may now shade with pen or crayon to suit the wants of the copy.

The small screws on the bars near the figures, are used in adjusting it to suit the size of picture required.

COPYING WITH TRANSPARENT PAPER.

ANOTHER method of transferring pictures to paper is by the use of a transparent paper, which is made by dissolving castor oil in absolute alcohol, and applying the liquid to the paper with a brush or sponge. The paper becomes dry as soon as the alcohol evaporates, which is almost instantly. After which lay the paper on the picture you are about to copy, and with a pencil follow the outlines of the picture until you have gone over the whole. As soon as done immerse the paper in alcohol, which will remove the oil, and restore the paper to its natural state.

PASTEL PAINTING,

WITH SUGGESTIONS FROM THE BEST ENGLISH AUTHORS.

"Exactly in proportion as an artist is certain of his end, will he be swift and simple in his means; and as he is accurate and deep in his knowledge, will he be precise and refined in his touch."—*Ruskin.*

PORTRAITS.

For the past few years a great improvement has been made in the **execution** of portraits in black and **colored crayons.** Crayon painting is much easier in its execution than oil painting, and pictures **may be** completed at one sitting, owing **to the fact** that dry colors are used instead of oil, which may easily be removed or changed at will, left and resumed again at any time desired. In this department of art *crayon takes the place of brush and paint,* in all the different places **where** colors are used.

Crayon painting is said to have **been** practiced for a century or more after it **came into** use, and during the past few years it has had a "big **run**" in this country.

Crayons, or Pastels, can now be purchased by the box, in all varieties of tint, each box containing a graduated series.

The Paper upon which the drawing or painting is made, **is** manufactured **for this** purpose in such a manner that the texture becomes loosened **and** forms a woolly surface, which **assists** the blending of the tints, and receives the crayon.

As soon as a crayon picture is completed it will necessarily have to go under glass, for so slightly tenacious is the crayon, in some places where it may have been repeatedly applied with a view to brilliancy, that it may be blown from the surface of the paper.

Exposure to the Sun, which may brighten pictures painted in oil, will in a short time destroy the delicacy of crayon colors. They must also be kept free from *moisture* or *dampness*, as it is sure to *change the color and produce spots* on the face of a portrait, or the sky in a landscape.

Colors. The colors employed in pastel painting are about the same as used in oil painting, with some exceptions. The best for crayon work are the following:

Oxide of Zinc, White Chalk, Spanish White, Naples Yellow, Mineral Yellow, Chromes, Cadmium Yellow, Gallstone, Soft Red Chalk, Chinese Vermilion, Venetian Red, Chrome Red, Carmine, Lakes, Indigo, Prussian Blue, Smalt, Cobalt, Terre Verte, Cobalt Green, Brunswick Green, all the Greens from Copper, Green Oxide of Chromium, Lampblack, Umber, Ivory Black, Blue Black, Black Chalk.

Color of Paper. In regard to the use of paper, any color may be used, it being wholly a matter of taste with the artist.

The prevailing colors are Blue, Drab, Grey, Straw, Buff, Olive and Stone Colors.

A yellowish tint, you will find, produces the best results.

Mounting the Picture. Before commencing upon the drawing it must be mounted upon a stretcher, after which, with a firm crayon, trace the outlines, with either red, brown, or grey color. The beginner will find the Pentagraph of excellent service for outlining where you are working from a copy.

Sketching in the Outlines. This must be done lightly, in order that the crayon does not enter into the texture of the paper, so as to render the marks difficult to be superseded subsequently by the necessary colors. When the outline is completed, the breadths are made out by means of a brown crayon, and a stump, working for the degrees of shade.

Applying the Crayon. When the likeness is satisfactory in the sketch, the complexion may be commenced on, beginning with the lights. The whites, yellows, reds and greys must be worked in, and blended to an imitation of the reality of nature. From the highest lights, proceed in regular order to the deepest shades, and, in order to secure substance, these must be put in equal in strength to nature; after which the middle tones must be carefully blended, so as to unite the lights and shades by imperceptible gradations. The markings must be definitely made out, and the reflexes also, if there be any. As the fresher tints occur principally in the lights, it would be well to keep the color rather high, and of a warm tone, in order to reserve the brightest and most effective tints till the last.

When all the tints have been laid in, and the head is in a satisfactory state as to form, color and expression, then, with the finger, pass over the whole, working and blending the colors in harmony. In this operation the finger is used instead of a stump, and nothing else will answer better. When this operation is concluded, the crayons will be again used to bring up the colors, and tone to those of the life—to modify and correct those which may require retouching.

Those parts which are heavy must be relieved, and those which may be too cold or too warm, must be reduced to harmony. Working with the finger will be found the most available method of managing the crayons.

Having laid in the tints, according to the natural complexion, it will be necessary, before touching the work with the finger or blender, to be certain that all are laid in the proper places; a little experience will enable you to judge; there remains but little work for the fingers to perform, and the less the colors are worked upon the more fresh and transparent they will remain.

Colors and the Composition of Tints. The shades of flesh tints are warm or cold, according to the warmth or coldness of the breadths of the light. If the lights be of a healthy hue, the shades may be warm, inclining to brown, mixed of va-

rious colors, broken with light red, carmine, yellow, blue or grey.
Some artists represent nature as violet or green, in shade; but
this is untrue and must be guarded against.   It is advisable generally to follow the Italian feeling of leaving the dark passages
warm.   When the complexion is strong in color, the effect is
most agreeable; if worked without hardness, opacity or black-
ness.   In feminine portraits the work must be brought up to the
utmost brilliancy of color, by the brightest and freshest hues,
composed of White, Naples Yellow, Vermilion and Madder,
mellowed with Yellows, or slightly purpled with Lake or Carmine, according to the prevalent tint of the subject.   In the
masculine subject the colors will be stronger, and the half-tints
more positive.   Great care must be observed, lest the high and
delicate passages be soiled or stained.   They must only be approached by, and blended with, other shades at their extremities; and these shades are, in most cases, half tints.

It will be clearly seen by the artist, that if the intermediate
tint be too cold, it must be treated with the reds or yellow; if
too warm, reduce by grey or blue.   The lights and shades should
be carefully graduated, and harmony prevail throughout the
work.

Backgrounds.—For backgrounds there is no established rule;
a head may be relieved by a light, or dark background, either
producing good effect.   A dark background is not always suitable for female loveliness.

Backgrounds are not to be rubbed in mechanically, with the
idea that any dark shade will relieve any light, or that any middle tint will suffice.   As a general rule, the background around
the head should be lower in tone than the half tints of the
face, and lighter than the shades—to disengage the head.

Where the paper becomes greasy or glazed by the too frequent
application of the pastel, or the finger, it may be necessary to
rub it with pumice pounce, or with cuttle-fish, lightly.

If the paper stretches by constant pressure on it, you can remedy it by wetting the back with a light solution of alum water.

LANDSCAPE PAINTING

WITH

CRAYON COLORS.

HE crayons used are much harder than the soft kind required in portraits; they are manufactured expressly for landscapes, and resemble firm chalk. The following is a list of the most useful crayons: White, Italian chalk; straw colors and light yellow, blue, grey, vermilion and Indian reds; blacks, conte crayons Nos. 1, 2 and 3. The white Italian chalk is used both for light touches and blending all the other crayons into which it may be worked.

The black conte chalks are also of the utmost importance; Nos. 1 and 2, the harder degrees, are used for outlining, and the softest degree, No. 3, may be blended with many colors to reduce their tones.

The Paper. The paper must be a good quality of drawing paper, such as will take the crayon, and it must supply a good middle tint, as the color of the paper appears through almost every passage of the finished work. A soft paper of a low-toned olive tint, which has been found by long experience to be better adapted than any other for landscape drawing, as affording an agreeable neutral, upon which warm or cold tones, lights or shadows, may be placed with the best effect.

Arranging the Paper. Attach the paper to a drawing-board with thumb tacks, in order that it may be kept smooth and level while the *flat tints* are rubbed in. It is well to select paper some larger than your design, so as to give the picture a margin.

The Drawing. With conte crayon No. 1 the design must be outlined, showing enough of the objects to guide you in the *flat tints* of the sky and distances.

The difference in the crayons used in portrait and those in landscape painting is, that the latter is much harder, which is essential, as will be seen when applied to the paper. The breadths of the composition are not laid by working with the point of the crayon, but a part of the crayon, sufficient for the purpose required, is brokenoff and applied flat to the paper. Work it lightly over those parts of the drawing that it is desired to tint, and the light-ness of the tint is derived from the hardness of the crayon, which is "bitten" by the surface of the paper, and leaves on it a quantity of the color. This tint is rubbed vigorously with the fingers, so as to work the colors well with the texture of the paper; as the operation leaves but little color these tintings are repeated until the necessary strength of tone is obtained, varying and blending the colors by working them into each other from different directions with the fingers, as the subject may require; *draw the remote forms* with pieces of crayon, held flat or lengthwise. Blend the tints in and repeat where necessary. The distant ridges of the mountains being made out, the middle distance and the nearer objects are approached by the nearer tints; still drawing with broken pieces of crayon, working obliquely or otherwise. The black conte Nos. 1 and 2, are used in the near parts of the

picture; all the striking features of the foreground, such as trees, rocks and buildings, are drawn, and the material used in the manner described. When any fine lines are necessary, they are not made with the crayon cut to a point, but by the sharp edges of the fracture of the crayon.

Using the Colors. Each object having been drawn in with the conte, it is now tinted or colored by working over the black markings with the necessary colors. It is like the operation of glazing in oil painting, as under the light lines of the tracing of the colored crayon the conte drawing is still visible. By blending and again drawing with conte, and again glazing as often as may be necessary, we approach the finish of the picture, which is completed by sharp touches of light put in with sharp points of the broken ends of colored crayon. The color should be used sparingly, and the black chalk should appear prominent in the drawing. Do not rub in the colors in finishing or you destroy the effect. The beauty of the work depends upon the paper being perceptible through the final finish. Any markings too sharp, may be worked down by the finger or *blender*. These retouchings are repeated until the desired effect be obtained.

As crayon painting is liable to become changed or removed, even by blowing upon it, we must present some method whereby it can be fixed permanent.

Fixing the Drawing. Infuse an ounce and a half of isinglass in five ounces distilled vinegar twenty-four hours; add to this one quart of hot water, keep at a light heat, stir often until the isin-glass is dissolved, when you filter it through paper; pour it into a bottle with the same quantity spirits of wine, shake a few minutes and you have the fixatif ready.

Place the picture face down (avoid having the colors touch anything), and apply the liquid to the back with a brush until it has penetrated through to the crayon and all the colors become moistened and bright. The first application will penetrate very quick. After this apply another with great care and evenness, and not so plentiful as at first. When done lay it with face up until dry. The picture is now completed. After this process of fixing the colors, they can be cleaned any time without injury to the painting.

MATERIALS FOR PASTEL DRAWING.

Crayons, square black conte, Nos. 1, 2, and 3. Square white, red, and grey, Nos. 1, 2, and 3.

Round black conte, Nos. 1, 2, and 3.

Round white and red crayons.

Conte crayon pencils in wood, Nos. 1, 2, and 3.

Charcoal in sticks.

Hard and soft pastel, containing 130 shades.

Crayon holders. (Brass and German silver.)

PREPARED PASTEL PAPER.

Royal, super-royal, double elephant, colombier.

STUMPS USED.

Chamois skin, cork, paper, (grey).

DIRECTIONS

MONOCHROMATIC DRAWING.

TAKE pasteboard or drawing paper, size with isin glass, or paint with pure white lead. When thoroughly dried, smooth it down with sand-paper, and paint again. Before this coat is perfectly dry, sift upon it pulverized white marble, through muslin. When dry, shake off the loose marble that remains. Monochromatic board can be found already prepared at the book stores, where artist materials are kept. The materials needed for this work, is a thin-blade knife, crayons, fine sponge, pencil, cork, rubber, blender, &c.. Commence painting with the dark shades first, and blend gradually into the light. For very dark shades, rub the crayon directly upon the surface with a light hand, and blend off carefully. Paint the sky first, as in water colors. It is well to shade distant mountains *very light* at first, and be sure to have the edges soft and faint. For water, scrape some black crayon into a powder, and lay it on your board with the blender, working it horizontally, making the lights and shades stronger as it comes nearer. Use the pen-knife for making sharp lights. Dark subjects work to the best advantage, such as moonlight scenes on the water, old ruins, etc. The foliage requires a great deal of attention in showing it up. Draw in the figures last. One familiar with crayon or pencil drawing can acquire this branch of art very easily.

WATER COLORS.

N this branch of fine art we will avoid all preliminary remarks in regard to its advantages, and direct you at once to the method of treating it, in as clear and comprehensible a manner as possible, and at the same time omit nothing that will in any way facilitate the progress of the learner.

INSTRUCTIONS.

Arrange the paper for the painting, after sponging it, by stretching upon a drawing board, and then turn to the mixing of the colors.

Colors Used for Skies and Distances.

FOR BLUE OF SKY.—Cobalt Blue, lowered with Pink Madder and Gamboge, to the hue required. Ochre may be substituted for Gamboge.

CLOUDS.—The same mixed so as to form a variety of warm and cool pearly greys.

FOR EXTREME DISTANCE.--Cobalt and Venetian Red.

FOR LOCAL TINTS.—Blend the colors so that the tints produced may incline toward yellow, red, or any tint required.

FOR MIDDLE TINTS, use Indigo, Pink Madder and Ochre on the same principle for

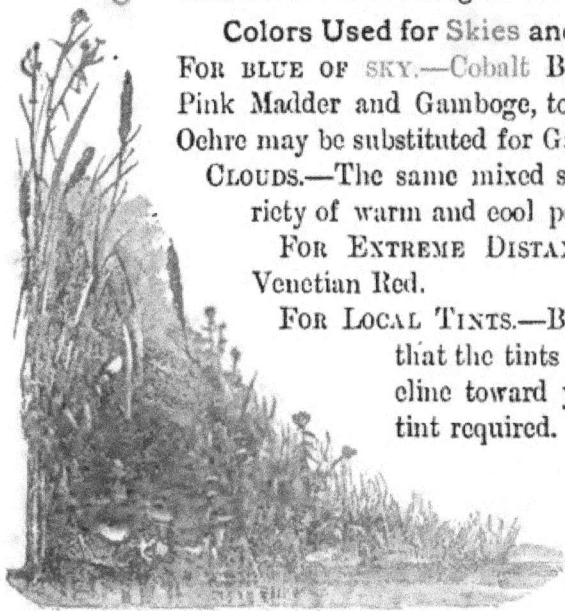

the light parts, and Indigo, Pink Madder and Gamboge for shady portions.

SETTING SUN.—Use Yellow Ochre and Pink Madder, or Venetian Red and Yellow Ochre; sometimes Vermilion and Gamboge or Indian Yellow in small proportions, when a strong effect is to be given.

TREES.—In painting trees use Indigo, Burnt Sienna and Gamboge. These colors will make tints for the light; Indigo mixed with Vandyke Brown becomes a fine deep grey, of a green hue. Purple Lake may be added when you want the tint more neutral.

FOREGROUND.—Green in foreground is made by mixing Sepia with Olive Green in the shade, and Olive Green and Burnt Sienna in the lighter parts. A light transparent yellow, raw Sienna or Italian Pink may be carried over the foreground where herbage is to be represented, when a bright sunny effect is desirable to give fullness and richness to the colors that come afterward; it also answers for high lights upon leaves, and the brilliant specks which are left sharp. Indigo, Indian Red and Ochre for the ashy grey of loam; Burnt Umber alone, or mixed with Burnt Sienna, pure Ochre, and Ochre mixed with Sepia alone, and mixed with Purple Lake for dark parts; also, Vandyke Brown and Purple Lake, or pure Brown Madder for very dark touches.

Indigo, mixed with Gamboge, makes a cold green well suited to dark leaves; Purple Lake may be added for cool reflected lights; Indian Red mixed with Indigo to a pale tint for willow leaves or foliage stained with dirt, or for the grey back of a leaf.

These cold greys and greens are of great value in foregrounds to repeat the cool greys and cold lights of the sky in pictures composed of much warm color in the middle distance, as midday effects, sunsets, etc. The foreground should show a great deal of relief, distinctness and accuracy in the drawing of these small objects which are particularly marked, but are merged into masses when further removed. With regard to *roads* in your painting, Yellow Ochre, mixed with Burnt Sienna, and lowered with Indian Red and Indigo. Indigo and Brown Madder being transparent colors, will allow a wash of Cobalt Blue and Pink Madder to alter the hue without danger of opacity.

WATER.—The same as for clouds, blended with the local color of the water (greenish) and with the reflected objects.

DARK SEA is indicated by combining Indigo, Vandyke Brown and Lake.

DARK SKY.—Indigo, mixed with Pink Madder and Gamboge.

IN BRICK WORK.—Mix Ochre with French Blue and Indian Red, Indigo and Venetian Red, Ochre and Pink Madder for bright part of brick work. When the color is more of red, Vermilion may be used, with caution, and in small quantities for lights. For shades, mix Sepia and Purple Lake, or Sepia and Indian Red; Sepia alone is used for light shadows from trees.

We will now paint a landscape, the foreground composed of rocks lying near and dividing a stream of water from a road; the margin of the river skirted by trees; beyond a range of hills, and still beyond another range of mountains with high points extending above all else; cattle standing at the foot; flock of sheep coming along the road, cottage, etc.

Direction. Cover the entire surface of your board with a tint of Yellow Ochre of moderate strength; when this is dry a tint is formed from the mixture of Cobalt Blue and Pink Madder, the blue predominating; use it in a very diluted state, on the side whence the sun is supposed to shine, graduating the tint as the opposite part of the sky is approached, so that the ether may appear of a clear and rather strong color; the lights of the cloud to be left, and care to be taken to diminish the strength of the tint in the lower part of the sky. The same tint may be carried over the mountains, leaving small, brilliant lights if there be any.

A wash of Pink Madder and Ochre, or Venetian Red and Ochre may be given to the lights on the clouds, afterwards they may receive their middle tint, composed of Pink Madder, Yellow Ochre and Cobalt Blue.

THE CLOUDS may be finished by shading with Cobalt Blue and Venetian Red; the water should receive its tints at this time; any very bright lights should be left. Clouds that are darker than the ether, lay on with Venetian Red and Ochre. If the clouds are meant to show lighter than the blue of the sky, they should be left. Mix in one dish Ochre and Pink Madder with more strength than the sky tints; and in another Cobalt, Pink Madder and Gamboge, with as much strength as possible, so that it will work freely. Having the brush charged with the first paint, proceed to lay in the light parts of the mountains, varying the color by the addition of Cobalt Blue where a greenish line is wanted, Pink Madder where the granite prevails. Now, with a brush filled from the other saucer, lay in the shady parts, varying the colors. These opposite tints of light and shade should be made to blend imperceptibly where they meet. Indigo, Pink Madder and Gamboge, mixed, will be found useful for dark touches in shadows, and Cobalt mixed with Indian Red may be used for the same purpose in the lights.

FOR THE HILLS, mix Indigo and Yellow Ochre, so as to make a light green; lay in the light parts with this, adding Ochre when a brighter and warmer light is to be expressed, and Pink Madder when the surface is broken by rock. Any bright projecting rocks may receive a touch of Yellow Ochre and Indian Red, mixed. A few broad touches will bring this sufficiently forward; they may be given with a brown, produced by the mixture of Indigo, Purple Lake and Gamboge, inclining to Orange or Purple.

THE TREES, skirting the stream, should be covered at the same time with the first and lightest tint, varied in the same way and brought into the water, leaving a sharp strip of light at the edge for a bank or path. Any very light stems of trees should be left. When this has become quite dry lay in the trees with Gamboge, Burnt Sienna and Indigo, mixed, for the light; Purple Lake, mixed with Indigo and Gamboge, for stems; stronger and browner for dark touches. The rocky masses lying in the water near the promontory may be covered by a tint of Indigo and Brown Madder, mixed; a little Olive Green will vary the tint, if a greenish hue is wanted. Gamboge, mixed with Indigo to a light green, and varied with Purple Lake and Indigo, will serve for the parts of the rising ground seen through the branches of the trees, which may receive a tint of Indigo mixed with Burnt Sienna and Olive Green.

The Foreground may be laid in with Indian Red, mixed with Yellow Ochre, and broken by Sepia or Indigo; shadows across the road may be rendered by washes of Indigo mixed with Brown Madder, and Lampblack mixed with Purple Lake for cool slate colored rocks in shade.

Birch trees should be covered with a tint of Indian Yellow and Burnt Sienna, and shaded with Brown Madder and Indigo mixed, or Sepia and Purple Lake. *Bring out the stems* by dark touches of Vandyke Brown mixed with Purple Lake, in shade. The dark greens about the foreground should be composed of Sepia and Indian Yellow. The figures in the landscape may have some red in the drapery; the sheep, a little Yellow Ochre. In mixing the colors always incline towards warmth, because a little more coolness and atmosphere may be given by a wash of Cobalt Blue mixed with Pink Madder or Indian Red. Reflections in water should be painted similar in hue to the objects, but lower in tone and more transparent. Large stems of trees may be colored effectively by applying varied greys, browns (made by a mixture of Indian Red, French Blue and Ochre), for light sides, leaving any very bright features shown in the bark. Brown Madder and Brown Pink, and sometimes Vandyke Brown mixed with Indian Lake, will be found of service for markings. When laying on the blue in the sky, be careful to leave the shape of the light parts of the clouds, then with another brush wash in the middle tint and suffer it to blend with the blue on the shady side of the cloud. Add a little Venetian Red, as the tint is carried down to the horizon; mix more Cobalt for distance. Give a first color to the road and cottage; pure Yellow Ochre for the light of the plaster, with white paper left, and with very small portions; the shade, Sepia or Brown Madder, mixed with Indigo; the hedge by the cottage, brown-pink, olive-green, mixed with Burnt Sienna.

WHEN THE DRAWING IS DRY, begin with the sky, and heighten or subdue as seems best; give the shade to the clouds, taking care that the indications of shadow, and feature generally, grow lighter the nearer they come to the horizon; the country is distinguished from the sky by outline—a dark touch of blue in the shadows, from the clouds. Dark touches on the roof, chimneys and windows of the cottage, will give it relief from the sky, and give distance to the small objects; they may be made with Vandyke Brown, mixed with Purple Lake. Brown-pink, mixed with Purple Lake, gives a very dark transparency to water.

FOR MOONLIGHT SCENES, *wash in* the general effect of sky with Burnt Umber, mixed with Cobalt Blue and Pink Madder, and Cobalt Blue for dark clouds and distances; Indigo, mixed with Vandyke Brown and Pink Madder, for the general landscape. The learner, before commencing at once upon a landscape, will do well to practice upon blending colors; commencing with Cobalt Blue and Pink Madder you will produce a purple; add Gamboge, the purple will be grey, etc. In the combination of the following colors, a great variety of tones adapted to skies and distance may be found: Sepia and Gamboge, Sepia and Indian Yellow, Sepia and Italian Pink, Lampblack and Indian Yellow. Chinese White is of service when tinted paper is used for sketches.

IN SELECTING THE PAPER it should be as natural as possible, either cool or warm in hue, according to the effect intended. The tint may serve as middle tint in light of buildings, stems of trees, banks, etc. Cold pressed imperial paper is the best for landscape. There are several other kinds of paper which are used, such as Whatman's extra thick, of 140 lbs. to the ream; or Creswick paper, if white; or pale cream color, are good ; but if much opaque color is used in the picture, any common paper will do, especially if of a warm grey or brownish color ; and very good pictures are painted on the ordinary brown paper used for wrapping. The most convenient form of paper for sketching in the outlines of a scene is that made up in blocks or tablets.

BRUSHES should come to a fine point of their own accord, and not bulge out in the middle. Sables are the best for general use. The brushes necessary are two or three red Sable, or goose quill size, and a black Sable of large swan-quill size for flat washes ; or where these are too high price for the beginner, a large swan-quill French camel's hair with good points. Do not allow the color to dry on them, or they are spoiled ; but wash as soon as used and allow them to dry with the hair in its natural position.

OTHER MATERIALS, such as a drawing-board, a sponge, an HH pencil for outlining, India-rubber, a sharp penknife for mixing up opaque colors with Chinese White, a tin water-bottle to hold water when sketching, prepared ox-gall to use in small quantities where the paper is greasy or woolly, a quill pen, will also be found useful.

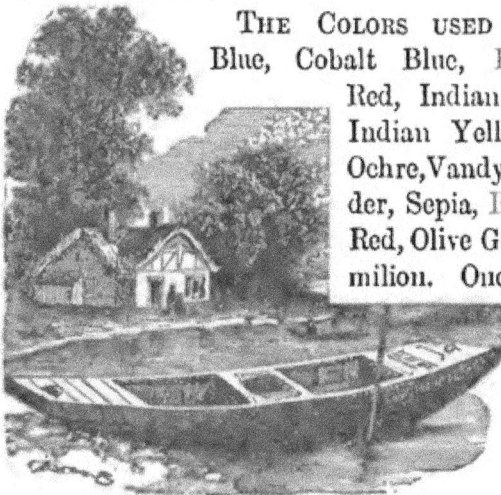

THE COLORS USED ARE Indigo, French Blue, Cobalt Blue, Purple Lake, Indian Red, Indian Lake, Pink Madder, Indian Yellow, Gamboge, Yellow Ochre, Vandyke Brown, Brown Madder, Sepia, Burnt Sienna, Venetian Red, Olive Green, Brown Pink, Vermilion. One of the principal points in which water-color painting differs from oil, is the laying on of the flat tints by means of washes.

THE ART OF

LANDSCAPE PAINTING

IN

OIL COLORS.

TECHNICAL NAMES AND MATERIALS USED. MIXING OF TINTS, AND HOW TO APPLY THEM.

———

No doubt you are sufficiently acquainted with the general principles of Drawing and Perspective at the time you reach this branch of art work, as to be able to apply them with facility and certainty to the representation, in outline, of a given view or subject. The rules here laid down will place within your reach the power of securing to yourself one of the most delightful and agreeable of accomplishments.

In the production of a painting in Oil Colors, there are certain modes of operation, in introducing a beginner to the practice of the art, the operations are distinguished by the technical names of glazing, impasting, scrumbling, and handling.

A GLAZE is a thin transparent film of color, laid upon another color to modify the tone, or to aid the effect of the latter, the work thereby appearing distinctly through the layer of glaze, from which it receives a characteristic hue. This process of glazing is effected by diluting proper transparent color with megilp, or other suitable vehicle. Thus diluted, these colors are

laid upon portions of the **work,** either in **broad flat** tints, or in **touches,** partially and judiciously distributed. **The** object **is to** strengthen shadows, and give warmth **or coldness** to their hue, to subdue lights that are unduly obtrusive, or to give additional color and tone to those that are deficient in force and richness.

IMPASTING. In oil painting, the dark shadows, or dark portions of the picture, **are** painted thinly, while the lights are laid **on, or** "impasted," **with a full** pencil and **a** stiff color. In the lights of the foreground, and of parts not intended to be remote **or to** "retire," the impasting should be bold and free; **while** in the more brilliant lights it **cannot well** be **too** solid. The palette **knife** has always **been** a favorite instrument of this "impasting," **or** laying on of color, **capable** as it is **of** producing an agreeable brightness on, **and** of giving an appropriate flatness to, **the** pigment. A clear and appropriate tint, skillfully swept across a **sky** by these means, **often produce** a brilliant **and** charming effect which **is** surprising.

SCRUMBLING, **the** opposite **process** to that of glazing, is done **by** going **lightly** over the **work** with an opaque tint, generally produced **by** an admixture **of** white. **For** this purpose a hoghair **brush** is used, charged with **color** but sparingly, and with it the tints are drawn very thinly, and somewhat loosely, over the previous painting, which **should,** as in the case of glazing, be dry **and** firm.

The judicious combination of glazing and scrumbling will **produce** richness, brilliancy and transparency.

HANDLING. By "handling" is **meant** the mechanical use of **the pencil or** brush, exhibiting the artist's **power** of adopting certain modes and processes in the expression and representation of the different textures of objects, such as foliage, wood, water, etc.

Light. The position of a painter at his **easel** should be such that his work **may receive** the light from his left, falling upon it only **from** the **upper part of the window of** his room, the lower

part being darkened by a piece of green baize. A light proceeding from the north is the best, it being most uniform through
the day.

The first thing to be done in painting a landscape is to select
a canvas of moderate size, let the design be drawn upon it with
a firm and well defined outline. This being done, tint the lower
part of the canvas in a clear, warm tone with a mixture of Yel-

low Ochre and Venetian Red, or with a pale hue of Burnt Sienna,
in water colors, mixed with a little ox-gall to make it adhere to
the oil ground.

The upper, or sky part of the canvas, being left clear, commence the work lightly about where the horizon will appear, and
gradually strengthen the tint as you descend. The sketch being
laid in, the painting of the picture may now be commenced.

Have near your easel a slab of ground glass, on which you can prepare your tints to a proper consistency or hue. A set of tints, of the hue of the sky, and for the distances, is now mixed, and you commence with the blue of the sky, working downwards, and securing a proper gradation of color; then follow the distances, mountains, &c. This being done, the work is left to dry. The mode of applying the color to the canvas is chiefly by touches, or pats of the brush in succession, from left to right. The color should be tempered with a proper quantity of vehicle, that it may work crisply, and above all, that it may be laid sparingly upon the canvas.

Short hair brushes are best adapted to painting with little color. In laying on, or "impasting" the lights, the brushes should be rather longer than those used for general painting—such a brush will yield the color more readily. Unless the colors be allowed to harden between the first and second painting, also between the second and third, they will be liable to be rubbed off by the application of the oils and glazing used in the after painting.

When the first painting is dry, the picture should have a damp cloth passed over its surface. Being then wiped dry, let it be rubbed over with a small portion of poppy oil, for this makes the after painting unite with the first. It is a mere moistening of the surface that is required—no excess of oil to remain. All that is not necessary should be removed by the moderate application of a piece of silk or linen.

In the second painting we advance by giving more attention to the details of various objects; their drawing, light and shade, reflected hues, and various tints in coloring are more elaborately made out; the relative distances of objects from the eye are most carefully preserved, and the shadows, which are yet painted thinly and transparently, are carefully united, with half-tints, so as to produce a roundness.

The third, or finished painting, is commenced by wiping and oiling the picture in the manner before described as necessary for the second painting. We then proceed to complete the details of form and color, which were brought forward in the former painting, employing for this purpose delicate touches of glazing and scrumbling alternately, not to conceal, but improve and render as perfect as possible what has already been done. Sharp, vigorous touches where the markings of the details require them. These touches must be made with freedom and decision, or they fail in producing the desired effect. They should be of a warm tone, not cold—not grey. In this stage of the work do not attempt too much at one sitting. It is best to allow the colors to dry gently, and to repeat the operation when necessary.

Lastly, a mode of aiding the finish is by passing over a portion of the work with light, delicate tones, which are left only on the projecting touches of texture objects.

MATERIALS USED.

Many of the pigments which change color by the action of impure air, and are, therefore, useless in water-color painting, may, nevertheless, be safely used in oil painting; for this reason: In water color the powder colors are mixed with only just enough of some binding cement (called a *vehicle*), such as gum, size, sugar, etc., to prevent their being easily rubbed off the paper, and are, therefore, freely exposed to the action of the atmosphere, or of the colors with which they may be mixed; but in oil colors the powder colors are ground up in oil, so prepared as to oxidise rapidly in the air into a kind of impermeable leathery resin, which, completely enveloping each particle of color, effectually protects it, not only from the action of impure air, but also of neighboring particles of different colors. And it thus happens that pigments may be used in oils with tolerable safety which in water color might turn black in a few days. Indeed, the white which we invariably use in oils—flake white—is certainly one of the most unstable of colors in water colors; and nearly the same

may be said of the chrome yellow, Naples yellow, emerald green,
etc.

The colors named below **will be found** a useful set:

Flake White,	Lamp Black*	Cobalt Blue,
Ultramarine,	Cappagh Brown,	Madder Brown*
Prussian Blue,	Raw Sienna,	Burnt Sienna,
Yellow Ochre,	Cadmium Yellow*	Pale Cadmium Yellow*
Carmine (in Powder)*	Rose Madder*	Indian Yellow*
Indian Red,	Emerald Green*	

The colors marked with an asterisk do not dry quickly, except
when mixed with much **flake-white.** To these it is necessary to
add a very little *drier*—a **mixture of** sugar of lead and boiled
oil.

BRUSHES.—After the **colors, the brushes are** the most **impor-**
tant part **of the** artist's materials. **Flat** hog's-hair brushes **are**
the most useful for general purposes. **These** should **have** polished handles, and the hairs should **not** straggle **at the** point,
but keep together, so as to form a **straight,** thin **edge. The**
small sizes are most convenient when **made very short and very**
thin in the hair, it being **difficult to make the** long-haired ones
keep together at the point. For fine touches, sable brushes are
the most convenient, some flat and some **round ; the former**
thin and short-haired, **the latter** coming to a fine point.

Badger's-hair softeners **are** used, as their name implies, to
soften broad tints in skies, **etc.,** but require the greatest caution
in their use, or they will **certainly** produce a disagreeable " wool-
liness," or smudginess. **They are** made with the hair radiating,
or spreading out, towards **the** point, and are used by dabbing or
jobbing them lightly over the work, and should always be used
clean and dry.

The brushes should **always** be cleaned as soon as they are done
with for the day. The easiest **way is to rinse them in a little**
spirits of turpentine, **and,** after drying them **on** a rag, wash
them out clean by rubbing them in the palm of the hand with
thick soap and water, and **then** rinsing them **in** clean water, and
allowing them to **dry** with **the hair in its** proper position. It

happens sometimes that, leaving off in a hurry, one has no time to wash out the brushes carefully. In that case they may be laid by for a few days, dirty as they are, with their ends under water. The paint will keep under water without drying.

CANVAS.--This is the best material for painting upon. It is sold ready stretched on frames, and is kept of all sizes at the artists' color warehouses.

PREPARED PAPER is perhaps the most convenient material for the beginner, occupying so very little space when the picture is dry. It must be fastened, when in use, to a board by means of drawing-pins. It is also kept bound up into blocks, like those used for water-color sketching, and this is, perhaps, the most convenient form in which to buy it, though not the cheapest.

MILLBOARDS seem to me to possess no advantage over paper, and are very heavy, and liable to break at the corners.

PANELS are heavy and rather bulky, but are peculiarly well adapted for works requiring high finish.

PALETTES are usually made of mahogany or satin wood. The latter are the best, the colors being better seen on the lighter colored wood. The rectangular shape is the most convenient, and packs best into the lid of a color-box. A wooden palette should have plenty of raw linseed oil rubbed into it before being used, and be allowed to dry. This will prevent the colors sinking into the wood and staining.

A DIPPER is a small tin cup made to fix by sliding on to the palette, to contain oil, turpentine, varnish, or any other vehicle used.

THE REST STICK is used to rest the right hand upon, while painting those parts of the picture that require great steadiness and care. It should be as stiff and as light as possible, and is held in the same hand as the palette.

PALETTE-KNIVES are necessary implements for mixing and manipulating the colors on the palette. It is convenient to have two of different stiffness.

EASELS are inconvenient usually in proportion to their cheapness. They should be tolerably firm and heavy, and should allow the picture to be raised easily and quickly.

VEHICLE is the diluent used to temper and thin the colors for the purpose of bringing them to a proper state. Linseed oil, rendered drying by boiling with certain metallic oxides, is the vehicle generally used. Drying oil should dry quite free from stickiness in two or three days, in ordinary weather. Copal varnish is also an excellent vehicle, but dries so rapidly that it will not do where the colors require considerable manipulation with the brush—as in skies and broad tints generally. Colors used with varnish will require frequent thinning with spirit of turpentine. Megilp is a most pleasant vehicle to use; so pleasant, indeed, that one is apt to use far too much of it. It is made by mixing strong mastic varnish with drying oil.

The beginner should bear in mind that all oils and varnishes have a strong tendency to turn dark brown with age, and should therefore learn to use *as little as possible*; indeed, the colors, as generally sold, are ground with sufficient oil for use with a hog's-hair brush; and it is only where greater freedom is required, and when using sable brushes, that an addition of vehicle is of use. It is absolutely necessary, however, in the process called "glazing," which is where a transparent color is rubbed thinly over parts of the picture, the general tone or color of which it is desirable to modify. And in this case, too, as little vehicle as possible should be employed.

MIXED TINTS.

The following are given as examples of some of the tints that may be obtained by mixture of the more important colors.

Rose Madder and **Cobalt.** With these colors a variety of delicate tints of great purity and permanence may be produced; of general use in distances, skies, water, etc.

Yellow Ochre, Rose Madder, and Cobalt. Being made up of the three primaries, are duller or greyer, but will produce a greater variety. Of use in distances, middle distance, etc.

Vandyke Brown and Cobalt, Brown Madder and Cobalt. Of use in the same cases as the last. Good for middle distance foliage.

Yellow Ochre and Orange Vermilion. Of great use in obtaining warm, sunny effects in distances, skies, clouds, and for brilliant tints in foregrounds. Will give beautiful flesh tints with Chinese white.

Yellow Ochre and Prussian Blue. Pleasant, cool, greyish-greens may be produced with these colors; especially useful in middle distance trees. May be saddened with black or Vandyke brown

Rose Madder and Prussian Blue. A variety of useful and permanent sober greys and purples may be thus obtained. Of great use in cloudy skies and distances, etc.

Vandyke Brown and Prussian Blue. Useful in the same cases as yellow ochre and Prussian blue.

Vandyke Brown and Yellow Ochre. Gives good tints for earth, etc., in foregrounds.

Vandyke Brown and Gamboge, Vandyke Brown, Gamboge, and Prussian Blue. Give colors of the greatest use for foreground and middle distance foliage.

Burnt Sienna and Carmine, Gamboge and Burnt Sienna. Warm, rich, transparent colors. Of use in autumnal foliage, and for bright tints in foregrounds, such as the shading of draperies, etc., and cattle, birds, and flowers; in fact, in all cases where very rich transparent color is required.

Burnt Sienna, Gamboge, and Prussian Blue. Of the greatest use for foreground and middle distance foliage.

Burnt Sienna and Yellow Ochre. Useful for the same purposes as Vandyke brown and yellow ochre.

Raw Sienna, Carmine, and Prussian Blue. With these three colors an immense number of beautiful transparent greys and browns may be obtained, useful in all kinds of foreground shadows.

Burnt Sienna and Cobalt. For distant and middle distant foliage.

Carmine and Prussian Blue, Carmine and French Ultramarine. Whenever brilliant and transparent purples of great depth are required in foregrounds.

Indian Red and Cobalt, Indian Red and Prussian Blue. Useful in the same cases as rose madder and Prussian blue.

Raw Sienna, Madder Lake, and Cobalt. Give quiet, semi-transparent greys for middle distances, cloudy skies, etc.

Carmine and Gamboge. For transparent deep oranges and reds in foregrounds.

Emerald Green and Gamboge. May be sparingly used where very bright greens are required in foreground foliage.

Orange Vermilion and Cadmium Yellow. Safe colors to use for all very vivid oranges.

Lamp Black and Cobalt, Lamp Black and Gamboge. Illustrate the use of lamp black in saddening other colors. The most beautiful greys may be thus obtained. Of universal use, whether for foregrounds, distances, or skies.

THE
OIL-PHOTO MINIATURE.

CALLED BY SOME

CAMEO-OIL.

IMPROVED METHOD.

HEN the photograph you desire to color is mounted on a card, first immerse it in *boiling hot water* This will soften the paste, and in a short time the print may be lifted from the mount. Do not hurry, but give the print a thorough soaking before trying to lift it from the card, and always use great care to avoid tearing the photograph. Rinse the picture in cold water to clean it from the paste and coloring matter that may adhere to it from the card. Let it remain in the vessel of clear water until ready for mounting on the glass. Prepare a little thin starch paste, as follows. Amylum (Refined Corn Starch) a teaspoonful, cold water 2 ounces, or nitrate strontium $\frac{1}{4}$ ounce; stir till dissolved, then bring it to a boil, stirring constantly.

Have the starch paste *thin* and strain it through fine muslin. Having cleaned your Convex Glass *thoroughly* with alcohol and a piece of cotton batting, take the photograph and blot off the surplus water. Paste the face of the print and the concave or hollow side of the cleaned glass with your starch, being very careful to cover both the print and glass smoothly. A wide bristle brush is most suitable for this work. Lay the print on the glass, the prepared surfaces together, and proceed carefully to work the bubbles out with your fingers, after which lay two or three thicknesses of tissue paper on the print, and with an ivory paper-knife, or flat stick, with curve about the same as the concave surface of the glass, work the print down to the glass, forcing out all the air. Work from the centre of the glass toward the edges, and with great care, using very light pressure to avoid breaking the glass. The mounting of the print should be done quickly, as the paste dries very fast. If any bubbles should remain, prick them through with a fine-pointed needle and rub over with the ivory knife. After mounting the picture on the glass allow it to dry thoroughly. Now fill the concave or hollow side of the glass having the picture on, with Castor Oil three parts, Oil Lavender one part. Allow the oil to remain until the photograph is transparent; this will take from three to twelve hours. When perfectly transparent, pour off the oil and wipe with a fine sponge until nearly dry. Your picture is now ready for painting.

The colors applied directly to the photograph are those that need no blending—such as the eyes, lips, jewelry, light ribbons, flower ornaments and neck-tie. Edges of ruffles and embroidery should also be touched up on the photograph. When you have finished coloring the picture on the first glass, pour Glycerine over it, being careful to cover the surface thoroughly. Drain off and then put the other convex glass to the back of the one having the print, and wedge apart from it by attaching little pieces of card-board to the second glass with mucilage.

Have the wedges very narrow and close to the edge. This separates the glasses and keeps the upper one from pressing the oiled and painted glass below. On this second glass you will color the face and other flesh, hair, drapery, and, if necessary, the background. The miniature is finished by using card-board to back up the picture, white being very effective.

Bind the edges of the glass and card-board together with strips of adhesive paper.

CAUTION! Don't use Silver Gloss Starch; it will not do nearly as well as Corn Starch.

Directions for Coloring.

The coloring of the eyes, lips, jewelry, ribbons, edges of embroidery, lace, neck-tie, flowers, and other ornaments, is applied directly on the photograph after it is mounted on the glass and made translucent with the oil.

EYES—Use small brush. BLUE EYES—Use Prussian Blue mixed with little Ivory Black. BROWN EYES—Use Vandyke Brown. GREY OR HAZEL EYES—Prussian Blue mixed with Vandyke Brown and Silver White.

LIPS—Use Rose Madder.

JEWELRY—Yellow Ochre for Gold, Silver White for Pearls, Emerald Green for Emeralds, Rose Madder for Rubies.

RIBBONS—Whatever color is required. Flowers and other ornaments the same.

The color for Flesh, Hair, Drapery and Background is applied to the concave surface of the clear glass which is placed over the mounted print.

FLESH—Use Vermilion, Silver White and Chrome Yellow; mix to suit. For children use Rose Madder or Carmine in place of Vermilion. For dark complexions dull the color by adding Vandyke Brown.

HAIR—For blonde hair, use half Naples Yellow and Vandyke Brown. For lights, use Naples Yellow. Brown Hair, Vandyke Brown. Black Hair, Ivory Black and Silver White, adding a little Prussian Blue. For Grey Hair, use Silver White, Naples Yellow, Black, Burnt Sienna, and a little Prussian Blue.

DRAPERY—Whatever color suits.

BACKGROUND—Your own judgment will suggest the proper color to use.

If you want to change the work in any way, take a small piece of cloth, dipped in turpentine, and remove the color.

For home work and adornment it offers special attractions. The photographs of relatives and friends can be made into

Oil-Photo Miniatures, done by your own hands, and handsomely furnished for the mantel and wall at small expense.

We have given you the *simplest* and *best* process for making the picture. It is claimed by some that when the oil is used it dries out after a time, and produces opaque spots. Should this trouble appear, it is easily overcome by using glycerine as previously directed. We herewith give you another method in use, and you can adopt whichever you see fit.

SECOND METHOD.

IVORY-TYPE OR MEZZOTINT.

For Mounting the Photograph.—Isin-glass (fish glue) made in the following proportion: One teaspoonful to half cup of water, dissolved by boiling; strain through fine muslin, and apply the same as starch. Pure Albumen, or white of egg, brushed over the glass and surface of the photograph, is used with great success by some. Equal parts Canada balsam and turpentine is also used for attaching the print to the glass. Rubber varnish, made with pure rubber, dissolved in benzole. Some add a little Cooper's glue to the starch when making it. Dextrine is a favorite with many.

After the use of the castor oil, castor oil and glycerine, poppy oil, nut, or any of the oils, the print may be covered with a coating of Damar varnish, which it is claimed holds the oil and preserves the transparency. Many artists after oiling or varnishing, use water colors mixed with ox-gall in coloring on the back of the print, then follow with the oil colors as directed. In adopting any of the methods herein noted, your judgment will dictate care in observing the results, and suggesting changes that may facilitate the work, and success of the picture. You will find this art very attractive, simple, and productive of both pleasure and profit. Ladies are occupying leisure hours, and making home attractive with their artistic work in producing the Miniature.

By the first process pictures have stood for years without spotting or cracking.

ANOTHER PLAN IS: After cleaning the photograph, blot off the surplus water and place it in alcohol, let it remain until transparent. Old, faded pictures can be brought out clear in this way. After placing it on glass, cover the print with "paraffine," and let it lie for a short time in the sun, until crystalized, when it is ready to receive the colors. You may use water colors on the first glass with good effect.

" By this simple process any person unaccustomed to painting, and ignorant of art, may color photographs, and produce with rapidity and little trouble, effective, permanent, and beautiful pictures, so soft and delicate as to closely resemble painting on enamel; may render the treasured family portrait doubly valuable by adding the warm tints of life to the faithful but cold and deathlike production of the photographer, and produce a pleasing as well as a truthful representation. The largest and the smallest work may be painted with equal facility, the life-size portrait or a miniature for a locket, the only qualification for success, even in very elaborate pictures, being taste in the arrangement of the colors. An objection to coloring photographs, as coloring has hitherto been practiced—that the delicate truthfulness of nature's drawing was injured, and sometimes a likeness wholly destroyed, through being obscured by the colorist in the working, that the only guarantee of fidelity was the talent of the artist—in the beautifully simple process under consideration with which all the softness, lights, and shadows of the photographs are preserved."

THE ART OF

COLORING PHOTOGRAPHS

IN WATER COLORS.

ELECT a well-defined **Photograph**, one of light color is preferable, and the background free from spots; it is also well **to have** a duplicate copy to refer **to** in case **of necessity—a** copy of two different sittings. **Always** select a good subject, as a good portrait depends much on a good model. In sitting for **a** photograph, take your own natural and easy position **several** feet in front **of the** background, **with your** eyes a trifle **above the** camera. Avoid all superfluous surroundings. such as fancy chairs, **table covered** with books and other objects, making **your face a** secondary affair in the picture.

Preparing the **Photograph.** Take **a** piece of White Glue about the size of a hickory nut, and about one-half the quantity of pulverized alum; dissolve in half a wine-glass of warm water and it is ready for use. Apply **the mixture with a** flat camel-hair brush to the photograph; cover the entire face of the picture, care being taken not to get it too wet. When dry, wash it in clean cold water with a sponge to remove any superfluous matter that may rest upon it. It may be necessary to go over it a second time, as it is essential that the paper be well hardened to work upon. You may test it by applying a drop of the color to one corner and if it washes off and leaves no stain the paper is in good condition for the work. Albumen paper can often be worked without using this preparation, but should be sponged off with cold water.

The colors used are in cakes: Dry Carmine, Rose Madder, Crimson Lake, Venetian Red, Indian Red, Vermilion, Chrome Yellow, Indian Yellow, Roman Ochre, Gamboge, Cobalt, French Blue, Emerald Green, Indigo, Prussian Blue, Burnt Sienna, Burnt Umber, Sepia (Brown), Vandyke Brown, Madder Brown, Ivory Black, Chinese White, Constant White.

Burnt Umber, mostly used for the hair; Vandyke Brown is one of the most used of browns, although Sepia may be said to be the *most* useful in black silk and satin, when mixed with Lake, Indigo and Gamboge; Sepia and Lake for the eyebrows and hair; Sepia and Indigo form a gray, very nice for background. Of Red, Carmine is the most brilliant; Rose Madder the most useful in flesh, especially in youths; in older persons add Vermilion; Crimson Lake is very useful for flesh tints; Light Red, Venetian and Indian Red can be used for nearly the same purpose.

Coloring. Commence upon the face with the flesh tints, using for this a good size Sable brush; go over the entire face and wait till dry. Use for the lips a little Vermilion and Lake. Now go over the background, and then the draperies. Deepen the Carnations, touching the eye and mouth with Lake; also the hair with the proper color. Touch the under lip with Rose Madder enough so as it may look natural. The white of the eye in youth is nearly blue, in old age it becomes yellow, in middle age it is white. You must vary your tints to correspond.

The iris must be laid in with transparent color, then shaded, then finished with Chinese White. The pupil is touched with a dark color and the speck of white laid on last. Use the same color for black or brown as used for the hair, viz.: Light Red

and Chinese White, and neutral or Purple tint and White for
the latter. The face is now nearly finished; it only remains to
add a few touches to the eyes and mouth, and impart life and
expression to the countenance. If the person be dark, use Sepia and Purple Lake, equal proportions; but if fair, dispense
with most of the Sepia. Next complete the background, after
which finish up the hair over the background; after the last
shaded parts of the hair lay on the high lights. Burnt Umber
is most useful in brown and auburn hair; Indigo, Sepia and Lake,
or Lake, Indigo and Gamboge, are the colors used for high
lights, the lights inclining to a purple tint, the blue predominating. Keep the hair in masses; a good sized brush
is needed. In painting cloth fabrics it will be well to use
the local color at first very light, much more so than you
desire it to be when finished. A black coat: begin by laying in
a weak local wash as directed, and when it is dry go over the
folds with a thin shadow color, which will prevent them being
obscured by the next local wash. Having repeated this two or
three times, you will find the garment to be as dark as necessary,
but the shadows will be feeble; you may strengthen them with
Sepia and Lake. A good black for gentlemen's drapery is made
of Indigo, Lake and Gamboge. When a blue-black is required,
first make a purple-blue and then add the Gamboge till the tint
is changed into black. In shadowing, always carry your pencil
the way the folds run, instead of across them. The colors for
backgrounds for fair people are blue, purple and greys. Dark
complexions should have dark background. Stone is represented
by a tint formed of Carmine, Indigo and Yellow Ochre, and the
more distant you wish it to appear the more must the Indigo
prevail. A background made of Cobalt, Burnt Sienna and a
little Rose Madder works well. Madder Brown and Cobalt answers for the same. A purple cloudy ground is made of Indigo
and liquid Carmine or Lake. An opaque ground, of a choco-
late color, is composed of Lampblack and India Red.

Paint curtains over the background and put on the lights with
body colors.

RUSSIAN,

OR

EGYPTIAN METHOD

OF COLORING PHOTOGRAPHS

WITH TRANSPARENT INDELIBLE COLORS.

THIS is the "biggest little thing" in painting that probably has ever been presented to amateur artists. For beauty of arrangement, ease and simplicity in its execution, no branch of art work of a similar nature has ever met with like success. With a fair idea of colors and their application, you may increase the beauty and enhance the value ten fold of any ordinary photograph, by following these instructions. To produce a first-class picture, you must necessarily have a good subject to work on. A photograph that will take a variety of colors, is best adapted for a showy picture.

Before applying the colors to a burnished or finished photograph, soften or cleanse the surface with the tongue until the saliva wets the picture evenly, without crawling; oxide gall is good, but saliva is the best for this purpose.

For a palette on which to mix or dilute colors, the bottom of a plate or saucer will answer. Always have a piece of blotting paper at hand to take up or remove superfluous paint from the picture, and use it after each application of color to the photograph.

It is not necessary to mix paints on a palette, washing one color over another will produce better results. A tint is a color absorbed in the picture, and washing or wetting will not remove it. A surface color remains on top, and water will remove it. You can use colors stronger over the shadows. Use just what liquid

you will find on the cork of the bottle, added to about one teaspoonful of water, for flesh; for draperies you can use it stronger,
or as you desire.

The liquid colors are mostly used, and consist of twelve one
ounce bottles, and are very powerful. Therefore, make your application very weak, a mere tint only is required. Repeat the
washing or tinting until the desired shade is produced. The
colors used are as follows: Black, Red, Blue, Green, Carmine, Gold, Brown, Violet, Orange, Purple and Lemon, all of
which are transparent, soluble in water, and used as tinting colors. White is a surface color, and opaque.

For Flesh—Use first a weak wash or tint of gold; over this a
tint of red, a little stronger for the lips.

White—This is always used last for high lights; you can make
the white any tint by use of other colors.

Black—Can be used for a natural tint if toned down; valuable for all kinds of shading.

Red—Takes readily, and produces all tints from rose to scarlet;
used in flesh.

Carmine—A delicate pink to magenta.

Gold—Takes readily; is a substitute for yellow; used for jewelry,
flesh, blonde hair, etc.; use weak, and wash over with red for
deeper results.

Brown—Takes readily; darkened by tinting over with violet or
black.

Violet—Takes on touch, and is very powerful; first application
very weak to insure even coloring; it makes all tints from lilac
to purple, etc.

Blue—Takes slowly; repeat the washing for deep results.

Green—Takes easily, lighten by washing over with gold; darken
with the blue; always let your first wash or tint be very weak;
increase as desired by repeating.

The colors in moist cake form are often used, but the liquids
are preferable. Sable brushes, about Nos. 3, 8 and 12, are sufficient for ordinary purposes.

HOW TO MAKE PHOTOGRAPHS

BY THE

GELATINE DRY-PLATE PROCESS

THE latest and most rapid advance in the art is due to the discovery of the sensitiveness of a gelatine film. This knowledge has been practically applied in the introduction of plates prepared with such a coating; they are called "dry plates," to distinguish them from plates which must pass through the silver bath, and be used while wet. The gelatine-bromide dry plates are now in general use for taking pictures of out-door scenes, landscapes, houses, groups of people, etc. To make photographs,

First Procure an Outfit from a dealer in photograph requisites, costing from ten to twenty-five dollars, consisting of a view camera, for making 4x5 or 5x8 inch pictures. This camera is so constructed as to make either a picture on the full size of the plate (5x8 inches), or by substituting the extra front (supplied with the outfit), and using the pair of lenses of shorter focus, it is admirably adapted for taking stereoscopic negatives. Also, by the same arrangements, two small pictures, of dissimilar objects, can be made on the same plate. Included in the outfit, are also one patent double dry-plate holder, one large achromatic nickel plated lens, one pair "Waterbury" achromatic matched stereoscopic lens, one Taylor folding tripod, one carrying case.

Filling the Plate Holder. If this is done in the daytime, a closet or room is selected, and all white light excluded from it.

It is difficult to make this **exclusion absolute. One ray of white light** will spoil a sensitive plate, and therefore **the evening is generally** chosen **to** develop negatives, and **for illumination, the light** from a ruby lantern is employed.

Gelatine Plates are glass, with **one** side coated with gelatine, containing a haloid salt. Place one of them in a dry-plate holder, with the sensitive (or the coated) side facing outward. Handle the plates by the edge, between **the** thumb and fore finger, without touching the sides. **After** putting into the holders **as** many plates **as are** needed for the day's work, pack the outfit so that it can be carried about.

Taking the Picture. For field service a camera, a **number of** plate holders, filled **with** sensitive plates, a lens, tripod, carrying case, and focussing cloth are needed. When **these** have been taken to the place which **you want** to photograph, fasten the camera on the tripod, **throw the focussing cloth** over your head, gather it **under your chin, draw** out the back of the camera, thus extending **the** bellows, and continue the movement until the image on **the ground** glass appears distinct, then fasten the back of the **camera.** This is called "focussing." At the first glance, an inexperienced person **sees no reflection** on the ground glass, but the eye **soon becomes practiced** to perceiving the inverted image there. Substitute a plate **holder** for the ground glass, see that the cap is **on the** lens, pull **the** slide out of **the** holder, place it on the top of the camera, **or** in a convenient place. If everything **is now** in readiness, and the time for exposing the sensitive plate determined, uncap the lens, **re-capping** it at the end of the allotted time, and replacing the slide in the holder. After you have picture impressions on each sensitive film, pack **your** outfit and return home.

Making Negatives. Amateurs may content themselves with making the exposures, **and sending their plates** in a light, tight, negative box, **to some** photographer, **who** will produce the finished picture, and mount them on cards. It is not **necessary that this**

should be done at once, months may elapse, and these dry plates be carried hundreds of miles.

The chemical outfit for making negatives comprises the following items: Two vulcanite trays, a glass graduate, a set of small scales, and weights for weighing chemicals, a ruby lantern, a bottle of varnish, a package of dry plates and of chemicals, a small quantity of bromide of ammonium, neutral oxalate of potash, protosulphate of iron, hyposulphite of soda, alum, and sulphuric acid. These chemicals are not dangerous, neither will they injure any one who handles them, and they do not emit offensive odors. Silver stains, and the disagreeable smell of collodion belong to the old or "wet" process.

At a convenient time take the plate holder into the dark room, illuminate it with ruby light, take the sensitive plates out of the holders, being careful not to touch their surfaces. Hold them by the edge. Place one of the sensitive plates, film side up, in a tray partly filled with water. While it remains there, mix this solution: Neutral oxalate of potash, 5 ounces; bromide of potassium, 20 grains; water. 20 ounces. If the solution does not turn blue litmus paper red, add a few drops of oxalic acid, enough to make it do so. A graduated glass is used to measure out the liquids. After rinsing the glass out, mix a second solution made as follows: Protosulphate of iron, 5 ounces; water, 20 ounces; and acidulate it with 20 drops of sulphuric acid. Both of these solutions keep well. Now combine a quarter of an ounce of the latter solution with two ounces of the former and mix them well. Pour off the water in the tray containing the gelatine plates. Be certain not to touch the sensitive side of the plate. Flow the combined developing solution over the plate and displace, by a touch of your finger, any air bubbles that may form. After a short time traces of the image on the sensitive film will appear. If they do not, pour the developing solution back into the tray and add a quarter of an ounce more of the iron solution. Pour the strengthened solution over the plate and look at it intently. In a short time the details of the picture may be dimly seen. Wait patiently till the milky white appearance is changed to a grey color, and then pour off the developer into a developing bottle, if you have one. Wash the plate in two changes of water. In the unused tray mix a solution composed of 4 ounces of hyposulphite of soda and 20 ounces of water. (Label this tray "Hypo.," and do not use it for any other purpose.) · A plate lifter is a convenient device for taking plates out of the solutions or baths. Change the plate to the hypo. tray, and let it remain there until every vestige of the milky white appearance has vanished, even from the under surface of the plate. The plate can now be examined by white light, which has no effect upon it at this stage. Wash it thoroughly. A negative washing box will be found to be of great assistance. If this washing of the plate is not done thoroughly, the hyposulphite of soda crystals will adhere to the plate and mar the picture. Meanwhile rinse out the tray first in use and partially fill it with a solution consisting of 20 ounces of water and all the alum it will hold in solution. Allow the plate to remain in the alum bath five minutes. Cleanse your hands from any adhering soda solution. Again wash the plate, and set it on edge to dry in a negative rack.

All the preceding instructions can be briefly summarized.

1. Put some sensitive plates into dry plate holders.

2. Make the exposure.

3. After taking a plate out of the holder, place it in a tray filled with water.

4. Drain off the water and put the plate in the mixed developing solution.

5. Wash the plate and place it in the soda solution.

6. Wash the plate and give it an alum bath.

7. Wash the plate and set it in the rack to dry. When perfectly dry, coat the plate over with negative varnish, and have that coating dry and hard. Now it may be touched by the fingers.

Making Prints from Negatives. At this point the work ceases to be one of faith, as the results are now to appear. An outfit of printing requisites comprises a printing frame, a porcelain pan, a vulcanite tray, some ready sensitized paper, a bottle of French azotate, a bottle of chloride of gold, a glass graduate, some hyposulphite of soda, a glass form, a Robinson trimmer, some sheets of fine card-board, a jar of parlor paste, and a bristle brush.

Sensitized Paper Prints. In the morning prepare a toning bath sufficient for the prints to be toned that day. Put 7½ grains of chloride of gold into 7½ ounces of water. Label the bottle "Chloride of Gold Solution." Take 1 ounce of French azotate, 1½ ounces of the chloride of gold solution, and add 6 ounces of water, and you have a toning bath which keeps well. Where the prints do not give the required tone, the bath must be strengthened by adding to it some new solution. Place the glossy side of a sheet of sensitized paper upon the film side of the negative in the printing frame. *Do this in a very dim light.*

The printing has gone far enough when the print looks a little darker than you wish the finished picture to appear. Make as many prints from the negative as you desire. Wash the prints in several changes of water. Take seven ounces of the toning solution and change the prints to the pan containing it, where the prints should be turned over and over to make the toning even. The toning process should go on until the dark part of the pictures have a very faint purplish tint and the white portion is clear. Wash the picture, but preserve the toning solution. The pictures should now be left for twenty minutes in a solution composed of 4 ounces of hyposulphite of soda, 1 ounce of common salt, ½ ounce of washing soda, and 32 ounces of water. This solution should also be prepared a day or two in advance. Give the pictures a final and effectual washing. After they are dried, lay them out one by one and, using the Robinson trimmer, cut them to the desired size. Now spread over the back of each in turn some parlor paste, and lay them down with the center on the sheets of card-board. This operation is called "Mounting Pictures." Press with a paper cutter upon the pictures and toward their edges until you are satisfied that they will lay flat.

DRAUGHTSMEN'S SENSITIVE PAPER,

FOR COPYING DRAWINGS.

PROCURE a printing frame, such as photographers use; lay the tracing, **face** down, upon the glass, upon which place the sensitive paper, prepared side down, then several thicknesses of cotton flannel for a pad to equalize the pressure, and cause the sensitive paper and tracing to lay in close contact, and then close in the back. If, on turning the frame over, any wrinkles appear, that side of the hinged back may be opened and a piece of paper laid in just above the spot, when all will come smooth on closing the frame, (this should be done in a dimly lighted room), then expose to direct sunlight, care being taken that the whole frame comes under the light, without shadows; let the exposure be from five to ten minutes, according to the brightness of the day. Remove again to darkened room, examine by opening one of the hinged backs; if the lines have slightly turned in color, it has been highly exposed; it can be removed and washed in clear water, with two or three changes, then hang up to dry. You will have an exact copy of the original, with white lines on a blue ground, at a cost of about one tenth that of tracing, with absolutely no error. The paper must be kept in perfect darkness until used.

THE NEW

WOOD PAINTING.

TRANSLATED FROM THE GERMAN.

THE term wood painting has, through the numerous designs invented for the purpose, found such a widespread use that it would be wasted pains to attempt to substitute a more fitting one. Not everything that is painted upon wood, falls under the knowledge of wood painting. No one would think of counting an oil painting, executed upon wood, under the category of wood painting. But if the colors were the distinguishing sign, then wood and water color painting would fall together, or wood painting could be only an aquarelle painting applied upon wood. Wood painting permits itself to be thus defined, inasmuch as the character of the material and the choice of its objects differ, so *wood water-color painting* differs from the actual water color. While it is possible for the water-color artist to produce upon paper the softest tones and most brilliant phenomena of nature, so that the painting inspires the observer through its life-like freshness; if the same picture, by the same artist's hand, were reproduced in exactly the same manner upon wood, it would appear raw and unfinished,—yes, even wholly incorrect.

The prepared wood takes the softest tint, as well as paper, but the texture of the wood shimmers through the transparent tones, and though the fibres and pores of the same have taken another hue, they still act as wood, and thereby destroy the effect which the artist intended. For it is originally the task of the artist to thus deceive the human sense of vision in such a manner, and so faithfully imitate the appearance of things in nature that the observer must believe himself transported in the midst of reality and actual life, through the activity of fancy; in short, the artist must reproduce true to nature, and his pictures have the effect of nature.

If one was to try with exclusive body colors which do not allow the grain of the wood to penetrate, to attain this ideal of painting, and attempt to create upon wood an actual life-like picture, we would not conceive such an aquarelle, that never can compare with a picture upon paper in softness, just as little as an oil painting upon wood, as wood painting in the general sense.

Therefore, neither the material to be painted nor the colors applied are the criterion of distinguishing reasons for wood painting on one hand, and the oil or nearer related aquarelle painting on the other.

The difference in a measure lies herein, that the characteristic peculiarity of wood does not subdue, but is drawn upon for the effect of the painting, partly in the nature of that which painting upon wood represents or should represent.

Wood painting, as far as we have touched upon it, cannot and does not intend to create natural pictures; it only serves to ornament objects in wood, which through colored and tasteful designs are to produce an agreeable charm to the eye. It is not an object in itself, like a painting, the frame of which serves as a folio, but an external addition, like the ornaments of buildings, to make an otherwise monotonous surface interesting.

Wooden articles admit of being ornamented in various ways,

through sculpture work, by inlaying of colored woods and metal, and by painting.

The choice of ornamenting is naturally dependent upon the purpose the object to be decorated is intended for ; a table, which must naturally have a smooth surface, we would not think of making useless by carving the top.

Wood painting, as it is now *en vogue*, is of a recent date, and originally sprang out of the idea to imitate the mosaic work of art cabinet-makers.

It may, with consideration for the purpose of the objects to be ornamented, also imitate carving, but must not go beyond the wood tones and the production of the effects of light; it may even attempt to imitate enamel work by the application of strong, bright colors; but it ought at the same time be in keeping with the purpose the object in hand is intended for, and never involve itself in contradictions.

Its refined field should always remain the imitative, and should therefore confine itself as near as possible upon the application of ornaments with a surface where effect is flat, and consequently do not mar the surface. To apply figures, modest, decorative additions for the ornamentation of surfaces, is allowable, as long as they do not clash with the character of the surface ; but here the limits that are drawn by the nature of the article are not to be overstepped. For every perspective representation of a figure painted with the application of light and shade intends to deceive the observer; it lifts itself off the surface and no longer works upon our fancy as a part of the surface, but as body. Cases, chests and other large pieces may be decorated in this manner; tables, portfolios and similar pieces which in themselves are required to have smooth surfaces; smaller objects to be handled, where the sense of touch can at every moment convince itself of the attempted deception intended for the eye, one will do well to take heed in not painting these with figures of a plastic effect. Such contradictions are not to be tolerated in principle and should be avoided in the selection of patterns and designs.

To create a real picture in the beginning lies outside the province of the art of wood painting, and therefore the practice of the same, as far as it does not reach into the professional art, must always be confined within the circle of amateurs. Good, correct drawings of the outlines, cleanliness in coloring and a proper combination of the colors, is the highest aim the art of painting upon wood may achieve; for the artist is greatly answerable for the composition of ornaments, where designs are used as patterns.

But even in the narrow limits in which the art of painting upon wood moves, it accomplishes much that is beautiful, that the acquirement of the same cannot be too strongly recommended.

This is especially intended for young ladies, who, in the occupation of painting upon wood, find just as agreeable and remunerative diversion as the tedious, sense-dulling work of embroidery.

General Preliminaries. The first essential requirement to paint upon wood is, without a doubt, practice in drawing.

One is easily inclined, inasmuch as there is no self-inventive gift employed in connection with it, to consider painting on wood as a purely mechanical work, because the design is traced and transferred upon wood, by means of tracing paper; yet there remains, up to this easy beginning, the further embellishment entirely to the free hand, and it is just here that difficulties meet the painter unskilled in the art of drawing.

The difficult point in wood painting lies in the conscientious, artistic execution; the more pains taken in that direction, the stronger the lines of beauty and harmony in coloring, the more certain it is to obtain something excellent in this work.

The simplest design, when correctly and cleanly painted, has a more agreeable effect upon the observer than the most beautiful pattern that has been faultily produced through a series of shortcomings.

Requisites. The possession of a good and complete set of

instruments, in a measure, assists in the success of the work.
The following utensils are used in wood painting: Lead Pencils, (Faber's B, HB, HH), a pen knife, a lead pencil file, an
eraser, a horn protractor upon which to rest the compass upon
round articles, a ruler, a square, a porcelain palette with six cells,
several good fine and coarse water-color brushes on handles with
metal ferrules, several sheets of extra fine tracing paper or cloth ;
the latter is more expensive than the paper, but far more durable,
in such cases where the drawing is gone over again. For the
drawing of fine outlines, pens (Gillott's crowquill pens are best) ;
for heavier outlines or large designs goosequills are best. It is
desirable to possess a complete outfit of drawing materials, of
which the following are indispensable : A drawing pen, a compass with pen and pencil pieces.

The Colors. It is advisable to use only the genuine India
ink, as the ordinary India ink nearly always discolors the soft
tints that are painted over it, which sometimes spoils the entire
work. The ordinary water-colors, not the covering or Gouache
colors are to be used. The prepared wood just as readily takes
the Gouache and covering colors, as a large number of designs of
natural flowers show, yet this method should not be indulged in,
for this reason, because it completely covers the texture of the
wood, thereby giving the art critic an opportunity to censure.

Since wood painting is mostly an imitation of inlaid wood
work—mosaic—as a rule the preference should be given to the
application of the fitting colors to the stained wood tones. Who
does not possess a complete outfit of colors, ought at least secure
the following : sepia, dark sepia, burnt sienna, light ochre, dark
vermilion, carmine, cobalt blue, Indian red, olive green, Roman
brown, lampblack and white.

The best colors are the Dusseldorf (Schonfeld or Winsor &
Newton's) moist water-colors, in metal tubes or porcelain pans.
Gold and silver is generally painted from shells, this is to be used
sparingly, and is polished when the work is finished with a steel

instrument, a knitting-needle, glove buttoner, or an agate burn-isher. Red gold has a dark effect, retreating; green gold, on the other hand, stands out and has a light appearance. Black-lead is to be had in lumps, and is most effective for bright or red ornamentations. Bronze powder is prepared with a little gum water. The possession of a magnifying glass is of importance in going over the work when finished, and subjecting the same to a severe scrutiny. It also greatly assists in the correction of faults that may have crept in.

Transferring the Drawing upon Wood. A design should be chosen that corresponds with the size and shape of the wood article. A design is seldom spoiled by extending the outer lines, yet we should be cautioned against the reverse case, in trying to force a large design upon a small space by omitting the outer lines that serve as a frame.

Enlarging and Reducing Designs. If a design is to be brought within the compass of another, reduced or enlarged, take a proportional divider, or draw a net of equal squares, the original or a drawing of the same with a lead pencil, in proportion required for the wood surface, which are numbered. In each square ex-actly the same parts are drawn from the design which are con-tained in the corresponding square on the wood.

The Divisions of the Wood Surface. At the beginning of the work, the surface to be painted is divided by distinct pen-cil lines into halves, quarters, sixths, etc., just as the design admits of; these lines serve as a starting point for the traced design to be placed upon this, where halves, quarters, etc., must fit exactly into these. The measuring is done by means of a compass or a strip of paper the length of the object, which gives the center point by cutting the same in two. In painting round articles, such as lamp plates, table tops, etc., a sheet of paper of the exact size is cut out. This is folded once, in halves and quar-ters, as the case may be. It is spread upon the surface of the article, then prick through the creases where they cross each other. To avoid injury to the center of a round wooden plate by the repeated application of a compass, a horn protractor is fastened to the center with thumb tacks, which leaves the center transparent, upon which the compass may be. applied with considerable pressure. In the absence of a compass with an extension where large circles are required, a strip of pasteboard is substituted; this is fastened to the center by a needle. For every cross line a hole is made into the strip, the pencil is inserted and drawn around by moving the strip in a circular motion.

The Tracing and Transferring of Designs. The design is carefully drawn upon tracing paper or tracing cloth, by means of a medium soft pencil; the more perfect the drawing is made, the more it will lighten the work. If the drawing obtained is perfectly symmetrical, i. e., the right half of the same exactly like the left, it will save much time and labor by transferring it upon the surface by rubbing. If the symmetrical design is accompanied in the center by a monogram, motto, figures or flowers, these are for the present omitted and traced in a manner which will be explained further on.

The tracing of an entirely symmetrical design is reversed, with the drawing turned downward upon the wood and carefully observed that the center of the tracing lies completely in correspondence with the center line of the division line of the surface. The tracing paper is fastened with wax, and held as firmly with the left hand as possible, that it cannot be displaced, and rubbed with a paper folder or the thumb-nail of the right hand over all parts of the design, until the same is plainly transferred upon the wood. For figures, flowers, monograms and all not strictly symmetrical designs, the following manner is applied: The tracing paper is laid upon the surface, design upward, under which a piece of colored transfer paper is placed and the design is retraced with a hard lead pencil. For this somewhat slower and more tedious manner it is advisable to fasten the tracing and transfer paper with thumb-tacks. Those parts of the surface are selected for the thumb-tacks that are afterwards to be painted with black or other ground colors, so that there will be no visible traces left after design has been transferred.

Fixing the Transferred Design. After the design has been transferred, all the straight and intersecting lines are carefully measured and compared with the compass from the center or the dividing middle lines; then with the drawing pen and India ink the entire design is gone over in fine lines. In figures and light ornamental designs, that come upon a dark ground, the India ink line is not put over, but closely to the outside pencil mark, or such figures will become too faint in the beginning, and are lost in the dark ground, whilst it can always be remedied by the subsequent removal of parts that have been drawn too heavily. The entire article is now cleaned from all pencil marks left by tracing, and the coloring begins.

The Coloring. Spread upon the palette, before beginning to paint, all the different colors, in sufficient quantity, that are to be used. A good rule in coloring the design, is not to apply the colors in too dry a state, so that the separate brush strokes may not be visible. The coloring is just that part of the work which cannot be explicitly enough described and taught in written instructions, and can only be thoroughly comprehended through the practical knowledge gained by experience, and thereby perfected.

Upon the most delicate tinting of entire surfaces the middle tones follow, lastly the dark ground colors, black, and the metals. Allow each color to dry thoroughly before beginning with the next, or going over it. The colors must stand out boldly from each other and should not be too lightly applied; this must be particularly observed in the dark body tints, as the colors lose a little of their depth in the process of polishing.

When the work is completed, the entire drawing is gone over

again with a fine brush or pen; all the outlines lost in painting are reproduced with India ink.

Clear white upon light wood is to be avoided as much as possible; on the other hand, a mixture of white serves to make the light colors stand out more effectively upon gray or black wood.

Retouching. If there are any weak points in the painting, the spots are to be carefully removed with a damp sponge, and the dampened parts scraped clean with a penknife. If visible holes are left by the thumb tacks used in the tracing of the design, a small drop of clear water is applied to them, when they will gradually draw together. Paint in good light, have a steady table, and keep the design constantly before the eyes during the work.

In painting boxes and other high objects, it is necessary to place on the right and left of the same some other objects, such as books, to reach the plane of the surface being painted, in order that the hand and arm may rest with ease.

The Wood Articles. Wooden articles ready for painting are procured from the cabinet makers, or at the art stores.

There are over 900 different articles in wood for decorating, in all shapes and sizes, beautifully and tastily finished, for the artist and amateur to paint upon. A few of them may be mentioned here—tables, panels, workboxes, paper weights, fancy boxes, fans, hat brushes, glove boxes, albums, dust pans and brushes, photo frames, easels, trays and newspaper holders. What canvas is to oil painting, and paper is to color painting, the above articles are to the art of painting upon wood.

Not every ordinary smooth-planed piece of wood is adapted to painting. The wood must be prepared for the purpose it is intended for, or it would cause the color to flow or spread. Lime, maple, chestnut, ash and holly are the woods generally manufactured into articles intended for painting upon. Olive wood is also excellent for this purpose. In the south of France and

Italy, painted olive wood, forms quite an article of commerce, being closely allied with the inlaid work.

Polishing. Procure a bottle of the wood varnish (prepared for this purpose); in a warm room, with a soft flat brush, go over the article as rapidly as possible, with a thin coat. Leave this first coating until the next day to dry, in a place entirely free from dust. The varnish is applied twice more in the same manner; then have at hand a small bottle of white shellac polish and one of linseed oil. Make a small ball of flannel; put upon this a few drops of the oil; then cover it with a piece of linen, which is moistened with the polish, and the article is rubbed in a circular manner, without resting upon the article when the rubbing is discontinued. If the linen should adhere during the polishing, put a drop of the oil upon it. It sometimes requires from one to two hours of constant rubbing until the surface is completely smooth and polished.

Designs recommended are those by Minna Laudin, Hermann Schaper, E. Wendt, Emil Zschimmer and Elizabeth Hubler. They are lithographic color plates, and come in the form of sets.

Minna Laudin's designs are among the newest. The two sets contain over twenty patterns, each fitting exactly in size and shape the wooden articles already mentioned.

Schaper's designs are intended for larger pieces, such as table tops, music holders, lamp trays, etc. His first series (entirely new) is divided into five sheets, with as many sheets upon which the outlines of the designs are clearly printed, to facilitate the transferring of the same upon wood.

E. Wendt's designs are both unique and rich in their way, and contain considerable ornamental work in gold and silver. His designs for table tops are extremely handsome.

Emil Zschimmer's and Elizabeth Hubler's are acknowledged as standard works, and favorites of the artists engaged in painting upon wood.

⟶ TRANSPARENCIES. ⟵

HESE transparencies, or window pictures, are of late very much used and admired, and are purchased by those who have no knowledge of how they are made, at exhorbitant prices. They are made upon glass, perfectly transparent, and require a good light to see them. The way these pictures are produced is simple, and the process easy to learn. In it lies the secret, or fundamental principles, of all glass pictures.

Instructions. Procure a fine, clear, French plate glass, size required, to receive the picture, and make it perfectly clean with alcohol. Select the picture you may desire from the list of fine steel engravings contained in magazines, etc. Go over the face with a damp sponge, in order to remove the dust or spots that may have accumulated upon it, and smoothing it out. Apply to the face of the print, with a brush, a paste made from amylum, a teaspoonful, and nitrate strontium, $\frac{1}{8}$ ounce --sometimes albumen is used. Now go over the glass in the same way, evenly and smoothly. When this is done, lay the picture, face down, upon the glass, and press with dry cloth until every part of the picture has adhered to the glass, and all the air bubbles pressed out. Lay away the glass for a few hours, until perfectly dry, when you wet the paper and commence rubbing it off; if it works well without any further wetting, continue the process until every vestige of paper has been removed, and nothing left upon the glass but the outlines of your engraving. Oil it now with castor oil three parts, oil of lavender one: if too thick, add turpentine. It is now complete, and by holding it to the light it will present a beautiful, steel-like engraving transparency.

You can add a border if you like, by pasting around the margin a tinted paper; or to give them still a better finish, back them up with a pane of ornamental ground glass, and place in a transparency metal frame, with rings to hang them by, which can be found at any art store.

THE

Crystal, or Oriental Painting.

INSTRUCTION.

Ay the glass over the pattern or copy you wish to paint from, such as flowers, birds, wreaths, etc., then with a fine pencil brush, or a common writing pen, trace all the outlines of your pattern as well as possible on the glass, using for that purpose black paint made from lampblack and copal varnish; if too thick, add a little turpentine. When this is done, paint all the glass outside the picture, or that part not occupied by your drawing, with the black paint, same as used in making the outlines, only a trifle thicker. This will give your picture a neat background; other colors can be used, but this gives the best body, and is the most appropriate, contrasting well with the other colors to be used in the picture.

Let it lay until well dried, so the black will not unite with the colors you are about to use. Now, with the glass still remaining over the copy, you may commence applying the paints, if the tracing lines are dry. If you are painting a red rose, use carmine and flake white, Prussian blue, and chrome yellow for the leaf, etc., using a small camel-hair brush. Continue in this way until you have used all the colors which appear in your copy or picture underneath, which remains there to guide you, and the pen lines upon the glass to separate the colors. When the first color is perfectly dry, apply the second, and so on until you have completed all the work which the copy demands, using your own judgment in the matter, applying them as they appear in the picture you are working from.

When the painting is done and dry, cover the back of the transparency with *copper or tin-foil* crinkled, which gives it a sparkling, crystal-like appearance. It is now ready for framing. In placing it in the frame, be careful and not press the back-board too close on to the foil, or it will destroy the brilliant effect in the picture.

The colors used in this kind of painting must be *transparent* oil colors, with the exception of the background.

For white, use ground silver or flake white; for blue, Prussian blue; for pink, mix scarlet lake and silver white; orange, mix chrome yellow and scarlet lake; for red, use scarlet lake, crimson lake, or carmine; for green, mix Prussian blue and yellow lake; for purple, mix red and blue. Use the best tube paints and camel-hair brushes.

No style of painting has yet been produced which shows transparent colors to such advantage, and never fails to attract attention and admirers wherever introduced.

It is called Oriental from the fact of its producing effects of coloring equal to the colors of Oriental flowers, and the plumage of Oriental birds.

Italian Landscape Painting

ON GLASS.

LL honor to the worthy sire who produced the first pictures upon glass, paper or canvass, with oil; and, although those pictures have passed from sight of the present generation, we live to enjoy the knowledge given to us through history, that many a fine artist did live long enough to give to the world the highest productions of his artistic hand; and, although passed to "that bourne from whence no traveler returns," his teachings are still practiced among men. And no man, however original he may be, can to-day sit down and paint the form or ornament of a house, but that it will be the development or degradation of forms practiced by the artists of early days. The style of painting which is given below is somewhat ancient, but very ornamental and useful; and, although to an extent it passed from existence years ago, the lovers of decorative art have again revived it in the East, and it is now being sought after and practiced by thousands on account of its being cheap and easy to attain. This plan of transferring the engraving from paper to glass, and discarding the paper wholly, is simply wonderful. We give it below:

Procure a fine quality of French glass, make perfectly clean with alcohol, then apply with a stiff brush a coat of damar varnish; after drying about an hour, apply another coat, evenly and smoothly; this allow to dry about ten minutes, or just long enough to make it sticky. Procure an uncolored steel engraving that you may desire to see painted, and trim off all the paper not connected with the picture. Dampen it with a sponge or wet cloth, and while yet damp place the engraving on the glass with the face to the varnish, rubbing with your dry hand or cloth until every part adheres to the surface, and all air has been removed, rubbing from the center.

Lay this away a few hours, until it is perfectly dry, then dampen the picture again, and commence rubbing therefrom the paper; continue this until you have removed every vestige of the same, nothing remaining upon the glass but the face of the engraving. Now apply a coat of boiled oil, let it dry fifteen or twenty minutes, and apply another, or a coat of varnish, evenly and smoothly; after laying an hour or two it is ready to receive the paint. As the paper has been all removed the colors will strike through readily. Arrange the glass to the light in such a manner that you may see through it, and apply the colors to the engraving on the back, as in the Grecian oil. The outlines and shades are already produced by the engraving, and all that is necessary now is to place the colors where they belong, which, with a little practice, can soon be acquired.

The paints used are, yellow lake, yellow ochre, chrome yellow, chrome green, Prussian blue, burnt sienna, Vandyke brown, ivory black, verdigris green, silver white, mixed with damar varnish. Use brushes as in Grecian oil.

GRECIAN OIL PAINTING.

GRECIAN OIL PAINTINGS are made from engravings and lithographs. There is but little of it done in this country; and, although there was quite an interest manifested in it here a few years ago, it did not live long, and this is the first time I have seen the instructions in print since or before.

We select the engraving most desired to hang upon our walls, (regardless of size), and place it upon a frame or stretcher with small tacks or glue; this prepares it for the work. When ready, commence by sponging it with clean water; when dry, saturate it well with turpentine, applied with a large size paint brush; when this is done, apply Grecian varnish in the same way, spreading it smoothly and evenly over the surface, until all the dry spots in the paper have entirely disappeared. The application may be made on either side of the picture. When done, let it lay level (with the face down), twenty-four hours, and it will then do to paint, if free from spots and perfectly transparent. When you commence upon the back to paint, follow the lines with those colors necessary to make it look natural; the shading being made by the engraving, nothing is necessary but to apply the colors required. Suit your taste in choosing those colors. Mix the paints with varnish made from balsam fir three parts, alcohol two parts, and spirits turpentine one part; or use *tube paints*, which are already prepared.

In painting the figure of a person, if the eyes are blue, mix Prussian blue and white; for dark eyes or hair, Vandyke brown works with good effect; for flesh color, mix red, white and a little yellow, adding a little more red for lips or cheeks. You may suit your own taste in regard to the color for background, but I will suggest equal parts of blue, red, green, and Vandyke brown, covering all that part which is not connected with the object you have painted. Don't apply a second color until the first is perfectly dry. When done, give the face a coat of varnish.

The colors suitable for this painting are chrome yellow, yellow lake, emerald green, carmine, Prussian blue, burnt sienna, raw sienna, Vandyke brown, ivory black and silver lake.

The brushes required are one large varnish brush, with two or three small to medium size camel or sable hair paint brushes.

ORNAMENTAL

GLASS SIGN WORK.

FOR LETTERING DOOR PLATES,

ORNAMENTING GLASS WORK BOXES, Etc.

How this art may be applied to making signs of every description, numbers of dwellings, door plates, ornamental borders for pictures, ornamenting work boxes, etc., which are made at a trifling expense, and unsurpassed for brilliancy.

First. Clean well the glass to be used, with alcohol. Second. Wet with your tongue the side cleaned, and immediately lay over the whole of that side a coat of gold or silver leaf. Third. Let this dry on—it will take from two to four minutes. Fourth. When the leaf has dried on the glass, polish it with a ball of cotton. Some of the leaf may possibly be rubbed off by the polishing, but this is of no consequence. Fifth. After polishing, wet again with your tongue the whole side you have polished, and lay another coating of leaf over it. Let this dry. Sixth. After the second coat of leaf is dry, polish it as before, with the ball of cotton, and then your sign or door plate will be ready for lettering.

As a border will add much to the appearance of the plate, I will now instruct you how to make one. Rule with the point of a needle two lines around the edge of the plate, the outside line one-quarter of an inch from the edge. After the lines have been ruled, wet your pencil brush, and with it moisten the leaf laying outside of the space between the lines you have ruled, and remove with the brush the leaf thus moistened, working gently from the lines. Your border is now made.

Your next step is to put the lettering on the glass. To do this, first measure the height of your letters, then rule with the needle two lines as far apart as the letters are high. When this is done, lay the letters on the leaf, one at a time, beginning at the right hand, and placing the back of the letters up, or backwards. Hold the letters on firmly with your left hand, and with your right mark around them with a needle. When you have marked around all the letters in this way, wet with your tongue the pencil brush, and apply it to all the leaf on the glass, except what is needed for the letters and border; then remove the leaf thus wet by rubbing it gently with the brush.

The next process is to apply the Japan. Do this with a small paint brush, and cover the whole of the side which has been covered with the silver leaf. It will require two coats, and after these are dry you have an elegant plate.

All that now remains to be done is to place the plate in a frame, to do this apply a little putty to the edges of the glass, and set it in the frame; then lay upon the back a piece of paper of the same size, and over that a piece of tin, and fill up the remaining space with plaster of Paris. Your door plate is now complete.

To ornament glass work boxes, flowering, etc., proceed as above.

Articles Used. A small camel-hair pencil brush, cost three cents; blue or black enamel, or Japan, per gill, 25 cents; selected silver leaf, per book, (24 sheets), 24 cents; patterns for letters, per set, 37½ cents; patterns for numbers, per set, 25 cents.

[NOTE.—A gill of Japan will answer for fifty signs. A book of silver leaf will answer for six or eight door plates.]

VITREMANIE.

FOR THE EASY AND INEXPENSIVE

DECORATION OF WINDOWS, CHURCHES, PUBLIC BUILDINGS, AND

PRIVATE HOUSES.

———

VITREMANIE is the process by which glass of all kinds may be easily, durably, inexpensively, and elegantly decorated by any person. Diaphanie, which this art supersedes, was a great success, (no less than 250,000 sheets of designs having been sold in England alone). It had, however, its defects; the sheets being applied with transfer varnish, bubbles of air sometimes remained between the design and the glass, which in the subsequent process of rubbing off the paper, resulted in holes; this rubbing off, moreover, required much time, patience, and care, and was rarely perfectly performed. These defects are obviated by Vitremanie. By this method the designs, after being covered with Glucine, may be applied to the glass with water only, and the paper removed entire, a few minutes sufficing for the operation, and nothing being left upon the glass but the design in colors of unclouded brilliancy and transparency.

The Materials Required are as follows: The printed designs, three brushes, (two of camel's hair and one of hog's hair), a bottle of each, Glucine and enamel varnish, a roller, a sponge, a little blotting paper, and a pair of scissors.

The instructions are very simple. With the camel-hair brush pass a coating of Glucine over the colored face of the designs that are proposed to be used, care being taken that the Glucine does not touch the plain side of the paper; the sheets of the designs should be laid flat to dry, they should be left two or three days before being used, and they will remain good for three months, or even longer.

To apply the design to the glass it should be wetted with water on both sides, the glass should also be wetted; lay the design on the glass, and roll well down—all air bubbles will be easily removed by this means—keep the plain side of the paper wet for a few minutes, then, with the point of a knife, carefully raise a corner of the paper and pull it gently off; the work is now to be washed with a camel-hair brush and water, and afterwards dried by placing a piece of blotting paper over the work, and rolling it; leave it now for a few hours, then coat it with enamel varnish, and the work is finished. In removing the paper it is sometimes better, particularly when the design is large, to carefully scratch a hole in the paper, and tear it off in pieces from the center. The work is more easily performed on free glass, cut to the proper sizes, and afterwards fixed over the glass already in the window, by means of a bead; it may, however, be done upon the window as it stands.

The designs may be arranged to fit any window, strips of lead foil applied with gum being used for the purpose of covering the edges of the borders, groundings, etc., where they join. For circles and other shapes the strips of lead may be stretched with the thumb and fingers to any pattern desired, the creases being smoothed by the handle of a knife or paper-cutter, slightly wetted.

DIAPHANIE.

HE Diaphanie prints for transferring to glass are very similar to the Decalcomanies; they are colored lithographs arranged on paper for transferring to glass, to represent stained glass, and is equally as pretty, and not so expensive. By this plan you may ornament your church windows, lamp shades, glass work boxes, or wherever stained glass is employed.

The materials required are a bottle of fixatif for fastening it to the glass, one or two medium size brushes, a bottle of transparent varnish, a plate of glass, and your design.

The Application is as follows: Lay on a coat of the fixatif to the face of the design, and place it upon the glass, pressing it closely and evenly, that it may adhere perfectly to the entire surface of the glass. In order to do this, it may be well to lay over the design a piece of heavy damp paper, and then roll it to the glass with a small roller used for that purpose; when this is done, and it is dry, apply a coat of transparent varnish with a flat camel-hair brush.

Some of the designs used are as follows: There are the Japanese and China figures, autumn leaves, Grecian and Egyptian heads, birds of paradise, soldiers, national figures in bronze, butterflies, angels with wings, roses, fruits and flowers, buildings, landscapes, etc., besides ten thousand other choice selections which can be furnished to you by mail, at catalogue prices.

PAINTING ON

SILK, SATIN AND VELVET,

WITH THE ENGLISH OIL COLORS.

ROM all the different styles of modern painting, we select this as the most admired, and seemingly the most sought after by ladies of taste, fashion, or wealth; for nothing will aid more in beautifying the dress than a beautiful flower or butterfly painted upon the little satin or silk scarf which surrounds the neck, the collar or cuffs; your monogram on one corner the pocket handkerchief, or any other portion of the dress desired by the lady artist and lady of taste.

Transferring. First get the outlines of the picture you wish to paint, by use of transfer paper, or in the following manner: Lay the picture upon the silk to receive the painting, and with a needle-point prick through the picture, following closely the outlines, until you have passed over the whole, holding it to its place with one hand—with the other rub over the perforated part a black powder or fine crayon. For this purpose use a piece of velvet, rubbing it sufficiently to pass the powder through the holes. On raising the picture you have the outlines of it left on the silk, which is now ready to receive the paints. This method is merely given to aid the beginner in getting started; those more familiar with painting can commence at once upon the silk, without the aid of transferring.

The Painting. Stretch your silk upon a board, and lay the board flat. After you have the outlines, proceed with fine pointed brush, the same as other fine painting. Do not place a brush full of paint upon the work at once, but use paint lightly at first, otherwise it may crack and harm the picture.

In painting on velvet, with oil, place such colors as are intended to be used, on blotting paper for a couple of days, until the paper absorbs the oil. This will leave the colors in better condition for this kind of work. Use colors lightly—a great deal of stippling is needed. For raised work, or what is sometimes called Kensington painting, use sugar of lead, with the colors as a medium.

N. B. Use for this painting the *English Oil Colors*, and mix with gold size or opaque mixture.

After the work is completed, if it looks dull, you can bring it out again by using the sicatif gently upon the surface.

Staining Wood

AND IVORY.

YELLOW. Diluted nitric acid will produce a fine yellow on wood; sometimes it makes a brown, and if used strong, it will be nearly black.

MAHOGANY COLOR Is produced by a mixture of madder, Brazil wood, and logwood, dissolved in water and put on hot. The proportions must be varied, according to the tint required.

BLACK. Brush the wood several times over with a hot decoction of logwood, and then with an iron lacquer; or, if this cannot be had, a strong solution of nut-galls.

RED can be made by a solution of dragon's blood in spirits of wine. This stain is to be laid on the wood boiling hot, and before it dries it should be laid over with alum water.

BLUE. Ivory may be stained blue thus: Soak the ivory in a solution of verdigris and nitric acid, which will make it green, then dip it into a solution of pearlash boiling hot, and it will turn blue.

To stain ivory, black, the same process as for wood may be employed.

Purple may be produced by soaking the ivory in a solution of sal-ammoniac and four times its weight of nitrous acid.

TO PRODUCE A CRYSTALLINE SURFACE

ON PAPER, WOOD AND GLASS.

A CONCENTRATED solution of salt, acetate of soda, Epsom salt, etc., mixed with Dextrine in the cold, and laid on thinly as possible, with a broad, soft brush, and allowed to dry. The paper must be sized first, otherwise the formation of crystals will be irregular, on account of the absorption of the liquid. The coating on glass is rendered adhesive by brushing it with a solution of shellac in alcohol.

Colored glass arranged in this way makes a pretty transparency.

A beautiful adhesive coating of pearly lustre upon paper produces a very handsome card.

"Out of Art Culture grows Refinement."

CHINA PAINTING.

Colors Used, and the Process of Burning them in.

AT the present time this art is receiving a great deal of attention among the American people, and especially the intelligent class, who are taking every opportunity of informing themselves in regard to the plan of moulding the various ornaments for use, the art of decorating them, the particular kinds of paints used, and the operation through which they pass in the *burning in* of the colors. It would be useless for me to attempt a book on art that would meet the wants of the people, and omit China Painting, which is gaining universal favor among the higher classes in eastern cities.

The art is applied directly to the ornamentation of the house, which makes it much sought after by ladies, who take pride

in ornamenting their china and earthenware by the use of the
La Croix Enamel Colors, which are arranged especially for this
kind of painting.

After the paints are applied, the ware requires a certain amount
of heat to fix the colors, and prevent it from being effaced by
washing. Commence work by first

Tracing the Drawing. For tracing, details should be left
out as much as possible, or at any rate indicated soberly.

DIRECT OUTLINE. If the pupil can draw well, she will outline
her subject lightly on the object she wishes to paint, directly,
without tracing, by means of a lithographic pencil.

TRANSFERRING. When you want to make a minute and com-
plicated drawing, you are obliged to transfer, to avoid getting
double lines on the china.

Before transferring, prepare your piece of ware as follows:
Pour three drops of alcohol on the plaque or white plate intended
for decoration.

It is very easy to trace on a perfectly flat surface. We shall
mention several ways.

FIRST METHOD. *Tracing by Rubbing.* After having traced
from the engraving, or original model to be reproduced, the outline of your subject (figure, ornament, or landscape), with one
of the lithographic pencils, you reverse the tracing over a sheet
of white paper, and go over the outline again very carefully with
the same pencil; this being done, prepare your piece of china
with medium as we have just described. The vegetal tracing
paper is then fixed, by means of little lumps of modeling wax, on
the exact spot the subject is to occupy; and when that is done,
you have only to rub all over the outline with an ivory knife, to
make the lead that is on the vegetal tracing paper convey itself
distinctly on to the previously prepared oiled enamel.

SECOND METHOD. *Tracing with a Tracing Point.* Take
either black, blue, or carmine transferring paper, according to
the tint of the painting that is to be done. The carmine gives

all security for the success of the painting; it does not soil it. When the piece of paper has been rubbed with carmine from a soft crayon, after taking great care to remove what is superfluous it is cut to the size of the subject, or rather to that of the space you are to paint on.

To make sure of tracing on the exact spot, you must draw a horizontal line in the middle of your drawing, one also in the middle of the tracing paper, and one as well on the porcelain, with crosses and letters to each end as landmarks; two crosses marked A and B on the horizontal line of the enamel, and + + a b on the horizontal line of the tracing paper. The piece is *prepared* with oil of turpentine or spirits of wine. At the end of two or three minutes you place your drawing on the porcelain in accordance with the marks + + a b, taking care to place the middle lines one on the top of the other, a on A, and b on B; you fix the vegetal tracing paper by means of small bits of gummed paper, or else with little balls of modeling wax; the sheet of tracing paper being quite firm, you slide beneath it the piece of paper rubbed with carmine, blue, or black lead; you then take a porcupine quill with a fine point, and without leaning too hard you go over all the outline. You must be careful not to press your fingers on the drawing, for it often causes the deposit of powder to be of the same color as your transferring paper, which spoils the result and prevents careful painting. Before finishing all the work, lift up a corner of the overlying paper to see if the tracing does mark. It will be but an affair of habit to trace well, for it is by experiments frequently repeated that one comes to know exactly the amount of strength to be used so that the transferring paper may mark sufficiently. This paper lasts a long time, and improves as it grows old; you must prevent it from getting creased. For this, each time it has been used, it should be put away into a brown paper cover, wherein the tracing papers are also placed.

THIRD METHOD is by pricking the outline with small holes, and in making what is called a " Poncif,"

In a bottle containing alcohol the brushes and the **dabbers**
are cleaned after each day's work. To preserve these useful instruments it is indispensable never to leave any color in them;
you must take care to wipe them well after this washing, and
even to blow a little on them, to make the spirits of wine evaporate, for if any were to remain it would spoil the color and
take away the painting already finished. With a few drops of
spirits of wine, the most loaded palette can be instantaneously
cleaned, and the driest painting can be effaced. For this reason
I recommend that the little bottle of spirits of wine be kept always far away from you during your work; if a single drop
were to fall on the painting, it would immediately smear and
obliterate the work done.

Cleaning brushes with spirits of wine has to be done every
day. From time to time a more thorough cleaning with soft
soap is resorted to; the brushes are steeped in the soap, and are
washed the next day only.

PORCELAIN AND EARTHENWARE. — COMPOSITION, USE AND MIXING OF THE COLORS.

GENERAL INFORMATION.

E borrow from M. Lacroix his classification of colors,
which is very practical with regard to their employment in painting:

"CLASSIFICATION OF COLORS WITH RESPECT TO IRON.—
Iron plays an important part in the composition of a
great many enamel colors; for this reason I have taken it
as a standard for my classification of colors into three groups.

"FIRST GROUP.—Colors that do not contain any iron: First,
the white; secondly, the blues; thirdly, the colors from gold.

"A horn or ivory knife is preferable for the use of colors of
this group.

"A glass muller is still better than knives.

"SECOND GROUP.—Colors with but little trace of iron. This group includes the yellows and greens, several of which colors contain iron in small quantities.

"THIRD GROUP.—Colors with an iron basis, or of which iron is one of the coloring parts: First, the reds, fleshes, red browns, and violets of iron; secondly, the browns, yellow browns, ochres, blacks and a greater part of the greys."

The enamel colors usually designated by the name of iron colors are: All the browns; the greys, excepting platina grey; the blacks, minus iridium black; the ochres; the reds, and the violets of iron.

The enamel colors said to be with a golden basis are: The carmines; crimson lake; the purples, and the violets of gold.

TESTS.—The amount of flux added to the coloring oxides for the manufacture of enamel colors varies according to the color; this difference, joined to the diversity of the chemical elements, causes actions in the firing which may modify certain colors and even make them disappear entirely; it is said expressively that they have been *eaten up, devoured* by the fire. We shall cite, as an example, the mixture of ivory yellow with carmine, as one of those which decompose in the firing. Other causes act likewise on enamel colors during firing; the intensity, more or less great, of the heat, the thickness, and the amount of oil in the color, the way it is used, etc.

In order to well understand the various influences, and to secure yourself against accidents, you must be continually making tests of the mixtures *yourself;* it is the only way to paint with safety.

It is indispensable for the test to be double, that is, on two small bits of precisely the same manufacture of china as the piece you wish to paint. The same mixture is made on both small pieces, they are both dried, and one only is fired in order to be able to judge what change is caused by the firing, by comparing it with the unfired test you have kept by you. Besides, you will be able to make sure of a satisfactory result by comparing your experiments with the test tiles and plates of fired colors.

Mixed colors should be stirred with the brush when used; without this precaution they would separate; light blue would rise on dark blue, yellow on green, ivory yellow on carnation.

Some hints follow which it will be advantageous to verify and to carry out by tests. They apply generally to painting on porcelain or earthenware for the ordinary muffle.

FUSIBILITY. **Hard** colors (those which require the greatest heat to make them fuse) spoil and often destroy those of a softer **flux** (that fuse more easily). The flux added by the manufacturer to the coloring oxide lightens the tint of the color; dark colors are therefore generally harder than light ones. In the palette of M. Lacroix the colors more fusible than the rest, although taking the same time to fire, are light sky-blue, light carmine A, pearl grey, warm or russet grey, and ivory yellow, all light colors.

THICKNESS. The tint of enamel colors get darker when you increase their thickness. But you must beware of doing it too much. Light and fusible colors used too thick, blister in firing; it is prudent to give them only a medium thickness.

You should apply in drops those colors only that are specially designed for the purpose; permanent white, permanent yellow, and relief. They hold on earthenware, but their use on porcelain is liable to failure.

MEDIUMS. Experience will prove that if too much oil of turpentine is added to the colors used, which is called adding "fat," they will craze in the firing. Make some trials by exaggerating this fault. You will remark nevertheless that colors applied very thin, although with much "fat," do not craze. The cracks caused in the firing, by the action of the resinous part of the oil, which evaporates and causes the white of the enamel to reappear, is called crazing.

CONDUCT OF THE WORK. It is very important in the first painting to use the most fusible light colors, and those most easily developed in the first firing, which is the strongest. Commence always on a lighter scale than the final tint, for in pottery painting any color made too dark in firing cannot be made light again. When the mixtures have produced, for example, some browns or russet hues which have not glazed in the first firing, the glazing is brought back by a little fusible light grey, applied before the second firing for retouches. These short general instructions will be resumed and developed in the following lessons.

SPECIAL INFORMATION CONCERNING PAINTING COLORS.

MODE OF USE — MIXTURES — CONCORDANCE OF ENAMEL WITH MOIST AND OIL COLORS, AND THEIR USUAL TECHNICAL NAMES.

WHITES, belonging to the first group. White is obtained by *permanent white*, (for high lights), and *Chinese white*, a color of very limited use in painting, it being preferable to keep the white of the china when possible.

Permanent white, alone or mixed with other colors for heightening, which is called *high light*, or *relief*, requires perfect grinding. It should be tried by repeated and well fired tests before using it for important works. It is lifted up with the point of the brush, and laid without spreading. It could not bear two firings; it is put at the second firing, which is always less powerful.

BLUES. (First group.) In his character as a chemist, M. Lacroix gives us, in his work already quoted, the general reason for excessive care in using blues · "All the blues, with very few exceptions, derive their color from cobalt. . . . **As the mixture of cobalt** and iron produces, proportionably, **tints varying from** light grey to black, it **is well to** take great precautions in painting when blues are used with reds, fleshes, **browns** and **ochres.** It follows as a natural consequence, **that** when you wish to have some beautiful shades of blue, you must avoid using brushes which have already served for one of the iron colors, and have not been properly cleaned."

Blues are laid on in very **thin** coatings, particularly blue green.

Ordinary oil medium.

The first painting is but little loaded, and is shaded with the same tint in a second coating, added to grey in the last firing for the darkest parts.

Here are some notes on the concordance of enamel colors with oil colors and their usual names.

Sky Blue—sky blue.

Light Blue—light sky blue.

Blue Verditer—two-thirds ultramarine blue; **one-third deep blue** green. **Slight** oiling.

Barbean Blue, or Smalt—Victoria blue.

Marine Blue (in oils)—half Victoria blue, half carmine No. 2.

Cobalt—deep ultramarine.

Prussian Blue—one-third **dark** blue; one-third Victoria blue; one-third ultramarine; **a** touch of grey No. 2; a very little touch of purple.

Indigo—dark blue; a touch of raven black.

CARMINES AND PURPLE. (First Group.) Carmines **must be** used very thin, lest they should turn yellow in the firing. **You** must put but little oil **to** avoid shrivelling. Never touch them with a knife; the brush **must** be sufficient. It is also recommended, when using purple, to fill the brush well and to turn it round and round to dissolve the little gritty lumps generally found at the opening of the tubes. When **a pink color has had** an addition of **purple to it,** spirits of lavender with **a drop of oil** of turpentine should be preferred to turpentine only.

All the carmines are shaded with the same tint. Purples are also used for strong shadows, and blues for reflected lights. If light tints or pinks are made with light yellows, these colors must not be spread one over the other, but side by side, otherwise the carmine tints would be injured. In the first painting, carmines and purples are to be laid on very light; it is only in the second firing that strengthening touches are made.

" When carmines are fired in the muffle at too low a temperature, silver takes the upper hand and the color has a dirty yellow tint; if, on the contrary, the temperature is too high, the silver shade is completely destroyed, and the carmine becomes lilac or violet, which explains the difficulty in firing carmines. The same thing takes place with purples, but in a considerably less perceptible degree, because of the shade being much darker and cassius being in a larger quantity."—*A. Lacroix.*

ENAMEL CARMINES AND PURPLES are equivalent to the oil colors of the same name.

Light Pink—Carmine A and carmine No. 1.

Deeper Pink—Carmine No. 2 with carmine No. 3.

Laky Red—Crimson lake.

Purple Lake—Carmine No. 1 and a touch of purple.

Peony Pink—Half ruby purple; half carmine No. 1.

Chinese Pink—Carmine No. 3; touch of ruby purple.

Lakes (in oils)—Carmines.

Crimson Lake (in oils)—Purples.

Red Purple—Deep purple.

Crimson—Crimson purple.

LILACS AND VIOLETS. (1st group, except the violet of iron, which belongs to the 3d group.) The same precautions are required in using lilacs as for carmines.

Lilac—Half carmine No. 1; half sky-blue; a touch of carmine No. 3.

Mauve—Half carmine A; half ultramarine.

Magenta—Two-thirds carmine No. 3; one-third deep ultramarine; a touch of ruby purple.

Violet—Light violet of gold.

Deep Violet—Deep violet of gold.

Light Pansy—Light violet of gold, with a touch of deep ultramarine.

Deep Pansy—Deep violet of gold, sustained more or less and with an addition of ultramarine.

REDS. (3d group, except the purples.) Red, a predominant color, is nearly always used alone. Thus, the reddish tips of **green** leaves are obtained by placing the red next the green, but not by putting it **over.** With the dark colors, on the contrary, it is red that disappears.

Chinese vermilion in **oils has an** equivalent tint in coral **for** porcelain applied thin; backgrounds **are** made of it, but it would be risking a great deal to **use it in painting,** on account of its extreme sensibility in firing; besides, it suffers no mixing. Scarlet vermilion is approached **by adding a touch of** flesh No. 1 to capucine red, and laying on this mixture in a moderate thickness.

Capucine Red—Capucine **red.**

Poppy Red—Half capucine red; half deep purple. **A** satisfactory result is obtained only **at** the third application of this mixture, which loses at each firing.

Madder—Capucine **red; a** touch of purple and of carmine No. 3.

Gules (in heraldry)—Capucine red and a touch of purple.

Venetian Red (in oils)—Violet of iron (third group).

YELLOWS. (Second group.) Certain yellows greatly destroy the colors mixed with them, and even make them disappear entirely. This disadvantage is perceived when too much ivory yellow is mixed with red, or when that yellow is placed abundantly over other colors.

"The yellow called silver yellow contains no silver; it is composed of jonquil yellow and orange yellow. Yellows that contain no iron (yellow for mixing and jonquil yellow) are generally preferred for making fresh greens. On the other hand, for mixing with iron colors, yellows that contain already this metal are used."—*A. Lacroix.*

Light yellows scale very easily; the dark yellows, being less fusible, need to be used moderately thin in the first painting, for the first fire develops them; at the second firing they increase in depth, and if they are too heavily loaded they cannot be made lighter again.

Avoid using yellows next to blues, which would produce a green tint. For the centers of blue flowers, which necessitates some yellow, the place must be well scraped before putting the color.

Permanent yellow, (half white and half yellow for mixing), serves for placing lights in drapery and yellow flowers, as well as high lights in ornaments.

Lemon Yellow—Yellow 47 of Sevres, with a touch of silver yellow.

Golden Yellow—Half silver yellow; half jonquil yellow.

Saffron Yellow—Two-thirds ivory yellow; one-third flesh No. 1; a touch of capucine red.

Salmon—Two-thirds ivory yellow; one-third flesh No. 2; a touch of carmine No. 3.

Straw Color—Yellow for mixing, used very lightly.

Yellow Lake—Yellow for mixing.

Dark Chrome Yellow—Silver yellow; a touch of jonquil yellow.

Light Chrome Yellow—Jonquil yellow.

Indian Yellow—Half jonquil yellow; half ochre.

Naples Yellow—Ivory yellow.

Orange Yellow—Orange yellow.

Maize—Half ivory yellow; half orange yellow.

GREENS. (Second group.) For foliage it is well to remember that dark tints placed in advance of light ones destroy the latter in the firing.

All the greens, whether in foliage or in drapery, can be shaded with browns, reds, and carmine tints.

By painting over for the second fire, foliage can be made purple or bluish.

Dark green, being very powerful, should be used with caution.

The blue-greens are used for the distance, but then excessively light; they are tinted with capucine red for the horizon.

Emerald-stone Green—Emerald-stone green.

Water Green—Half apple green; half deep blue-green.

Veronese Green—One-third apple green; one-third chrome green; one-third emerald-stone green.

Malachite—Apple green; a touch of emerald-stone green.

Blue-green—Deep blue-green.

Dark Green—Two-thirds chrome green 3 B; one-third dark green.

Bottle Green or Sap Green—Sap green.

Emerald Green—Two-thirds blue-green; one-third emerald-stone green.

BROWNS. (Third group.) The artistic browns for china which steady painters prefer, are vigorous browns, fresh when mixed, and resisting well the action of the fire, but which have not the brilliancy of the less coloring browns.

The warm browns in oils exist for china. The deep red brown and mixtures of violet of iron and of laky red correspond to the red browns.

Golden Brown—Golden brown.

Vandyke Brown—It is impossible to obtain it exactly. The nearest approach would be by mixing brown 108 with violet of iron.

Raw Sienna—Sepia.

Orange Mars—Uranium yellow and a touch of purple.

BLACKS. (Third group.) The blacks in oils are represented in the palette for pottery by raven, ivory and iridium black, which answers all purposes.

If these blacks fail, others can be composed by mixtures of simple colors, as dark reds and dark blues. It would be better to operate in two firings to avoid crazing.

The use of iron reds is not admitted on soft paste; the blacks are to be made with iridium black, which is ready made, or with purple and dark green. It is rare that black is needed for subjects painted on soft paste. It is sometimes used in decoration for surrounding ornaments with a line, but seldom for backgrounds, excepting on decorative vases of a certain style.

GREYS. (Third group.) A grey of some kind is always obtained by mixing complementary colors; reds with greens, or yellows with violets, violet being a combination of carmine and blue.

The greys obtained by mixing greens, ready made or composed, with carmine or purple, as required, are very frequently used by flower painters.

Experience on this subject can only be acquired by continual trials.

Dove Color—Dove color.

Ash Grey—Light grey used lightly, and a touch of sky blue.

Pearl Grey—Pearl grey No. 6.

Russet Grey—Warm grey.

Brown Grey—Grey and sepia.

MONOCHROME PAINTING ON PORCELAIN OR EARTHENWARE.

INSTRUCTION.

WE now come to painting. Begin on porcelain by a plate, and on earthenware by a tile. If the pupil has had no practice either in water colors or in oils—if, in a word, has no idea as yet of setting a palette, undertake first a monochrome, that is to say, a painting done with one color only, heightened by one or two other tones.

Monochromes are made in the following tints: Grisailles, green, blue-green, blue, violet of iron, carmine, purple capucine red, sepia, red brown, bitumen.

Deep red brown and violet of iron are the two colors easiest to be used.

Grisaille Monochrome: **Light grey No. 1**, touched up with brown grey.

Greys Nos. 1 and 2; mix a little carmine No. 1 to warm up the tints.

On porcelain the bodies of cupids are often done in grisaille, with a little carmine at the extremities.

Green—Emerald-stone green and deep green.

Blue-green—Blue-green, touched up with the same color.

Blue—Deep ultramarine; dark blue; permanent white. Or common blue, shaded with itself; any other blue would spoil it.

Violet of Iron—Violet of iron, and the same with a grey tint.

Carmine—Light carmine A; deep carmine No. 3.

Purple—Deep purple, strengthened by the same tint placed at the second firing.

Capucine Red—Capucine red: orange red; sepia. Or orange yellow and capucine red in juxtaposition; the capucine red touched up with red brown.

Sepia—Sepia touched up with the same shade.

Red Brown—Orange yellow for light and distant tints; the foreground deep red brown. Or deep red brown heightened with bitumen. Or else deep red brown and sepia.

Bitumen—Yellow brown; brown No. 3 bitumen; brown No. 4 or 17.

The design having been traced on to the porcelain or china, you take the tube of color and uncork it with care. Squeezing out the color from the extreme bottom of the tube, you set about the tenth part of its contents on your glass palette, which should be extremely clean. Grind it with the palette knife, (of steel or of ivory, according to the color), for about a minute.

Sketching In. Is done with the finest pointed of your brushes, dipped lightly into the little bottle of spirits of lavender, then filled with a little of the color taken from the edge of the lump, turning the brush meanwhile between your fingers to get a fine point. It is better still to work with the color diluted with water, and with the addition of a little dextrine, which gives it the advantage of resisting the oils. Indicate lightly the nose, the mouth, the lachrymals a little, as well as between the fingers. It will be useless to efface this sketch.

You will then begin to paint the head, taking a larger brush to spread the color broadly and quickly. Still very little medium. Put a rather light local tint; while the color is still wet deepen the tone beneath the arch of the eyebrows, the cheeks, the extremity of the chin, and the parts to be shaded, taking care meanwhile to leave out the bright lights, or those reflected, which should remain of the first tint, in order that the shadows may give an appearance of roundness. Take next a small dabber, with a flat top, and holding it perpendicularly, dabble lightly before the color has time to dry. Soften and mix well the two tints, keeping them distinct the while.

Do the hair after the flesh tints have been laid on, toning the locks more or less. Here, however, no more dabber; on the contrary, the strokes of the brush must appear and mark the hair.

Pass on to the drapery, and wash in broadly the principal shadows with a still larger brush. It will be effective to preserve the white of the porcelain or china for the lights of the draperies. In the first painting, spirits of lavender are used, so that the color may dry less quickly. You must not be afraid to paint the drapery with large strokes of the brush, the effect is all the better for it. Above all, let there be no harsh or dry marks; in painting there are no marks, but shadows and lights.

Before retouching, the painting must be allowed to dry, and the medium to evaporate, and you must not work again on it unless, lightly placing the tip of your finger on the painting, you feel scarcely any dampness left; some, however, must remain, for the color would easily be removed by retouching, if it were in a pulverized state. The dessication can be hastened by heating, either at a lamp of spirits of wine, or in an oven; but you must wait until the work is quite cold again before resuming.

The first painting must be taken great care of, and kept very clean. While it is drying, it should be placed out of the reach of dust and damp; if it be a plaque, place it in a flat box with a proper lid to it, shutting hermetically.

M. Lacroix's colors being perfectly well prepared, we will not dwell upon the disadvantages offered by the former badly ground colors. The inexperienced beginner used to put too much 'fat,' or too much spirits of lavender. In the former case the painting crazed in the firing; it was lost. With too much spirits of lavender the colors ran; fled in the firing. Therefore there must be no excess, but the three mediums must be used with management and discretion.

When you retouch your painting, before the first firing, you must model by retouching with flat tints, and you must do it very soberly, very lightly, not to remove what is underneath; work almost dry, that is, without much soaking the brush in the spirits of turpentine. If the color does not spread easily, the brush is wetted with the least possible quantity of oil of turpentine, a drop of which has been poured on the palette. Spirits of lavender are of no use for this second performance.

To finish the monochrome completely, it is necessary to stipple the shadows, using very little rectified spirits of turpentine. If the beginner will master thoroughly the shadows of the original, she will not find it more difficult to paint in monochrome than to reproduce a drawing either in black chalk or in stump; the brush will take the place of the stump or chalk: the only difficulty that can arise being in the use of the mediums, and in the lack of time for allowing the painting to dry.

I repeat it again, for it is of great importance, that with the colors of M. Lacroix one can work almost dry, once the palette has been set.

When the work is finished, it is submitted to the firing, either at home, (by the Gabelle process), or at a decorators. According to the result obtained, the parts which lack vigor are retouched.

In general few raised lights or reliefs are employed. Yet in accessories, they heighten advantageously the brilliancy of the painting. The paint for raised lights is taken from the palette in a particular way; the brush must lift up a lump of color at the point, that it may be laid on the easier. Raised lights are placed on small flowers, on jewelry, pearl necklaces, etc. A light in the eye is often marked with permanent white, but it should be used in great moderation, and placed at the second firing.

Photographs from casts, medals, bas-reliefs, afford excellent models for copying in monochrome painting. Copies of photographs on oval plaques are done with red brown, heightened with bitumen. Raphael's female figures on plaques for sconces, are copied in light grey, retouched with brown grey, on a ground of very light carmine No. 1.

PAINTING THE HEAD IN COLORS ON PORCELAIN.

SET on the palette, at intervals of about an inch, some ivory yellow, yellow brown, flesh No. 1, flesh No. 2, light grey, brown 108, blue-green, and the other colors.

The drawing having been traced with chalk, you proceed to sketch it in, which should always be done in the same color as the object. For the flesh take some flesh No. 1 at the tip of your brush, and indicate very lightly the outline of the eyes, the nostrils, the corners of the mouth, and the ears; but above all, take care not to make a line all round the face, as the effect produced in the firing would be exceedingly bad. Paint likewise the face, the neck, and inside the fingers, but especially not on the side of the light, *which must detach itself by the local tint only.*

With the ivory knife mix one-third flesh No. 1 with two-thirds ivory yellow; this forms the flesh color for the local tint. Prepare also a little yellow brown for the reflected lights. These two tints are to be applied almost simultaneously, one next to the other. Commence always from the top of the head, and only when the sketched outline is dry, otherwise the local tint will remove it. This tint must be laid on very thin; apply it quickly with precision and without deviation of the brush, that is, without discontinuation of tint; look at the china sideways, and if the color is deficient in any place remedy that at once. Finally, the tints are made even by dabbing, and the flesh color is gently blended with the yellow brown by means of a very small fitch brush.

For faces high in color, yellow browns should be used with the reds, and some violet of iron.

While the first tint is still wet, and before dabbling, the flesh color should be strengthened with some flesh No. 1 beneath the arch of the eyebrows, the cheeks, and the lower part of the chin.

Cast shadows are commenced with yellow brown, and retouched with brown 108. Strong shadows are made of violet of iron, and the edges of blue-green and light grey.

Paint the lips with flesh No. 1, retouch with No. 2, but above all, let there be no outline either to the upper or to the lower lip, nothing but a soft, flat, pale tint, strengthened a bit for the shadow.

Blue eyes are made with sky-blue and a minimum of blue-green, retouched with blue-grey. Brown eyes, with yellow brown retouched with sepia or bitumen. The pupil, raven black. The sparkle is left white, or is laid on with a dab of permanent white.

Fair hair is begun with ivory yellow. The shadows are made with yellow brown, and brown 108 graduated, and they terminate with grey and bitumen.

Colored draperies are begun like the draperies in monochrome, a flat general tint touched up again at once with the same tint to give strength to the shadows. There is nothing prettier than pink drapery shaded with blue, and yellow shaded with pink or capucine red. White drapery is begun with an extremely light grey, mixed with green. Whites are reserved, that is, the greatest possible part of the china is left bare without paint to form the lights.

The beginner will do well if she paints a subject with several figures in it, to ascertain which colors throw back, and which bring forward. In the foreground, light colors; white, pink, light blue, lilac. In the middle ground, blue, green, purple and red are used. For the background there are dark blue, brown and dark green.

The ground is made with ivory yellow (for the lights), bitumen, grey, and a little violet of iron. Trunks of trees are begun with yellow-grey, greenish-grey, and bitumen.

The palette, set complete for figure subjects, includes the following colors: Chinese white, sky-blue, light sky-blue, dark blue, deep ultramarine Victoria blue, blue No. 29, (special for porcelain scales on earthenware), brown No. 3, bitumen, brown No. 4 or 17, yellow-brown, deep red-brown, sepia, light carmine A, carmine No. 2, deep carmine No. 3, light grey No. 1, grey No. 2, neutral grey, russet or warm grey, silver yellow, permanent yellow, ivory yellow, (47 of Sevres), yellow for mixing, (41 of Sevres), crimson lake, raven black, iridium black, yellow ochre, purple No. 2, crimson purple, deep purple, capucine red, flesh No. 1, flesh No. 2, deep flesh, orange red, grass green No. 5, brown-green No. 6, dark green No. 7, deep blue-green, deep chrome green, apple green, sap green, violet of iron, light violet of gold.

STYLE OF BOUCHER, FLOWERS, FRUITS, BIRDS, AND LANDSCAPE ON PORCELAIN.

STYLE OF BOUCHER.

To paint the style of Boucher (Cupids) you begin by transferring your design on the china.

Then you sketch with flesh No. 1 the lines of the face, and the fingers and toes. When this sketch is dry, the reflected lights are marked with yellow-brown, mixed with ivory yellow.

The local tint of flesh color is laid on immediately after, the same as in the preceding lesson; the dabbling evens the two colors placed side by side, and blends them one into the other. Let it dry, then heighten by half a tone the extremities of the hands, feet, knees, etc. Sketch in the hair and accessories, the clouds and background, while the local tint is drying.

Retouching. When the first painting has lost nearly all its moisture, return to it again; work the shadows by stippling some brown No. 17, mixed with sepia, yellow ochre, light grey, and a touch of blue-green for the transparent parts. Where the flesh is brown, the reflected lights are made with yellow ochre throughout, and the scale of browns is more used. A touch of violet of iron warms up the shadows, and approaches nearer to Vandyke brown in oils.

Flowers. To paint flowers well it is necessary that the drawing should be exceedingly correct and sober in its lines, for the tints having to be very light and very **pure**, too many pencil marks would **injure** the painting. The little details of the petals are done with the brush, without previous tracing. The pencil must only mark the leaf's contour and central vein; the direction of the brush strokes is enough to indicate the smaller veins.

A general rule for the manipulation of the brush in flower painting may be laid down thus: The handling is always done the way of the petals, converging towards the center.

Leaves. Each plant possesses a particular kind of leaf, and even in the rose the leaves of different varieties are not alike. Thus, for the leaves of the Bengal rose, a semi bright tint, a shiny appearance without many veins, the young shoots tinged with carmine, or else purple mixed with silver yellow. The king's rose: the leaves of this rose are of a darker green than the preceding; they are done with grass green No. 5, the edges of the older leaves become somewhat russet, the young shoots light green. Red rose: the leaves deep green, heightened with brown, the veins dark green No. 7, the serrations carmine red, the fading leaves have a reddish brown hue. Yellow roses: shiny leaves inclining to blue-green, retouched with grey, mixed with grass green; the deeper tints made with dark green No. 7. Do not use this last color too freely.

Leaves have a direction, to paint them properly you must begin them from the top, that is, from the stalk end. Half the leaf is painted at a time, from the principal vein to the edge, making the brush twist in such a manner that the brushmarks and ridges done in the handling may represent the secondary veins. The leaves of bulbs are painted from the top downwards; so are the leaves of heartsease. The leaves of nasturtium are made almost of a flat tint, converging to the center, which is a light spot; their color is a very light blue-green, shaded with grey.

You must not be afraid to mix purple or carmine with green, to shade foliage.

Fruit. This style is done indiscriminately on porcelain, earthenware, enamel, and faience. It is very easy; the essential point is to match well the different shades of color, and to lay them one over the other while they are still wet. The softener flattens them and helps the tints to mingle. Leaves are not dabbled, nor are the stalks.

To describe in detail the manner of painting divers fruit would take too long, and would, in truth, have very little interest. We shall limit ourselves to one example.

PAINTING OF A PEACH. Flat yellow tints, graduated into green, and mixed with grey in the shadow. Dabble carefully. Be careful to add more oil to the red part, which is softened afterwards very easily with a dabber, and red blending freely with its neighboring color from the effect of the oil.

Birds. On faience birds look very well. They are also done on porcelain to imitate Saxony ware. There is nothing particular to be said about bird painting. With regard to fancy birds, the merit consists in the servile copy of ancient and exotic types. Good examples of natural birds are not scarce. General information sufficient for the use of the colors will be found in our lessons.

Landscape. Landscape is not traced; it is drawn very lightly, so that the pencil may form no obstacle to the painting.

This is how the painting is proceeded with: On a square ground-glass slab of moderate size set your "palette" with green tints, in the following order: yellow for mixing, yellow ochre, apple green, grass green, chrome green, blue-green, brown-green, dark green, sepia, bitumen, violet of iron, etc. Take care to leave a space of about three-quarters of an inch between each color, in order to be able to mix them, for they ought not to be used pure; the effect would be bad and inharmonious.

Commence by the sky, using sky-blue and excessively light ultramarine; the lighter parts of ivory yellow, also very thin, and the distance blue-green, with the slightest touch of carmine. Skies are to be done with a very large brush, and the mixing of blue and yellow, which would produce impossible green clouds, is to be avoided. Skies are worked from left to right; they are washed in very rapidly, covering also the place for the trees. A dabber may be used after.

The sky being dry, the trees are massed. Inasmuch as light tints would disappear in the firing if they were put beneath dark colors, fresh tints of apple green are commenced first, which are retouched or darkened at once before dabbling. When these tints have been laid and are dry, the foliage is done by manipulating the brush from left to right with little strokes close together, to imitate the leaves. Autumn tints are preferable to greens that are too bright. You obtain them by sepia and the ochres. *Trunks of trees*, light grey and sepia. *Branches*, bitumen. For strengthening touches use violet of iron.

Houses, ivory yellow mixed with grey; shadows, violet of iron. *Ground*, the lights of ivory yellow, and sometimes yellow ochre; shadows, bitumen; strong tints, brown mixed with black. *Water* is done with very light blue-green, retouched with grey, and occasionally revived with fresher green to reflect grass or trees.

Strengthening touches are given at the second firing, and a glaze is passed over the tints altered in the first firing.

DIRECTIONS FOR PACKING DECORATED CHINA,

When it has to be shipped away for firing.

Have the work *perfectly* dry; if necessary, drying in oven, which may alter the color, but firing will restore that. Wrap each piece separately in fine paper, and pack in a box large enough to admit sufficient excelsior straw or paper to keep all steady, particularly the corners. Allow good layers at the bottom and top of the boxes. By sending directions in the box with the china, its prompt return is assured. In giving instructions with the china, be explicit as to pieces requiring gilding, and amount desired. Prices quoted on list refer to simple lines only. Gilding costs extra.

FIRING GENERALLY DONE TWICE A WEEK.

AVERAGE PRICES FOR FIRING DECORATIVE WARE.

1 Cup and Saucer, 15, 20 and 25¢.	Gilding inclu'd, 25, 30 & 35¢.
6 " " (12 pieces), 75¢.	" " $1.50
1 doz. Individ'l Butters, 50 to 60¢.	" " 1.00
Plates, single, 10 to 15¢	" " 20 to 25¢
1 doz. Plates, $1.00 to $1.25	" " $1.50 to $2.00
Pitchers, 10, 15, 20, 25 and 50¢.	" " 20 to 50¢.
Fruit Dishes, 25 to 50¢.	" " 50 to 75¢.
Covered Dishes, 25, 50 and 75¢.	" " 50¢ to $1.25
Placques. 10, 15, 20, 25 to 50¢.	" " 20 to 75¢.

Tiles, 6x6...10¢.

Tiles, 8x8...15¢.

Plates Banded in any tint desired (Gilding inclu'd), per doz. $3.00

Other pieces according to size and amount of Gilding.

Ladies who wish their China gilded must clean the edges of the same.

TERRA-COTTA PAINTING.

ENAMEL PAINTING ON TERRA-COTTA.

IRST outline with a lead pencil the subject to be painted; if tracing is preferred, use tracing paper, and transfer the design upon the article, by means of a colored transfer paper. The terra-cotta is now immersed in water; when thoroughly saturated, take it out, and with a soft sponge absorb all the superfluous moisture. If, during the process of painting, some of the parts become too dry, moisten them with a flat brush dipped into water.

Have on hand a sufficient quantity of white enamel powder, and with a glass muller grind this upon a ground glass slab until perfectly smooth, with water, adding a little gum water (dissolved gum arabic), until it assumes the consistency of cream. Apply this to the surface to be painted, going over it a second time, so as to cover the tint of the ware. The enamel should be put on heavy enough so that it appears raised from the flat surface, being careful to spread it on very evenly, that none of the parts are coated lighter than others of the design. Enamel will stand firing several times, and such parts not brought out sufficiently can be restored by retouching the same, and subjecting the article to a second firing.

If the design is to be in natural colors, these are painted over the enamel after having been fired, proceeding in the same manner as in china painting. Some colors will bear mixing with the enamel before firing; in such case the dry enamel colors (China) are used, thoroughly mixed with the white enamel. Steel grey, neutral grey, blues and yellows are among the colors that bear mixing. The first three are best adapted for mottled or clouded backgrounds, if such are desired. The glaze contained in the colors and enamel when vitrified by firing, produce the effect of Limoges ware.

For ornamental work the relief enamel colors can be used successfully in the way of bead work, as well as in the entire design, they being already mixed in a powder state, consisting of about twenty-four different tints.

In doing larger pieces, where a quantity of color is used, the former instructions are to be preferred. If vases are decorated, intended for use, the inside should be washed with a mixture of enamel and color to give it a glaze, and thus prevent the outer decoration from being injured by the penetration of liquids.

Before taking the article to be fired, place it where it will become thoroughly dry, as it cannot be fired in a moist state. The Barbotine ware, which has lately come into the market, can be effectively decorated in the above manner.

OIL PAINTING ON TERRA-COTTA.

Upon terra-cotta of a light tint the design is drawn with a lead pencil; upon that of a dark tint, use the colored impression paper.

Place the article between piles of books, or fill a box with sand, and lay or stand it into this in the position required; see that the right arm rests upon an even plane with the article to be decorated.

A terra-cotta medium is made from a small quantity of gum

arabic dissolved in water, to which is added a little syrup; go over the entire article with a flat brush dipped into the medium; when dry, repeat the wash. The article is now ready for the oil colors. Mix these with flake white, and use McGuilp instead of turpentine; lay the colors on fairly thick, and let them dry for some hours, then tint and finish with the colors necessary, without the flake white, but still using McGuilp. When finished and quite dry, varnish with best copal or mastic.

The artist should have at hand two or three fine oil brushes, a flat brush, and the necessary colors. Those being indispensable are the following: black, burnt light ochre, terra di sienna, Indian red, and flake white.

The artist is reminded that vases of antique shape look best when decorated in antique designs.

WATER-COLOR PAINTING ON TERRA-COTTA.

Outline or transfer the subjects as before mentioned. Moisten the terra-cotta, and absorb the superfluous moisture with blotting paper. Mix the colors with Chinese white, and use with them the terra-cotta medium already mentioned. For the blues, yellows, carmines, and the bright colors, coat the parts thickly with Chinese white, using plenty of medium; when quite dry, add the pure, bright colors. Wash them carefully over the white, mixed with medium, in order not to rub the latter up, which would lessen the effect. When finished and thoroughly dry, varnish with copal or mastic.

BURNING IN,

— OR —

✳MINERAL DECALCOMANIE.✳

A NEW AND BEAUTIFUL ART OF INSTANTLY TRANSFERRING
PICTURES TO CHINA AND OTHER WARE TO IMITATE
EXACTLY THE MOST BEAUTIFUL PAINTING.

DECALCOMANIE has now been successfully before the
public for a number of years. The above is still a
later invention, and never before brought to the market. It has long been a question whether the durability
of a transferred article, particularly on glass, porcelain,
china, etc., could not be improved upon. This has at last
been accomplished, and the choicest designs are now likewise printed with mineral or china colors, thus meeting a demand often made. Articles ornamented in this manner, and
after going through the regular process of burning in, will be
found as durable and impossible to deface as those painted by

hand from the celebrated potteries of Europe. By this, the art of Decalcomanie is brought to perfection.

DIRECTIONS.

1. Place the mineral subject which you wish to transfer (about ten to fifteen minutes before being used), between some blotting paper slightly moistened. The object of this is to give flexibility to the paper, which thus moistened will give itself easy to the object, either concave or convex, on which you desire to transfer.

2. Cover the object to be decorated with a coat of Vitrifiable Varnish, about the size of the design, with a flat camel's-hair brush; leave it to dry a few minutes, that is, until the varnish is nearly dry, and be careful to lay on the varnish as thin and even as possible, nor leave any spots bare. The varnish may be applied to the picture instead of the ware.

3. Press the picture on in a uniform manner, and rub at first with a clean piece of linen, then, with the handle of a tooth brush, or ivory handle of an infant's brush, or any smooth article suitable in shape, rub constantly for several minutes, until the entire paper assumes a polished appearance.

4. Place the transferred object in a pail of water, until the paper detaches itself, or can be removed without any difficulty.

5. Pass gently a soft brush, dipped in water, over the transferred picture, in order to remove the preparation off the paper. Press down the blisters of the picture with a soft pad made of silk or linen, instead of the above manner, if preferred.

6. Now lay aside the decorated article for twenty-four hours, to get thoroughly dry, and be careful in keeping it out of the dust.

This being all done according to directions, your work is now ready for being *burnt in* by the furnace. The *burning in* process for which the work is now waiting, is only to be accomplished in a *china burning establishment*.

Materials Required. 1. One flat camel's hair brush. 2. Vial of vitrifiable varnish. 3. Vial of clarified spirits.

Designs go by numbers, as follows:

301. Upright Flower Bouquets, 3x4, 30 on sheet $2.10
330. Scenes, Landscapes, 2x2¼, 35 on sheet.................... 1.50
351. Roman Heads, 2x2¾, 36 on sheet......................... 3.60
355. Celebrated Painters' and Female Heads, 2½x2¾, 20 on sh. 3.00
557. Ladies' Heads, small, 1x1½, 144 on sheet................... 2.40
401. Children scenes, Watteau style, 2x2¾, 42 on sheet........ 2.40
417. Ladies' Heads, oval, 2¾x3½, 20 on sheet................. 2.40
502. Flower Bouquets, assorted, 64 on sheet 2.40
505. Children's Heads, 1x1¼, 168 on sheet..................... 2.40
507. Roman Heads, 3x2, 36 on sheet ....: 2.40
508. Females, 4x3, 16 on sheet................................ 2.40
509. Female Heads, 2x2½, 42 on sheet........................ 2.40
510. Monkeys, 3x3½, 20 on sheet............................. 1.80
511. Roman Heads, one color, 48 on sheet..................... .75
512. Round Fruit Pieces, 5x5, 16 on sheet.................... 2.10
513. Classical Statuary Figures in groups, 6x9¼, 6 on sheet.. 1.80
515. Deers, full size, 15 on sheet.............................. 1.80

521. Oval Fruit Pieces, 3x3½, 36 on sheet.. 2.10
521. Bis. Oblong Fruit Pieces, 3x3½ and
        1x3½, 30 on sheet..................... 2.10
522. Bis. Children's Pieces, 3x3½, 18 on sheet 2.40
522. Children in squares, 3x4¾, 12 on sheet, 2.40
523. Chinese in groups, 6x4, 10 on sheet.... 1.20
524. Birds in squares, 2x2½, 24 on sheet.... 2.10
525. Oval Flowers and Fruit Pieces, 5x2½,
        22 on sheet........................... .65
527. Garland of Mosses, Roses, etc., assorted,
        28 on sheet........................... 2.10
530. Etruscan Figures, Emblems, etc., 31 on
        sheet 3.00
531. Female Busts, 4x5, 10 on sheet 2.40
532. Oval Landscapes, 5¼x4, 9 on sheet.... 2.40
533. Children's Heads, 2½x3¾, 21 on sheet, 2.40
534. Fantastic Warriors and Females, as-
        sorted, 14 on sheet................... 2.40
539. Female Busts, 3x3½, 21 on sheet....... 2.40
543. Figures in Groups, ass't'd, 8 on sheet... 2.40

The above designs are all to be burnt in on crystal, porcelain, etc., and cannot be used any other
way.

PRESERVATION OF

NATURAL FLOWERS.

WRITTEN ESPECIALLY FOR THIS WORK BY THE FIRST PREMIUM PRESERVER
OF FLOWERS.

"'Twas a lovely thought to mark the hours,
As they floated in light away,
By the opening and the folding flowers,
That laugh in the summer's day."—*Hemans.*

THERE are five distinct methods for preserving natural flowers, and no one method can be given proper for all varieties, and all families of the floral kingdom. Annuals, flowers of quick growth, of a succulent nature, cannot be preserved in their natural state. Balsams require the elaborate chemical method, and all flowers resembling the balsam require the same specific treatment To preserve flowers as they should be preserved, a thorough acquaintance with all five methods is desired. These, in combination, form one perfect system, which requires lessons and experimental practice.

There was a process patented, and practiced for some years, which was found, after a year's time, that the flowers grew dark, spotted, and were a distressing souvenir. This was the

Hot Water System.

All flowers of a fibrous, woody nature, are susceptible of preservation. The fibrous nature of the wood enters into the composition of the flower.

Roses, camelias, japonicas, tube roses, and azalias, also carnation pinks, (white), were preserved in boiling water, as below:

Take a few crystals of oxalic acid, pour on them boiling water, perhaps a pint to a half dozen crystals, thoroughly dissolving the crystals; after separating carefully with the sharp point of a fine moulding pin the flower petals, drop them into the boiling water, each flower separately—replace it over the fire and let it boil a few seconds, watching and removing each petal as soon as the waxy substance of the flower is gone, and the transparent fibre of the petals remain. Coat the back of the petal with sheet wax, pressing it down until incorporated with the fibre, and put back the flower precisely as it was taken apart, using a wax bud for the foundation of the flower, and using cotton covered wire for the stems.

At the Centennial Exposition held at Philadelphia in 1876, a white transparent camelia attracted my attention. Being possessed of every receipt in the known world, and some of my formulas being combinations resulting from experiments under the instructions of the celebrated chemical professors at Leipzig, I requested permission to examine this flower closely, and to do so, was obliged to get special permission. This camelia was transparent, clear, pure, without flaw, and close examination showed it to be a composite of several different flowers, all of the same variety, done by the hot water system, and instead of wax on the back, varnished with a fine transparent white spirit varnish. These flowers look well for a while, but I do not commend its general use. It will do where the flowers are to be worn in the hair, or on the breast, for a few times only, but after a year they grow discolored, spotted, and are unpleasant souvenirs.

The Sandwich Island Process. In the Sandwich Islands the ferns are preserved green and fresh for months by those who sell collections to visitors of the Islands. These are prepared carefully, and picked in a dry atmosphere, (remember, *that* is indispensable to good preservation), the fronds selected perfect in shape, brilliant in tint, and fully seeded. The fern fully spored is in its prime. The paper used for pressing should be an absorbent, not letter paper, or any satin surfaced or calendered papers. The collector should carry the book to the ground, and not depend on bringing them home in a botanist's case, or heated by hand bringing. You must pick them dry, and place them directly in the book, bringing them home only in that manner. Arrived home, roll a small bit of cotton batting around the cut end of the stem, and seal the end over with red sealing wax, leaving as small a wad of cotton and wax as possible. Then transfer the ferns into another fresh book of papers, changing them every morning and evening until dry. The warmer the books are kept the greener and fresher the ferns after drying. Then ferns can be used ten years after pressing, cutting off the waxed end and setting the ferns into water, they will in twenty-four hours, fill out again and look like freshly picked ferns.

A preserver of flowers said once to me that ferns could *not* be kept green by any known process. This Sandwich Island process is splendid, and a complete success.

By dissolving benzoic acid in alcohol one oz. to a pint, coloring with aniline green, shaded up by mixing brown or black and yellow, all anilines, and dipping *old* ferns, browned by time, the ferns can be used for decoration, in hanging baskets, or on the window curtains, but they do not bear close examination. The coloring matter is perfectly perceptible on close inspection.

The Sand Drying Method in preserving small flowers is good, and no process is complete without the addition of this important part of the instruction. It is within reach of every lady, and the flowers so dried will retain their colors a long time. To every 25 lbs. of fine glass blower's sand add 1 oz. of spermaceti and 1 oz. of calcined borax, thoroughly mixed and incorporated with the sand. The sand must be kept perfectly dry, the flowers must be dry, and from all flowers where the honey gathers at the bottom of the cup, it must be removed before the sand bath is attempted. This is a delicate operation, and effected by the use of a crotchet hook, with a little cotton batting twisted around the point. Introduce it delicately in the flower, remove the honey, dew-drop or water drop, and your flower will preserve dry, in shape.

Sweet alyssum, daisies, candytuft, can be beautifully preserved and keep their freshness for a long time, under the sand drying process. Some flowers need a varnish before the sand bath, some need to be varnished after removal from the bath. All labiate corollas, all flowers cup shaped, should be first stuffed delicately and carefully with cotton batting before putting them into the sand. This knowledge is obtained only by a regular course of instruction, as the family of flowers, or the floral kingdom is so extended. After preparing the flowers, (all flowers should stand after being plucked a short time, their stems immersed in cold water, so as to give full life and strength to the flower, and if it is to be varnished it should be done while standing in the water), have ready your sand in a box with a draw bottom. This bottom is drawn out after the process is completed, leaving the dried flowers intact in the box.

Fill your box partly, with sand perfectly dry, without mixture, clip off the stems to within an inch of the flower cluster, and dip it into hot sealing wax, sealing up the end of the stem carefully and thoroughly, then immerse the stem in the sand up to the flower cluster, taking care to space between the flowers—no two touching. After filling your flowers in the box, commence by pouring in softly and gradually the sand prepared for them. Cover them perfectly, and set the box in a dry place, where no dampness can get into the sand. A single drop of water, or a particle of sap, will ruin the whole of the box of flowers.

In some white flowers a little chloride of lime mixed with the sand can be used once, but as soon as the lime slacks it must be removed. Flowers require from two weeks to thirty days in an even heat of 80 degrees, not more. As soon as the process is complete, pour off carefully the sand from the flowers, and if found to be brittle, expose them a few hours to a dry atmosphere. The ordinary atmosphere of the room will be all that is required.

For the five methods combined, regular lessons are required, but it is not necessary for any excepting those who desire to make floral preservation a business. The sand drying can be followed by any lady for winter bouquets, and the usual flowers of the garden, beautifully preserved in this method, for winter decorations, hanging baskets, etc. Jardiniers are a lovely winter ornament, with green ferns floating, one could not tell but what these flowers had just been plucked from the garden.

The Last Process is: Clip from the bush, without injuring the stem, the buds just as they are opening, allowing two or three inches of stem with each bud, and immediately cover the ends with hot sealing wax. When cold, wrap them up in cotton batting, separately, and lay them away in a cool place in a box, where nothing can rest upon or injure them.

At any time you wish to make use of them, bring them forth from the place of concealment, cut off the end containing the wax, and place the stems in a vase of cool water, containing a little salt. Allow them to remain in a moderately warm room for a few hours, and you will perceive the buds commencing to expand and open, and soon after you can have the opportunity of beholding a full-blown rose, representing all those beautiful colors with which nature has so wisely endowed it, and sending forth, in all the sweetness and purity of its nature, the most loving and fascinating odors, which is so much desired and sought after by lovers of flowers.

These flowers in winter command exceedingly high prices, so much so that some are making it a business of preparing them, and are making money by the operation.

PAPER-FLOWER MAKING.

THE ARRANGEMENT OF BOUQUETS, MATERIALS USED, ETC.

UCH of the success in making paper flowers depends on the quality of the material, and the *form* of the pins, moulders, pincers, etc.

The paper should be carefully selected, reference being had principally to its color and texture. As a rule, it cannot be too thin, and must be soft and strong. Avoid highly glazed papers, excepting when such a flower as the peony is to be copied. In passion-flower and fuchsia there is a thickness of texture only to be imitated by placing a sheet of thin waxed muslin between two sheets of paper. For many flowers, especially roses, a shaded paper is used, so colored as to allow of its being doubled, that a number of petals may be cut from it, leaving the dark shade in the part required. Many flowers will need painting, and for this purpose powder color is employed, using it with a tinting brush, a separate one being kept for each tint. Many flowers, such as tulip, geranium, picotee, etc., require a second or third shade of color; for these, moist or transparent colors are to be used, violet, lake, carmine and sepia being most useful, but for a complete list of colors the reader is referred to page 142. The moist colors must be applied with a sable brush. They should all be mixed with water, in some cases adding a little gum, for the purpose of more completely fixing the color on the paper.

Avoid using the powdered color too wet; it should resemble a thick paste on the palette. Sometimes use the color dry, rubbing it on with the finger, but this only on rare occasions.

Several kinds of wire will be wanted, some flowers having soft and some stiff stems. In some—not many—a very light springing stem is necessary, as for poppy; fine soft wire for the stems of fuchsias, etc. I am led to insist on particular attention being paid to the stems being imitated carefully, as so many otherwise good specimens have been spoiled by having stems hard looking and unlike the natural flower.

Wire covered with cotton is generally used, also fine steel wire for the tendrils of passion-flower, or for the light and graceful stem of the common field poppy.

Floss silk is useful; this must be fine, strong, and soft. It is used as a fastening to many of the petals, to nearly all the leaves, and when a joint of many stems is to be formed.

Black tying wire, for greater strength and larger work, is sometimes necessary.

Gum water is used for fastening the work together; this must not be too thin.

The proper tools will be found at an art store, both as regards size and form, numbering from 1 to 8, but practice alone will enable the learner to judge which is best suited, some finding a large, some a small tool the more effective.

The pincers are required to arrange the petals of a flower, as for a rose, clove, etc.

Scissors adapted to cutting the paper, having a nipper-like contrivance at the bottom of the blades for cutting the wire.

As nearly all the leaves will require some painting, to give them a *warmer* or more natural tint than is to be found in those usually purchased, mix a small quantity of the proper color, use it with a tinting brush, and having carefully painted over the surface of the leaf, leave it to dry, then hold it to the fire ; or should a glossy appearance be required, as in a camellia leaf, the polishing brush must be used.

To obtain the pattern of a natural flower, proceed thus: Select one or more petals, as the case may require. Take a geranium, for example ; this has two sizes, so that one of the large, or painted petals, and one of the smaller, will be required. Place these on a sheet of thin cardboard, trace round the edge with a pencil, then cut out to drawing, allowing a little additional length for fixing them. Mark on each the number necessary for the flower.

In some cases petals are cut in a circle or star, as in clove, rhododendron, or passion-flower. This is done by getting one petal traced on paper, as above directed, then cutting the required number for it, and so arranging them on the cardboard as to represent, as in the passion-flower, a star of five. Take for example a

CRIMSON RHODODENDRON.

This most effective flower should be made thus: Select about twelve petals, gum the edge, draw over edge, let them dry, then gum the small bulb at base of pistil and stamens (called the "heart,") pass the stem of this through the opening of petals, draw down tightly, and let remain for a few minutes to dry, cover the stem with pale green paper, slightly bend the pistil and stamens that they may incline towards the central petal of the flower. A piece of strong wire about nine inches long is required on which to mount the flowers and leaves ; arrange three flowers on the top of this with their backs to each other, leaving the flower stalk about two inches in length, tie this with silk, roll a little stem paper round and then place on three scales, cut from palest brown stem paper ; other three flowers should be placed between those already fixed a little lower down. This order of arranging the flowers to be observed until the truss of flowers is complete. Cover the stem with brown stem paper and arrange the leaves, beginning with the small ones in the same manner as directed for the flowers, only that each leaf should be a little lower down than the last; they will require coloring, and for this use burnt sienna and Prussian blue, applied with a tinting brush, afterwards using the polishing brush; this will give them the gloss observable in the natural leaf. Many of the rhododendrons are made of plain colored petals, but their beauty is much enhanced by spotting them; the process is simple, and the direction for one will do for all, only varying the color used. Select the crimson with dark spots. Take in the hand a stamped flower, and having mixed some carmine, take a tinting brush and apply to the three uppermost petals, taking care that the color becomes lighter towards the edge and deepening towards the center. Now mix a little violet (moist) with carmine, and mark the spots as desired; this must be done with a small sable brush. White rhododendrons spotted with yellow and brown, or lilac with green spots, make very striking varieties.

WHITE CAMELLIA.

For this flower use white tissue paper of medium thickness; no other paper will so nicely imitate the texture of this well known flower.

Cut from a pattern, to be obtained as before directed, (which may be purchased when the flower is out of season), the proper numbers of petals; place each set or size separately on the hand, deeply curl the edge with the same pin used for the rose, and then press down the center with the steel stem, so as to give the deeply indented vein seen in the center of each. The larger petal will require turning on the fingers previous to using the stem of the pin, so as to cause the edges to turn backwards. 'Tis well here to remark that while you use the head of the pin on the edge or other part of a petal placed on the palm of the hand, always place the petal on the fingers when the stem of the instrument is to be used.

The stem of cotton wire No. 2. On this roll some pale-yellow wax; make it about the size of a small plum stone, the three smallest petals so placed that the edge turns inward and the points meet, leaving the base of each petal just touching the wire stem; three of the next size must now be placed on between the preceding, slightly raised. It is found that the most expeditious method of fixing the petals of this flower is to take a small piece of white wax, as large as the head of pin No. 2, used as a wafer, only without being wet. Place this at the bottom of each petal, it will then only require carrying to its place and firmly pressing with the finger or point of the ivory pin to make it adhere; this is both quicker and more easily performed than with gum water. The three following sizes may be arranged in the same order, and each set standing higher up and spreading open as the petals increase in size; all the remaining petals placed on in rows, gradually getting them to bend over, so that the last stand at right angles with the stalk; the calyx cut from pale green stem paper, thickened by the use of wax, this requires the edges to be curled, so as to give a rounded appearance. The edges should be shaded with brown, which may be applied with a small sable brush; a bud placed close to the flower, and some good dark leaves being added, we have one of the most perfect representations of nature to be obtained in paper.

ROSE.

(*Gloire de Dijon.*)

Cut from pale yellow shaded paper, petals Nos. 1 (the outside petal) and 2, and from shaded paper of a lighter shade, but having pink in the middle of the stripe, so placing the pattern on the paper as to bring the pointed end of it to the darkest part of the paper, and so fold it as to allow of eight petals being cut at once. Sixteen of each size will be required. Cut off a proper length of the medium cotton wire, bend over the top of it several times, so as to make a head to it about the size of a pea, on this tie a few of the proper stamens, and around it roll a small quantity of pale green wax. All the petals should be treated as follows, as a preparation for other moulding. Take eight petals of a size, place them on the palm of the left hand, so that they can be held in their place by one of the fingers of the same hand, holding in the right hand pin No. 1, so that it may revolve easily round the edge of the petals, held as described in the other hand. The object of this rolling of the edge is to overcome the hard or unnatural look of the paper, and is *essential* as a preparatory step to all other modeling. This done, turn the bunch of petals, press them in the center with the finger, after which roll over all parts of it excepting the edge, with the head of pin No. 2, this will leave the edge of the petals turned backwards, and this moulding must be continued until sufficient roundness has been obtained.

Separate the petals. This is best done from the points, so as not to disarrange the form already given to them. Take five of the smallest petals, place each on the hand as before described separately, and with the head of pin No. 2, indent it deeply down its center, *beginning at the top*, so as to curve the petal, that when placed on the foundation already prepared they will curl over and nearly conceal it.

These must be tied on with silk. To form the groups of petals, take two of the smallest, and three of the next size; the smallest place in front, the larger behind, and so arrange that each petal should be slightly elevated above the one in front of it; hold them together by the points, and then open the petals from the top, so as to be able to insert the end of a fine gum brush; a mere spot of gum is all that is required, as much as possible in the center of the petal, so as to leave the edges perfectly free.

Place this bunch of petals on the hand, as before directed, and round it in the same manner, only not to the same extent. Five or more of the bunches or nests of petals are required. Each should be placed in its proper position, and tied with floss silk. The two next sizes of petals must be treated in a similar manner, and placed on behind the bunches already fixed, so as, in fact, to give to the center of the flower the appearance of being divided into five or more divisions.

Petals No. 3, require the same rounding as applied to the preceding, two or three being placed together, giving them a more open form; fix these round the petals already on. Elevate them, so as to produce the cup shape observable in nearly all good roses. As the petals become larger, the thumb is found more convenient than the finger, it more quickly produces the roundness on which the beauty of a rose so much depends. The larger petals must be treated in a similar manner, only the edges require to turn back with more freedom and boldness, and the petals gradually receding, so that those placed on last will stand nearly at right angles with the stem, in some cases being even more bent backwards. Two or three of the last may be slightly shaded with green at the base, and carmine and burnt sienna at the edge, so as to give the faded appearance of the outer petals. Frequent reference should be made to the illustration of the flower or its parts as the work proceeds; the calyx should then be passed up the stem, so as to fit close to the back of the flower, and the stem covered with pale green stem paper.

Add a bud or two. These should appear close under the outer petals of the flower. The leaves start from the junction of these stems, being set round, each a little lower than the preceding. They should be colored and polished as directed in "general observations," to give them the bold and waxy appearance seen in this deservedly popular and beautiful rose.

PINK FUCHSIA.

(Duchess of Lancaster.)

Place a sheet of pale yellow waxed muslin between two sheets of pale pink shaded paper. So arrange the pattern as to bring the points to the white, and the darker shade of color to come to about the center. Cut the four petals from deep cherry paper, made thick as before described. The sepals, to be placed on the hand, and with the head of pin No. 2, gently roll from the points, so as to produce a number of faint lines, and also to unite the paper and wax firmly together, giving at the same time the proper transparency and gloss. The petals require considerable working with the large pin, to give them the roundness necessary after they are formed. They will require shading with a mixture of carmine and "magenta," put on with a large tinting brush, the color being almost dry. The pistil made of a large white seed, which must be attached to a piece of fine cotton wire. About two inches from the edge of pistil roll round some wax or cotton wool, then add eight stamens. These will not be as long as the pistil; they must be shaded with pink; top of pistil of a pale green color. Stamens may have a small quantity of white pollen on them; and this being finished, fasten on with a small quantity of wax the four petals, and then tie them with silk. The neck of the flower can be made either of wax or wool, the former being the best. The four sepals having been properly bent, are now placed on, great care being taken in forming them perfectly on the neck before mentioned, which, if it is made of wax, can be done by rolling over each petal as it is placed on with stem of ivory pin; but should wool be used, the petals must be fastened on with gum.

ARRANGEMENT OR GROUPING OF FLOWERS.

The lighter flowers, both of form and color, should be so placed as to be at the top, excepting such flowers as passion flower, fuchsia, etc., which are drooping or climbing plants.

Aim at simplicity in coloring rather than too great a mixture, which gives a confused look.

The foliage is used as a background; there should be no stint of this. The great fault observable in the arrangement of bouquets, whether natural or artificial, is that they rarely have the leaves brought as prominently forward as they should be, consequently the bouquet loses both character and elegance.

Ferns, of which there is now so large and beautiful a collection, add very much to the elegance of the bouquet.

EXAMPLES IN GROUPING. *No. 1, Roses.* Gloire de Dijon, apricot; Geant de Bataille, scarlet and purple; Aimee Vibert, small white; pink cabbage; forget-me-not; maiden hair fern.

No. 2. Rhododendron, crimson; red spotted do.; deep pink do.; pale do.; white do. Some large ferns and orange azaleas of various shades.

No. 3. White camellias; red camellias; pale yellow azalea; pink fuchsia; deep blue cineraria; ribbon grass.

No. 4. Passion flower (various); fuchsias; thunbergia; hop; ivy leaves.

LIST OF MATERIALS, TOOLS, &c.

Moulding pins, moulders, pincers, tinting brushes, scissors, three sizes of cotton wire, silk for tying, fine wire for tying, gum water.

COLORS IN POWDER. Carmine, burnt sienna, Prussian blue, ultramarine, chrome 1, 2 and 3, white, magenta, violet.

MOIST COLORS. Carmine, lake, violet.

The papers most used are: White tissue, carmine, pinks (various), shaded for roses (various), stem paper (green and brown), violet, 3 shades, yellows, scarlet for poppies, etc.

THE FRENCH ART.

A BEAUTIFUL AND PRACTICAL PROCESS

FOR DECORATING WOOD,

LEATHER, SILK AND OTHER FABRICS.

IT is simple to perform, durable, and very effective. The designs are printed in colors, upon paper so prepared that after they are cemented to the surface of the article intended to be decorated, by simply dampening the back of the paper, it may be at once and entirely removed, and the finished work exactly resemble painting; nothing but the colored designs remaining upon the work.

Suppose that a white earthenware or porcelain plate is the object to decorate: Take the design, and after having cut off the larger portion of the margin of the paper, pass over the colored design, with a fine brush, a slight coat of *Fastening Varnish*, being

careful to cover the whole of the design and not go beyond the
outlines. When the varnish has partially dried, or has become
"tacky," which will happen in five or ten minutes, place the varnished surface in the position you wish it to occupy upon the
plate, and then press it well down with the roller; then take a
damp piece of cloth or sponge and press well the back of the picture, (if you were decorating a curved surface, such as a vase, the
ivory knife may be used for the purpose), and allow it to remain
for a minute or two, then thoroughly wet the back of the design
and raise the paper with the hand evenly and carefully. Now
wash the picture, which is transferred as gently as possible with
the water brush, to remove any soil; this done, carefully press
the work with a piece of fine linen slightly wetted, so as to absorb
the water and nearly dry the design, this prevents it from blister-
ing and causes the work to dry flat and evenly. Then after
having left it at least one day, apply a coat of retouching varnish,
and the work is complete.

To Decorate Silk and other Delicate Fabrics. Apply a
coating of fastening varnish, and allow it to dry, then with the
water brush, wash the paper surrounding the design carefully;
this removes from the paper the preparation which would otherwise soil the silk; now apply a second coat of the same varnish,
and when this has slightly dried, place the design upon the silk
or other fabric to be decorated, and with the roller press it well
down. With the water brush wet the back of the paper covering
the design and the paper may be at once lifted off.

Another Method. Cut out the design carefully and cover
it with a thin coating of fastening varnish, and allow it to dry,
then lay it upon the silk or other fabric, and roll thoroughly;
dampen the back of the paper with the water brush, and lift it
off as previously directed.

To Decorate Articles of a Dark Color. In decorating
Japanned goods, or any dark material, it is necessary to take the

prepared pictures covered with white lead or gold back, and follow the directions as before. Should there be any design you wish to remove, or any spots of varnish accidentally dropped upon the article decorated, you can easily remove it by applying the clarified spirits.

A few of the many articles which can be easily and advantageously decorated. Vases, trinket stands, and other ornaments in white china, with or without a border of gold; tea or coffee services in china, earthenware, or Bohemian glass; dessert services, flower pots and boxes, candlesticks, urn and jug stands, carriages, sleighs, wagons, furniture, tinware, and many other china articles which have been made expressly for decoration by this art; white wood articles, straw dinner mats, silk or cloth sofa cushions, scent bags, slippers, hand screens, fans, ribbons, articles in ivory, book covers; indeed it is difficult to say what ornamental article may not be thus decorated, from the panels of a room to the tiny articles of the dressing table.

To the house decorator this art offers a complete substitute for the costly process of hand painting for panels of rooms, and other portions of his work which require artistic embellishment.

As to the choice of subjects, of course that must be left to individual taste. The variety is large, comprising flowers, birds, figures and landscapes, of all dimensions and in every style, the beautiful products of Sevres, the works of modern artists, and inlaid woods.

The brushes may be easily cleaned with a little of the clarified spirits, as well as any accidental spots of the varnishes upon the dress.

As all designs are covered with gold, or plain, the latter will show on a white ground only, and are mostly used for ladies' work. The covered designs will show on any ground, dark or light, and are principally used for manufacturing purposes, such as tin, woodenware, etc.

WAX ART.

FLOWERS AND FRUIT

WITH INSTRUCTIONS FOR

MAKING THE WAX AND MOLDS, MATERIALS USED, ETC.

AX ART was supposed to have reached the height of perfection many years ago, but since the invention of the various machines for cutting and molding designs into form from wax, the rapidity with which the work is executed, and the endless variety of artistic productions in wax art, it is evident perfection has not yet been reached, and we are led to believe it susceptible of attaining a still higher degree of excellence. The reason of its being taught so little during the past few years is owing principally to the fact of its simplicity since the use of molds and cutters, so artistically arranged that the form of any desired leaf or flower may be chiseled out at will, from the varieties of colored wax before you.

Nothing in fancy work excels the art of making Wax Flowers for interest, amusement and fascination. Only a few tools are required. A good eye for colors and a little taste in arranging them. There are two distinct methods. First, ..

By Molding Them. All tubular flowers must be made by molds, viz: Calla lily, lily of the valley, iris, morning glory, scarlet cypress vine, stephanotas, and all other flowers tubular or labiated. A good set of *wooden molds*, carved carefully, is the best, but any lady can prepare her own molds in the following manner. Get your flower fresh as possible, and stand it in water to give it perfect strength. Fix a little pasteboard box, or any small cup shaped box; prepare these yourself with strips of pasteboard, some larger or smaller, just according to the size of leaf or flower you intend to mold from; mix the finest dentists' plaster paris, (practice alone can perfect one in the proper consistency), and pour it into the flower, having enough mixed to fill it and cover every little part of the flower, let it remain until hard, tear off the flower, and you have a *perfect* mold, every little vein and impression perfectly taken. With a sharp knife trim off all ragged edges and superabundant plaster, leaving your mold small as possible, and lighter to handle. These *leaf* molds are much better for all uses, even for *sheeted* wax flowers, than those *metal* molds that *cut* the wax, and never give the fibrous look needed for a *natural* looking leaf. The lily of the valley needs a *wooden* mold, the flower is so delicate a plaster mold cannot be made.

Preparation of the Wax for Molded Flowers. These recipes are of the times of our great grandmothers, who kept a few bees in their gardens, making honey from the fields of sweet clover, the apple and other fruit blossoms in the spring of the year, and buckwheat patches in the summer. The wax was brown, and they bleached it by melting it, clarifying it by selecting the whitest, running it off in thin sheets, and laying it in the hot sun to bleach. All bleacheries do this on a larger or smaller scale.

After bleaching the **wax** white as muslin, you can make your parlor mantel ornaments of it.

Keep a set of tin cups for your different tints of wax, your white cup being the largest.

To Mold a Calla Lily. Have ready a basin of hot soap suds, strong as possible of soap, and hot, so that your lily will be smooth, not lumpy or bubbly. Melt your **wax** by setting the tin cup in *boiling water*, as glue is melted. **To every** pound of **white** wax add a tube of Winsor & Newton's flake white paint, dissolved and thoroughly mixed with one tablespoonful balsam fir, or Venetian turpentine, and half table spoonful of **dissolved gum** mastic, the *whitest* possible. This **is a** *good* recipe for *sheeting* *wax* for your own use, and will be given below in preparations for sheeted wax flowers.

Your liquid being thoroughly mixed in two cups, your white and yellow chrome **cup, the yellow** prepared exactly like the **white,** only *yellow chrome* paint substituted for the white tube paint; **your** molds all **prepared** by standing soaked in the hot soap **suds,** you commence with the yellow cup, dipping **your** spadix mold, or the center of the lily, in the yellow cup, making as many spadix as you wish to make lilies. After finishing **dip-**ping **spadix,** you take **your** white cup and large mold, dipping once and letting it **cool a** moment, and then immersing the second time, **to give a** double thickness to **the** heavy portions of the flower.

A hundred **lilies** can be molded in an hour.

The stems of wire can be prepared next. Fasten the spadix **to** the stem, and slip the stem through **the** hole at the bottom of the molded flower, then with a brush dipped in the hot *green* cup solder the whole together, spadix, stem and flower.

All molded flowers are made exactly alike. All tools dipped **first** in hot suds for every flower, after in the hot wax. It is well, **as a rule, to** make all *white* flowers first—afterward, the colored flowers.

All variegated flowers are *painted* with a brush, using Winsor & Newton's moist *water colors*. All yellow flowers, like Thunbergia, spadix of lilies, etc., by dipping in the *yellow* cup. A scarlet cup for scarlet flowers, blue for blue flowers, rose colored for roses, Naples yellow for sofrano and tea rose tints.

All roses and double flowers are made of separate petals molded and joined together afterward.

All large leaves should be molded, and all small leaves, all dipped in the green cup.

Your green cup is made of all your refuse colors melted together, and the tube green tint added. Never use any darker tubes than No. 1 chrome green. Your olive and other tints are made by the refuse tints thrown in from the drippings of red, yellow, purple, and odd tints.

Directions for Sheeting Wax. To every pound of bleached wax, after dissolving thoroughly in an outer crucible of hot water, add 1 oz. balsam of fir, or Venetian turpentine, in which dissolve a little resin, white or mastic. If white wax is desired, one and one-half tube Winsor & Newton's flake white paint should be added—yellow, orange or rose, and just what other tints are required. All sheeted wax by machine is first molded into square blocks or bricks, and the machine slices off the sheets. But these machines are expensive, and no lady cares to have one who only makes wax flowers for pleasure.

Green wax is made from the drippings of all the other tints, and from the yellow unbleached wax, with green tube paint added.

After preparing your cup of melted wax, have ready a plaster mold made on a tea saucer or tea plate. Dip your mold in hot soap suds, for flower molding, and with a small ladle pour over its wet surface the melted wax, trimming off the sides and making even sheets, remelting the clippings and resheeting it.

A wooden spaddle size of ordinary sheet wax is sometimes made, and used instead of the plaster mold, called *paddle wax*, and a great many teachers use a bottle, dipping the bottle, and forming **wax** thin at one end, thicker at the other. Either plaster, wood or glass must be dipped in the hot suds between every dipping in hot melted **wax**.

Wax Fruit is made in molds, and **is always** used with the paints in preparing the crude wax, and painted afterwards with dry powder paint.

Almost all molds **for Wax Fruit** should **be** made in halves—pears in three pieces—and some fruits require the mold in several pieces. Unless the molds are perfect **the fruit will be** defective, and nothing can make it beautiful when it is once molded wrong.

Your fruit should be perfect, and in making your **molds care** should be taken that there are no open places or leaks in the molds. Grease your lemon, apple, orange, or whatever is to be molded, well first in every part. Have **ready** your pasteboard cup, made a trifle larger than your fruit, nearly filling your cup with the plaster, mixed with cold water to the consistency of pound cake unbaked. Your fruit being oiled, *be very careful* to sink it down *just half* in the dissolved plaster. If you do not get in half, or if you sink it in more than half, you will have an imperfect mold, and your fruit will be defective. A little care makes it perfect

As soon as the plaster is a little hardened, with a pen knife make four holes in the outer plaster rim, not touching the fruit. These holes, half an inch deep, are to hold the top of your mold; lock it into the lower half, blow off all loose pieces of plaster, and when completely hardened, oil the top of the fruit and the new half plaster mold, and the holes for the locks; then prepare the second half. Be sure and have your plaster fresh and strong, when thoroughly mixed to the same consistency as the first, pour over the fruit into the pasteboard cup, and even it all over. Leave it standing a good half hour, then remove the pasteboard cup, and if the mold seems hardened, carefully open it, being careful not to **break off the locks, for** upon the perfection of **these** consists the perfection **of the fruit.**

In a basket of **fruit, lady apples are beautiful, crab apples,** Seckle pears, Bartlett **pears, a lemon, an orange or two, Califor-** nia plums, two peaches, and grapes are desirable. **Two** pounds of wax **will make this elegant** variety. None of the fruit should be large—all **small, high colors, and** *perfect* in painting.

After preparing your set of molds, prepare your wax, as before directed, and there should be twelve gill, **or half-pint cups** kept ready for this work, with the different tints. A small sharp pouring spout on each cup is a great help. The **half-pint** cups being generally used **for** apples, peaches, pears, **oranges and** lemons; the plums, cherries, and little fruits are **made with the** gill cups.

All fruit makers, *masters*, will tell you to be very careful and not get too **deep tints; for a lemon use common** lemon chrome paint, **dry;** orange, orange chrome, dry, and after making those two fruits, you make **from the** same cups your apples, peaches and pears, because the solid, clear color is needed first, and after, you can paint them to their natural tint. 1st, Lemon. Match the color of the wax to the lemon you imitate. Dry patent powdered yellow, gives a splendid lemon tint.

After melting and tinting your wax, two cakes **for one** lemon, have ready **your mold—remember that every mold must** be soaked in hot, strong **soap** suds—have the upper half ready **to** put on as soon as your lower half is filled with the hot wax. Pour in the even half of the mold with the melted wax first. Never allow any to slop over the edge. Place on the upper half immediately and lock closely together, holding them clasped and turning them gently over and over, keeping every part in a slow, steady motion until the liquid sound has all ceased. About ten minutes is needed to every piece of fruit the size of a lemon or an orange.

Let them stand inside the mold for some time, opening very carefully. If your mold is perfect, very little trimming will be required. With a sharp penknife remove every trace of the rim where the fruit mold joined together, and wash off with benzine, rubbing a little dry powder over the lemon to give it a fresh picked appearance, and painting the stem end with water colors.

Orange is made precisely like the lemon, only orange chrome is used instead of lemon.

Apples are made from the lemon cup or the orange cup, with a little green chrome added to vary the foundation tint, and after molding, trimming and washing off with benzine, paint red with dry carmine, producing a splendid effect.

Peaches molded from the lemon cup, or orange, according to the tint required. The fault with fruit-makers consists in getting too deep a color in the cup, or melted tint, and that always produces the coarse effect of the fruits usually displayed. Peaches should be molded of a very delicate foundation tint, first trimmed while *hot* from the mold, as little rubbing as possible on them, painted hot, and after the carmine cheeks are rubbed on, (dry powdered carmine being used), white flock should be rubbed all over them, to give them the soft, downy effect.

Plums are painted with ultramarine or indigo blue added to the carmine.

Grapes are made over glass globes, blown for the purpose, first stemmed, then dipped in green or purple wax, and bloomed over with corn meal (sifted on them).

The California grapes are easy to imitate, for the green wax, after dipping, simply needs a little carmine painting outside.

No cross, piece of statuary, or vase, can ever be taken from the molds unless the molds are made in a number of pieces. After running the body of a cross, there must be a standard through the upright before it hardens, to support it. Pour the lower part on afterward.

Molds for Leaves, consisting of a great variety of beautiful formations, from almost every tree or shrub in nature's garden,

Among the number you have to select from are: Oak, maple, myrtle, lily of the valley, ivy, willow, currant, cherry, grape, orange, strawberry, blackberry, chestnut, etc., etc.

Wet the molds before placing them in wax, to prevent them from sticking. It will require but a little time for you to become familiar with the method of cutting and molding the leaves and flowers, and by the aid of your good judgment and exquisite taste you may soon be able to arrange in form almost any leaf or flower you may desire to see produced in wax.

Wires. The wire used for making the stems and branches is covered with silk or cotton, and of different colors, and can be had in coils or by the spool, each spool containing from twenty to twenty-five yards. Paper wire comes in bunches. Silver wire on spools or in skeins.

Steel Molding Pins. The molding pins are used for molding and changing the wax leaves and flowers into form desired, before placing them upon the stem. They are made of steel. with glass and porcelain heads. Sizes run from 1 to 8.

Moss can be had by the package, or small sprig, for moss roses.

Miscellaneous Articles. Glass shades, glass balls for imitating currants, grapes, cherries, and other fruit, small sable brushes, and dry or liquid colors for tinting.

The Wax, consisting of a great variety of colors, you can purchase by the sheet. The size of a sheet of wax is $3\frac{1}{4}$x$5\frac{1}{4}$ inches.

Having given those who desire to do wax work an outline of the art, with the materials used, and the method of applying them, I leave the rest with the learner, who requires taste for the art, and perseverance to acquire excellence.

THE NEW

SPRINKLE WORK

FOR THE BEAUTIFUL DECORATION OF

WOOD AND CHINA ORNAMENTS.

N idea of turning the standard accomplishments of the day into a remunerative, as well as an agreeable occupation for one's leisure hours, has in the past few years so asserted itself in the refined female world, that the study of wood painting, and etching with the pen, as well as the production of sprinkle work, are now all much sought after.

There is no other handiwork that offers such enjoyment, to those possessed of a sense of the beautiful, as the different methods of wood decoration. While the study and practice requisite in difficult etching, and the decorative embellishment of useful articles with stylish ornamentation, makes one an acknowledged artist, so through the medium of sprinkle work, with the ever new and beautiful effects to be produced by the aid of pressed leaves and flowers, or by the simple method of painting bouquets and landscapes upon wood, there is endless scope for the taste of the amateur.

Sprinkle work upon wood, the subject of this article, is easily acquired. In the manipulation of the materials required, good taste is all that is necessary, although a knowledge of drawing is of great advantage. Besides the possession of the necessary utensils for the production of sprinkle work, one should not fail to secure a rich assortment of leaves, grasses and flowers, adapted to the purpose. A walk in the country in the early spring or autumn will provide one with a goodly quantity of lovely material; or suitable specimens can be procured from some neighboring florist. There are so many fancy articles prepared for this work, upwards of a thousand, that it is well to have a great variety of leaves, grasses and other designs, such as figures, initials, monograms, mottoes, arabesques, butterflies, etc., cut from paper, so that one can produce from the simplest to the most elaborate arrangement.

The pressing and drying of leaves is so well known that we need not refer to it here, but it is well to select leaves of perfect form, as the correcting of deficiencies sometimes destroys the entire work. The leaves best adapted for this work are: Ivy, oak, clover, geranium, rose, myrtle, gentian, maple, edelweiss and ferns, avoiding the thick, fleshy foliage plants.

It is advisable for beginners to arrange their designs upon a piece of wood or paper beforehand, to judge of the effect. Bouquets are appropriate for the smaller articles to be decorated, wreaths for larger or round pieces. For those more advanced, Konewka's silhouettes are recommended. With these and the addition of a little painting, highly artistic effects can be produced.

Utensils. The necessary utensils can be procured in complete outfits, neatly arranged in cases of different sizes. The contents are as follows: One wire sieve, with handle, one coarse painting brush, one fine painting brush, three hundred pins, one small pair of pincers, several china saucers, one tube prepared Vandyke brown, one drawing pen, one Herbarium with artificial leaves and space for the preservation of natural leaves and flowers, one envelope containing initials, six models of leaves.

In working with the sieve and brush, an irregular distribution of color is made almost impossible. The principal colors used in sprinkle work are the following: Prepared sepia, Vandyke brown, black, and dark green. A mixture of black and brown will produce quite a number of shades. The colors used are water colors, specially prepared, and come either in tubes in a moist state, or in cakes which require moistening. Great care should be taken not to get the color too thick.

Process of Sprinkling on Wood. After the materials, leaves, etc., requisite for the work have been selected, take the article to be decorated and score it gently with a small quantity of powdered pumice stone, applied with a flannel pad, this frees it from any roughness or dust that may have come upon it through handling or transportation. Next take a clean cloth, and wipe all the powder off. Now prepare the color to be used in a small porcelain saucer, above all, being careful it is sufficiently diluted to flow freely, not muddy; about the size of a pea taken from the tube is sufficient quantity of color to a teaspoonful of water. The dried leaves or designs are then fastened to the wooden article, by means of pins; this proceeding must be carefully carried out, the points, sides and stems must be well secured, and lie perfectly flat upon the object. In wreaths, the stems should be so arranged that they come together in the center, in order to accomplish a pretty *ensemble*. Now take the sieve in one hand and the brush in the other, dip the brush lightly into the diluted color, that it may not be too heavily charged with the color, press it gently upon a piece of paper, and let it glide back and forth over the sieve, holding the latter in a horizontal position above the object. In this manner a fine shower is produced, which is kept up until the proper shade is acquired. Blots, and where the color has run together, should be removed immediately with blotting paper.

The final arrangement of the wreath should be such that the leaves and grasses which extend out furthest, and are to have the darkest shade, should be fastened last, over the others, so that they can be first and more easily removed with the pincers. After the top layer of leaves, etc., has been removed, where spaces are now perfectly white, the design should be examined, whether any of the others have been displaced, proceed with the sprinkle work as before, and remove from time to time, the leaves in such a manner that those which are to be left entirely white, are left to be removed last of all; the others are removed first, according to the shade required. The spaces of those removed last are also spattered, but very lightly, so that they may not be too glaring.

The beginner will no doubt content herself to produce only such work in one shade; with more experience a variety of shades may be attempted. Those having more practice will not be satisfied with these alone, but after the bouquet or garland is finished in different shades, will by means of carefully spattering the separate leaves, seek to bring out a fine shading and thereby produce a more perfect work; in this case, the entire design, with the exception of the part of the leaf to be shaded, must be covered with paper, after it is perfectly dry, so that the color is not distributed further than the part desired. Through this later and more difficult work the whole is brought out with a plastic effect from the surface, while on the other hand the separate layers of the leaves removed would appear flat and monotonous in their extensions.

Lastly, the pen is taken, and what the foregoing process does not supply, is put in by hand, to complete the work. Take the same color, only thicker, and draw in the veins, and if necessary the entire outlines, to bring out the work more boldly. This being finished, the cleaning of the utensils should not be overlooked. The dried leaves place carefully in the herbarium, the brush and sieve wash thoroughly in water, the finished article allow to dry in a room (not too warm), and after a day or two the varnishing and polishing may take place, in order to give it, aside from durability and practical purpose, a more brilliant finish and higher value to that which has been accomplished with such care.

Varnishing and Polishing. Procure a bottle of "wood varnish," prepared expressly for the purpose. This should be applied to smaller articles, as its peculiar properties make the polishing unnecessary. This varnish is applied by means of a soft flat brush, in a room entirely free from dust, and of warm temperature; the brush strokes should be made from the center of the article towards its edges, and according to its shape. Repeat from six to eight times. Flat articles more readily take the polish than round ones. Before putting on the separate coats, the previous one should be thoroughly dry. After the last coat is dry, apply a little powdered pumice stone, by means of a moist pad, and make the uneven places in the varnish smooth by rubbing. When a perfectly smooth surface is obtained, (this manipulation is omitted in varnishing articles that are turned, because unnecessary), then apply the varnish once more in the same manner, for the last time, and the article will thereby obtain a glossy wood polish. This is left in a temperate room, free from dust, for two days, when it will be thoroughly dry and hardened, and ready to be turned over for the object it is intended. As before mentioned, we advise this method only for articles of small compass. Tables, etc., we advise to have finished by a regular furniture polisher, for the smooth finish cannot be accomplished by an amateur. It is easily conceived that by this process really wonderful effects may be produced, when the artist has taste, and devotes care and time to the work.

Sprinkle Work on China. It may not be generally known that the same effects as produced on wood can also be produced on china ware, the manipulation being slightly different. Instead of water-colors, the ceramic or enamel colors are used, (Dresden or LaCroix). They come in tubes, in a moist state, and are diluted with spirits of turpentine, with a few drops of oil of anise or cloves. Those doing both wood and china sprinkle work will do well to secure an extra brush and sieve, which are to be had separate from the outfit boxes, and use these for the mineral colors only. The leaves and grasses are fastened by means of dissolved gum arabic, being careful to scrape off any particles of the gum that may adhere to the china after the leaves have been removed, before sprinkling over the blank spaces. When the leaves are placed upon the article singly, and the desired shade is produced, lay it in a warm place, over a register if possible. and the leaves will come off as the gum separates from the ware, when the sprinkling may be resumed, and the proper shading given to heighten the effect.

Veins are drawn in with a crowquill pen, but the color must be properly mixed to prevent it spreading. Really beautiful decorations can be made by using ferns and maiden hair to ornament tiles, flower pots, etc. If the leaves, such as the maple, and others that grow bright with the first frosts of autumn, are to have their natural tints, the piece is taken to be "fired," which fastens the background, so that their colors can be washed in without fear of injury to the groundwork. The most useful colors for monochrome work in the Lacroix colors, are the following: Brown, No. 4 or 17, sepia, brown-green No. 6, dark green No. 7, Victoria blue, and violet of iron. If the Dresden colors (Muller & Hennig's) are used, which are preferable on account of their rich and soft appearance, the following are recommended: Dark brown No. 30, chocolate-brown No. 36, sepia No. 28, olive green No. 11, shading green No. 10, and dark blue No. 13. When the work is finished, take it to the china decorator and have it "fired."

It is not necessary to use the best French china for sprinkle work, as it is almost entirely covered with color.

Ladies who do not paint on china, but desire something different from the ordinary stamped work, that is all that can be had in decorated ware for common use, will find this an easy and delightful way of ornamenting the white ware with some favorite flower or fern, and so have something original, and that can be readily duplicated, should any piece be broken, one of the objections to the stamped sets being the difficulty and expense in replacing old pieces.

To those affected by the odor of turpentine, we would recommend the use of Hancock & Son's Worcester moist and watercolors for china.

Faience. Ivory white and other soft wares will answer, and the result will always be a pleasing one if a little care is taken in the execution of this branch of decoration.

PEARL EMBROIDERY

ON VELVET.

N the imitation of pearl, nothing has yet presented itself so favorable to the writer as the beautiful and new method of preparing fish scales for embroidery. You may take the scales from a large size fish, the larger the scales the easier they are to handle. Lay them in salt water for a few hours, until quite well cleansed, after which wipe them clean, and place them between two sheets of writing paper, and lay a weight on them, allowing it to remain a whole day, until they are dry and hard, when they are ready for further use. Now draw the pattern of any favored leaf, or whatever you wish on the scale, with pencil, and cut it out with small scissors. If you are conversant with the form of leaves, you can save time by cutting out the leaf without first drawing the outlines. Draw in the veins of the leaves next with a needle. Stretch your dark velvet tightly to an embroidery frame, place the pattern which you wish to copy before you, and imitate it by sewing the leaves, one at a time, on the velvet with fine gold thread, and the leaf stalks and tendrils embroidered with the same. Wet the thread before using, to render it flexible.

FEATHER FLOWERS,

WHOEVER may be so fortunate as to have in their possession fine feathers can certainly make fine flowers. Have at hand gum in solution, French paper for winding stems, and wire of different sizes. Draw the under side of the feather gently over the edge of your penknife to bend it in the required direction; make a lump of bookbinder's thick paste or wax on the end of a wire for a stalk, and begin your flower by sticking the smallest size feathers into it for a center; place other feathers of the same kind, but larger in size, around in order. Choose green feathers for leaves and calyx, and pure white ones for japonicas and white roses. Twist the ends of the same on a wire, and make fast with gum, glue, paste, or other similar adhesive substance. Be careful to select feathers of the same kind for the same flower. Arrange in a vase, and cover to keep free from dust. In this, as in all kinds of fancy work, let taste and neatness govern the process.

It will often be found necessary to color the feathers to give the desired variety of hues; this can easily be done by attending to the following directions: Put the feathers into hot water, then drain them; rinse two or three times in clear cold water; place them on a tray, over which a cloth has been spread, before a good fire; as they dry, draw them gently into shape between the thumb and finger.

To Dye Feathers Blue. Into about three cents' worth of oil of vitriol mix as much of the best indigo in powder; let it stand one or two days. When wanted for use, shake it well, and into a quart of boiling water put one tablespoonful of the liquid. Stir well, put the feathers in, and let them simmer a few minutes.

Yellow. Put a tablespoonful of the best turmeric into a quart of boiling water, when well mixed, put in the feathers. More or less turmeric gives different shades.

For Orange, add a small quantity of soda to the preparation for yellow.

Pink. Three good pink saucers to a quart of boiling water, with a small quantity of cream tartar. If a deep color is required use four saucers. Let the feathers remain in this dye several hours.

Red. Dissolve a teaspoonful of cream tartar in a quart of boiling water; put in one teaspoonful of prepared cochineal, and then a few drops of muriate of tin. This dye is expensive, therefore use the plumage of the bird ibis.

Lilac. About two teaspoonfuls of cudbear in a quart of boiling water; let it simmer a few minutes before you put in the feathers. A small quantity of cream tartar turns the color from lilac to amethyst.

Bunches of orange blossoms can be made with good success of feathers; the buds are to be made of starch and gum mixed; the stamens of ground rice, colored with turmeric, into which the gummed ends of manilla grass have been dipped.

The inhabitants of the Pacific Islands make beautiful feather flowers, rivaling the natural ones in delicacy and beauty. Pinks, orange blossoms, and roses of exquisite workmanship are often brought from these islands. Old ostrich feathers can be made to look as well as new by holding over hot steam, then drawing each vane of the feather separately over a knife to curl it.

LUSTRAL

BRONZE PAINTING.

PREPARE your board for bronzing by first coating it over with a strong solution of size, made by dissolving isinglass in hot water; strain it, and coat over with a flat camel's hair brush while the size is warm. When dry, coat it over thinly and evenly with gold size; let it remain until sticky, then apply the powder bronze, with a soft dry brush. You may use a variety of shades of bronze if you wish; pale, blush and white. Blend them together to suit your subject, and allow two days for it to dry before commencing to paint. Make a drawing of your figure on thin white paper, rub some white on the back of it, fit it upon the picture and mark over with the sharp end of a stick, pressing on very lightly; after all is drawn in, remove the sketch, and mark over the outlines with a lead pencil, lightly. If you are copying from an engraving, notice on which part of the building the light rests, and select those parts for gold, coating them over with gold size, and putting on the leaf gold when sufficiently dry. If there are any parts of your figure which you want rich colors, do them with gold at the same time.

The painting must now be wiped with a silk handkerchief, to remove all the particles of gold and dust, and supposing the thimble palette ready, with all the colors, first mix a pale tint of purple, made with Prussian blue and a little crimson lake, and pencil over the mountains of the landscape evenly, then go over the water with a very pale shade of blue. After coating the mountains and water once, it is best not to touch them again until dry. Now paint in the foliage, making the tints with yellow lake and Prussian blue; if you want them bright for the different shades, add burnt sienna and Vandyke brown, or both, as your tints require.

Stems of trees are mostly done with Vandyke brown, and other tints added to suit; faces of figures do with white and a little sienna, mixed together; white drapery coat over with white, scarlet with scarlet, and yellow with chrome yellow; all other parts of the figures with white, except the parts you have already gilded. This will answer for the first painting.

The second shade upon the mountain is made with a neutral, composed of three primative colors, crimson lake, yellow lake, and Prussian blue. The tone you desire must predominate in making all your neutrals. If you want a greenish neutral, the yellow lake must predominate; if you wish a bluish neutral, the blue must predominate, and if reddish neutral, the crimson lake must predominate. Having selected your shade, be sure to have it about the right strength before beginning, as it is difficult to avoid a patched appearance on the mountains with varnish color, especially on the second and third coating, unless you are quick in your work. If the water requires more color, paint it in the darker places, then repeat the shades on the foliage, where it is required.

Your figures now claim some attention. Any part you wish to have crimson, paint over with crimson lake, repeat it when a little dry if you wish it darker, and for the shades add a little blue with your crimson lake. Blue dresses paint with a pale shade of Prussian blue on white or pale gold; for the shades, paint in with a little stronger Prussian blue, and when you wish to make any of these colors paler add varnish, and when you want to thin it use turpentine. Green dress, with yellow lake and Prussian blue on pale gold or white; purple dresses, with crimson lake and a little Prussian blue, on white or pale gold. Any part of the figure you do with scarlet, shade it with crimson lake; yellow, shade with burnt sienna, (pale shade). In faces, paint features in with Vandyke brown, and different tints with yellow lake, crimson lake, and sienna paled down, and repeat to suit the eye.

Parts of mountains may require a third and fourth wash, if so, do it with neutrals mentioned above. Sometimes we heighten the effects of the near foliage by touching the edges with a little opaque color, made of chrome yellow, white, and a little blue. It must be done very carefully, as opaque colors are powerful, compared with transparent ones. If what you do shows too abruptly, you have a remedy by putting on a little more of the transparent color. Parts of the figures may be heightened by touches of opaque color, and the faces also may require retouching. When the painting is completed, a full week should pass before varnishing, and great care should be taken not to touch the bronze, as it will leave a stain, bronze being so delicate.

Varnishing. In varnishing, care must be taken to have a clean brush, and the dust wiped from the painting with a silk handkerchief. Lay the painting flat, and with a one inch camel hair brush coat over with copal varnish, as evenly as possible, being careful to cover every part. Leave it flat down, as it is, for a couple of hours, or more, before removing, or the varnish is liable to run in streaks. Once varnishing is sufficient to preserve the painting, but if you wish to polish it, another coat of varnish must be given, allowing a week between; then after another week, it should be rubbed with pumice sand and water, in the following manner: Take a piece of woolen, put it over cotton, to make a rubber of it; wet the rubber pretty thoroughly

with water, dip into some fine pumice sand, and rub it backwards and forwards on your varnished picture, carefully. After you have rubbed for a short time, wipe the sand from a part of it, to see the progress. **If not sufficiently** smooth, rub again, care being taken not **to rub through the** varnish. When smooth, wash all the sand **off, wipe** perfectly **dry,** and give another coat of varnish, allowing the same time for it to dry, then rub again with water and pumice sand. When smooth, wash off the sand and proceed to polish with very fine powdered rottenstone, and rubber made of satin or silk. Saturate this with water, and rub **with the rottenstone** for a short time, until it shines, then wash **all off.** You can make it shine by rubbing with your hand, using **a** little sweet oil and a little **more** rottenstone.

When wood is used for **painting on, choose** that **which is close** grained, and coat **over** several **times with paint, rubbing down** with pumice sand **and water.** After the third **coat, give plenty** of time between **each coat to.get dry and** hard.

GILDING.

The part you wish to have leaf gold, cover evenly with gold size. Chrome yellow or white lead may be mixed in with the gold size to enable you to see the process. Allow it to dry until a little sticky. It can remain much longer than for bronzing, as leaf gold does not require so strong a sticking property as bronze. When sufficiently dry, put on **the** gold by means of the tip, or your fingers, from the gold book. **Be** careful to cover every part **of** the gold size with smooth leaf-gold. When all covered, press **gently a** piece of soft **chamois skin, on** all the gilded parts, and remove the superfluous gold.

JAPANESE ART.

An elegant, **easy and** profitable method **of** arranging autumn leaves **to** make beautiful household articles, such as flower vases, work boxes, etc. Gather yellow withered leaves, perfect in form, press them between the **leaves of a book.** Rub the surface of the article to be ornamented with fine sand-paper, then give it a coat of fine black paint. When this is dry, rub smooth with pumice stone, then apply two other coats. Arrange the leaves according to taste, gum them on the under side, and press them on the piece to be ornamented.

Now dissolve some isinglass in hot water, and brush it over the work while the solution is warm. When dry, give it three coats **of** copal varnish, allowing time for each coat **to** dry, and the work is completed.

THE ART OF PAINTING

STAINING GLASS.

GLASS-PAINTING is not only restored, in our day, to the perfect fullness of its ancient splendor, but also has acquired, through the giant strides of the science of chemistry, and the great progress latterly made in the arts of design, an amount of technical and æsthetical power far exceeding whatever could formerly be called to its aid.

Notwithstanding this advantage, however, the art has not yet reached that wide state of diffusion which, from the exquisite effects it is capable of producing, and deserves, and which it attained in the olden time, even with its then more limited capabilities.

The obstacles which, on the revival of the art, have interposed to check its further extension, and therefore to diminish also the general demand for its productions, are much rather to be attributed to those in whose hands it rests, than to anything properly belonging to itself; they originate in fact less in the art than with the artists.

One of the principal causes of the earlier decay of glass-painting was that its rules being based so entirely upon empirical principles, those who practised it were accustomed to consider the knowledge they had acquired in the thorny path of tedious and long continued experiment as their most valuable personal property, forming at once the means of their subsistence, and the foundation of their future artistical fame. They therefore not only kept the information they had gained profoundly secret during their lives, but even carried it with them to their graves, in preference to leaving it behind them to be made use of by their scholars.

Glass-painting or staining may be defined to mean the art of painting on transparent glass, (either colorless or already colored in the process of its manufacture), with vitrescible metallic colors, which are afterwards burnt into the surface of the glass on which they are laid, leaving it more or less transparent.

All colors used in glass-painting are oxides of metals, or other metallic combinations. They may be divided into two principal classes:

1. Those whose coloring base, or the oxide, is laid upon the glass simply in its original combination with an earthy vehicle.

2, Those whose coloring base, or the oxide, must be made to adhere by the help of a glassy body, namely, the flux.

The colors which require a flux may be divided again into,

1. Those in which the oxide unchanged, but only *mixed* with the flux, is attached to the glass.

2. Those in which the oxide requires to be vitrified, by previous *fusion* with the flux, before it is laid on the glass.

The last may be called *fused colors,* all others *mixed colors.*

The classification before given may be made clearer by the following explanatory remarks. Glass-painting is distinguished especially from other illuminating processes in that the colors and the foundation on which they are laid must, in this art, be fused together in the kiln.

Now, some few colors combine with the surface of the glass, at the temperature of fusion, without further previous preparation than the simple laying on, wherefore these give to the glass only a coloring cementation or stain. Others, on the contrary, in consequence of their peculiar nature, can only be made to combine with the glass by fusing them upon its surface, into another thin sheet or layer of colored glass. This is done by means of the *flux*, a vitreous compound, which fuses more easily (*i. e.* at a lower temperature) than the foundation, the glass plate.

The Process of Laying the Colors on the Glass. The manipulation and the process of laying the colors on the glass varies, in some measure, according to the different kinds of glass-painting, which therefore call for the first explanation.

Either the colors may be laid upon a single sheet of glass, upon which the whole figure with all its principal colors and intermediate tints are burned in (Peinture en apprêt); or,

The figure may be composed of various pieces of *pot metal* (glass already colored in its manufacture), and only the outlines and shadows painted on, the glass pieces giving the colors for the peculiar places where they are inserted (Mosaic glass-painting); or, both these methods may be combined in one and the same picture, by composing it partly of pieces of colored *pot metal* and partly of white and painted glass, fixed together.

Peinture et Apprêt. For painting on a single sheet of glass, the following rules must be observed.

A pure white glass must be chosen for the purpose, free from air specks or bubbles, and especially difficult of fusion, as the whole labor would be lost if it were attempted to burn in the colors upon a ground which fused as easily as themselves. It is practicable, as the examples of the ancients show, to paint on what would appear the commonest glass with a good result, provided that it does not contain too much lead, and thereby become too easily fusible.

Before the operation of painting, the glass plate must be rubbed to a sufficient extent with pure lime, slaked by exposure to the air, in order to clean it perfectly.

The ground or foundation must then be laid over the whole surface of the plate, which may be done in two different ways. Some artists simply dip a piece of clean linen cloth, or a flat camel-hair pencil, in oil of turpentine, and brush the pane of glass with it equally over its surface; while others give to the whole a thin clear ground of black glass-painting color, in such manner as not to destroy its transparency, but at most to give it the form of a dead ground glass. Both methods answer the purpose of covering the glass with a viscous surface, which takes the design and the colors better than a polished ground, the latter prepares the glass at the same time for the painting effects which are to be obtained upon it.

In both cases the ground which has been laid on must be most carefully leveled over, and brought to as thin a coat as possible with a large hair pencil, and must be dried quickly, taking great care to preserve it from dust, etc.

Painting on one sheet requires only one pattern drawing or cartoon, which, however, may be used in two ways. Either the glass sheet, grounded and dried as above directed, may be laid upon the drawing, and the outlines, as seen through the glass, traced lightly with a fine pencil, and with black or other glass color corresponding to the ground. Or the drawing may be placed reversed on the sheet, and all the outlines marked over with a steel or ivory style. If this latter method is used upon a ground of simple turpentine, the back of the drawing must previously be rubbed over with black lead, so that the traced lines may appear dark on the light ground.

In both cases, the drawing, whether it is placed upon or under the glass, must, for the sake of convenience, be fastened to it with pieces of wax at the four corners.

For properly carrying out the process of laying on the colors, a desk or easel is necessary, which should· be capable of being placed in an inclined position by means of props, and should be formed by fixing a glass plate in a wooden frame, so that the light may pass through the painting. Sometimes during the progress of the work, the glass which is being painted may be removed from the easel and laid upon a sheet of white paper, in order better to show the effect of certain colors.

The vehicle with which the pigments are laid on is generally oil. Some artists use exclusively water, but this alone is an insufficient medium for binding the metallic bodies to the glass, particularly if, as in the case of fused colors, they are somewhat coarse in their nature, and require to be laid on in thick layers. They then easily loosen from the plate before the firing, and render the process of laying on much more difficult. It is an important advantage, that with oil the edges are more sharply defined, and the parts already painted may be again touched over when dry without danger of loosening the ground.

It must be understood that when it is wished to make use of water, the plate must either not be grounded at all, or only with a glass-painting color worked up with water.

The most suitable kind of oil for the purpose is rectified oil of turpentine, somewhat thickened by standing, and to which a little oil of lavender is added. This preparation gives the mass the necessary degree of viscosity, and also prevents the color on the palette from drying up and thickening too quickly.

The palette should be of thick sheet glass, ground rough by rubbing with a glass muller and fine sand.

Preparatory to mixing with oil for laying on, those colors which require a flux must (unless a different process is specially indicated) be ground fine in water with the flux, and again dried. But the fused colors, i. e. those in which the oxide has already been **vitrified** with the flux into the state of a transparent glass, should **for the** purpose of laying on, only **be coarsely** granulated ; for the **finer** these are ground the more likely is their **transparency and** perfection to be impaired when burnt in.

Those pigments which are laid on in their simple combination with an earthy vehicle, and without flux, as for example the yellow and red colors prepared from silver, form an absolute exception to the use of oil, and must, for laying on, be stirred up with water to the consistency of a thick cream.

The first of these three kinds of pigments should, as a general rule, be laid on in a thin, the latter two in a pasty, state. The depth of tone of the color depends, with all three, upon the degree of thickness in which the pigments are laid upon the glass.

The laying on of the fused colors **is** accompanied **with** more difficulty than that of **the other** kinds. The latter **are** simply laid on with the pencil, in **the same manner** as with other kinds of painting, **and the** only care necessary **is** that the coat may be perfectly **even** and regular, therefore for large surfaces a wide smooth pencil or driver **is usually** employed. The colors prepared from silver must be treated differently, and laid on the glass at least to the **thickness** of the back of a knife.

But the **fused colors** must be brought upon the surfaces to be covered in **the state of a thick** flowing mass, moist enough to run, but consistent enough **to lie** upon the glass. For this purpose small portions must be **laid on** and spread out with a pencil or small spoon, and **made to flow to** the circumscribing outlines, by inclining the sheet **in the** proper directions. If any part of the surface thus **covered is** required to take a darker tone of color, the plate **must be kept for** some time at **an** inclination in the corresponding direction, so that **the** color may thus accumulate thicker on that part. By **this** process many gradations of tone may be obtained from one **and the same** pigment.

The remaining **rules for the laying on of the** pigments are **those which** principally **result from the** different methods of painting on **one sheet,** of which **there** are principally three.

Either the whole picture may be brought out in its outlines and shadows, on one side of the sheet, with black, brown or gray color, and illuminated with the proper colors in the proper places on the other side.

Or simply the manner of ordinary oil painting may be adopted with the glass colors, and the picture treated as by an artist in oil.

Or, as is now most customary, both methods may be united, the artist making use of each in certain places, according to the requirements of the object he has in view.

For these three methods the following common rules will serve.

The shadows and dark colored outlines, and that which is called in oil 'under painting,' should be drawn on the front side of the glass, or that which is turned towards the spectator.

The illuminating colors, especially the principal ones, should be laid on the back or reversed side.

Intermediate tints, and gradations by shading, should generally be placed on the front side, but sometimes, when they alternate with each other, necessarily must lie on both; as they cannot be put in contact on one and the same side without danger of running into each other, and making a false color.

The silver yellow and red colors, before alluded to, must always be placed on the back or reversed side.

In some particular cases colors may be laid on corresponding places on both sides of the glass, in order to produce certain effects by the light falling through the two together. Thus, purple on one side and gold yellow on the other, give a magnificent fiery scarlet; blue and yellow, according to their respective intensities, give different shades of green; the latter, again, with blue on the opposite side, serve for excellent distance colors. And finally, by the mixture of several colors, the most diversified intermediate tints may be obtained, so that glass-painting in its present state may be brought to assimilate with oil painting in its power of producing varied effects.

In order to put a new tone of color on a surface already marked with outlines, etc., it must first be dried by a gentle and equal heat, (to avoid the warping of the glass), and again painted immediately after it has cooled. Or the black lines first laid on may be at once burnt in, and where possible, with these any yellow shades also which may be required, after which the painting, then fixed, may be further worked upon without danger of damage. The residuum of the unfluxed yellow color may be removed after burning, and again used. This color must never be put over any other, nor over dark shadows, unless these are previously burnt in, but always require a carefully cleaned surface of glass to lie upon; otherwise it would combine with the flux of the under color, whereby the earthy residuum would be fixed, and the transparency and beauty of the whole destroyed.

All pigments must be laid on somewhat darker than in other kinds of painting, as they lose in depth by burning.

When a pigment has overrun its outline, the superfluous quantity must be removed, when dry, with a knife.

By taking away the ground with a style of fine grained wood, pointed in front and smooth at the back, (a tool used in etching), the most effective lights may be obtained.

Should the colors not appear quite dull and dry, but shining and greasy, after the drying of the picture, this is caused by the misuse of the oil, which is always dangerous to the beauty of the pigments in firing.

It is neither necessary nor advisable to allow more than one day for the drying of the colors; the burning in should be proceeded with at the expiration of the time named.

Lastly, during the work, the greatest cleanliness must be observed throughout, the pencil and palette must be kept perfectly clean, and the painting preserved from dust, etc., for which reason it is not advisable to paint in a laboratory or melting room, where the presence of vapor, dust, and impurities of many kinds cannot be avoided.

Mosaic Glass-Painting. The before mentioned rules for laying on the colors will apply also to the method of forming designs with colored pieces of pot metal, or partly with these and partly with painted white glass. It remains to say something more in reference to the employment of the cartoons, and the cutting and arrangement of the glasses in this branch of the art, which, however, is but little practiced, since the leaden bars in a picture calculated for a near view are detrimental to the effect.

Mosaic glass-painting requires two cartoons. One of these, a finished and colored one, is used by the artist as a pattern, and serves to determine the arrangement of the piece of glass according to their several colors, and the manner of introducing the

leaden ribs to fasten them together, according to the outlines of figures. Each piece of glass proposed to make part of the picture, must be distinguished by a separate number.

The other cartoon, which consists only of the black outlines of the lead jointing, and whose several parts are numbered to correspond with the first, is to be cut up in pieces according to the outlines, and the size of each piece diminished all round by one-half the thickness of the lead bar of the jointing, so that the pieces of glass may be exactly cut to the proper dimensions.

The cutting of the glass may either be done by the diamond, or by tracing the line of division with a red-hot iron, after having made a small incision at its commencement, or by cutting with scissors under water, which, however, is not a safe process.

With overlaid glass, *i. e.* pot metal, several sheets or layers laid upon each other from the frit, as for example, red and white, blue and white, etc., it is possible to produce many effects of shading by removing more or less of the colored glass sheet, according to the outline, by grinding with emery. Or the colored sheet may be ground through to the white glass, and thus colored ornaments may be given on white ground, especially for the representation of damasked materials. Also, the white parts thus exposed may have a color given them at pleasure on the opposite side, in order to produce many kinds of effects, or to avoid the necessity of using many pieces when the introduction of another color in that of the pot metal is indispensable for the effect required.

The colored pot metal may be painted with intermediate tints of its own principal color, or even in order to produce certain effects, may be covered on one of its surfaces with another color. Thus, a fiery red may be obtained by covering a red overlaid glass on its white surface with the yellow silver color, and burning it in, or a shade of green by a similar use of the same pigment on a blue overlaid glass. In these operations the widest latitude is left to the talent and practice of the artist.

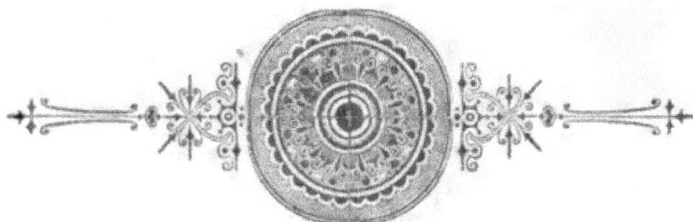

IN TRANSPARENCY, ANTIQUE,

AND OTHER GLASS PAINTING.

———

HE present art of gilding upon glass is an improvement on the method in fashion years ago. It is chiefly used for decorating the borders of prints in executing show glasses, and inscriptions for various purposes, also for ornamental decorations in a variety of elegant forms, upon different colored grounds; but as black is the most general one in demand, shall first treat on that, there being two ways of performing it.

Procure some fine isinglass. You will find white and transparent is the best, otherwise it will be unfit for this purpose. Dissolve it in very clean water, and strain through linen cloth. Put a piece the size of a pea into a tea cup of luke warm water, and let it remain until dissolved. Make the glass you wish to have gilded quite clean, and free it of any dust or grease, get some leaf gold, put it on a gilding cushion, and cut into pieces according to the breadth you wish to have your work gilt. Go over the parts to be gilt with a hair pencil, dipped in the thin isinglass water, and while moist lay on the leaf gold, piece by piece, until the parts are covered. The leaf will instantly adhere to the glass. Then place it near the fire, in a slanting position, until it dries, which will be in a few minutes.

While it is slightly warm, take a piece of cotton or wool and rub the gold to the glass, until you find the superfluous pieces of leaf gold gone, and likewise the back of the part gilt receives a kind of polish. Proceed to lay on a second coat of gold, in the same manner as the first, drying it as before, and polishing it, and so a third coat, which will be sufficient.

Then take the size of the print or drawing which is to be framed, and laying it on the gilt part of the glass, mark where the edges come to, with a hair pencil and some dark color, after which, being provided with a long ruler, and a pointed piece of ivory, draw two parallel lines out of your gold, and with a mahogany or deal stick, carefully pointed, work away the superfluous part, leaving the gold fillet which is to encompass the picture sharp and neat. If you wish to ornament it by any other lines, to appear black in the center, lay on your ruler, and with the ivory point scribe them, and then varnish, having some black Japan, to which a little lampblack has been added, to deepen the color. Paint it all over the gilt part of the glass, and the space between it and the edge, then set it to dry, which takes a few hours. When you are to lay out the breadth of the black line that is to be inside your gilding, scribe it with a sharp point, and cut away the waste black with a graver, or some sharp instrument.

To cut figures, or any kind of ornament out of your gold, after the glass is gilt, have a drawing of the design on paper, at the back of which rub some powdered red chalk, and the smallest quantity of fresh butter; lay the paper on the gold, and with a bluntish ivory point go over the lines of the drawing, and they will be nicely transferred on the gold, when you can with an ivory point trace them out of the gold, and shade them agreeable to your fancy, or from the drawing you have by you. You may, by mixing any other color you choose with white copal varnish, vary your ground as you think proper.

The most important secret in glass gilding is the following method : In an instant after your glass is blacked, taking away the parts where the gold is to appear, and the remainder of the black to stand fast, by which means the black gilding work is done in one-half the time, and with half the gold leaf. The process is simple, and is performed as follows : Obtain the very best black Japan carriage varnish, to which add a very small portion of burned lampblack, very finely ground in spirits of turpentine ; then with a large flat varnish brush give the glass one even thin coat, holding it between you and the light, and observing that it does not appear a thick dead black, but exhibits a degree of transparency not so much so as to prevent its appearing a good black at the right side of the glass. After this, have the letters and ornaments drawn on paper, as before mentioned, and trace it in the same manner on the black varnish when it is perfectly dry. The drawing will be thus very finely transferred to the black. Then take a needle pointed bodkin and finely mark the outlines of what black is to come out through the varnish ; take some thick brown paper, dip it in water, and squeeze it gently, spread it over the parts of the varnish you want to detach from the glass, and in a few minutes, by raising one edge of the black, it will instantly peel away clean from the glass. When all the black you want is taken out, lay the glass to the fire, and the remaining part of the varnish will instantly become as hard as ever, and ready to have the gold put on.

ETCHING ON COPPER.

OING this kind of work upon copper, in imitation of engraving, at a much less expense, is something worthy the attention of sketch-artists and draughtsmen, who will find it very useful in getting duplicates of their work. You first make a correct tracing with a black lead pencil of the drawing which is to be etched, then screw the copper plate into a small hand vice. It must be understood that the copper is perfectly free from scratches, or other blemishes.

Warm the plate from the back with a torch, which must be kept moving over it in all directions, until it becomes gradually heated. It should be just hot enough to allow your hand upon it for a second or two. Take the etching ground—which is inclosed in a silk wrapper—and rub it as evenly over the surface of the copper as you can. Before the plate cools, take the dabber and dab over the etching ground until it becomes perfectly flat, and indeed assumes the appearance of a thin transparent wash, through which the bright copper appears. The etching ground must be equally spread over the copper, not thick in one part and thin in another. Should the copper become too cold ere the dabbing has been finished, you may warm it again; be careful, however, not to make it so as it will burn the etching ground—this would be a great blunder, because it would not then resist the action of the biting-in liquid, which is aqua fortis of different degrees of strength.

Now take a wax torch and smoke the whole surface of the copper thus prepared; keep the torch at a fair distance from the copper, and move in all directions, until the whole plate becomes black with the smoke. Let the plate cool, then slightly dampen the tracing, and lay the penciled side upon the smoked plate, and run both through a printing press. Upon removing the tracing paper, you will find a perfect *fac simile*—reversed—of the drawing, transferred to the copper by means of the smoke.

Now place the copper on the table, which must face the light, and put up between the light and your plate a shade of tissue paper, which will cause every scratch you make on the copper apparent. The shade is simply a sheet of tissue paper stretched upon a common wooden strainer. Keep it constantly up during your work. The plate may be laid flat upon the table, or inclined a little, just as you please.

Now get a piece of thin mahogany, or common deal, longer than the copper, and sufficiently broad for your hand to rest upon while working, for the hand must not come in contact with the plate, otherwise the tracing would be obliterated. The rest for the hand must have two pieces of wood glued on each end, so as to raise it off the plate an inch or so; or you may place a book on each side of the copper—not on it—and lay a flat piece of wood across it, and resting on the books; all that is required being to keep the hand off the plate while etching in the outline.

Have a looking-glass near, and place the original drawing or tracing before it, which will thus be rendered just as the reversed outline on the copper. Now take an etching point and slightly go over all the outline, simply *scratching* the copper, not digging deeply in it.

When all the etching is done, put a border or wall, about an inch high, all around the plate, to contain the biting-in fluid.

The composition for bordering must be warmed, and laid **down** on the plate, taking care that it adheres sufficiently, or else the fluid will escape and burn whatever it touches. The aqua **fortis** is now to be laid over all the etching, and according to its strength so must its continuance be. It may be kept in motion with the feathered **end of a** quill, and when it bubbles up, **you** may be sure it is in active operation.

When the distances and delicate lines have **been** etched in sufficiently, pour off **the liquid**, wash the plate with cold water, and when dry, cover up **with the** preparation—made for the purpose of resisting the action of **the** fluid—all the parts which, according **to your** judgment, are sufficiently bit in. Lay on the fluid again, and rebite the **next** delicate parts, then pour off as before, and wash the plate **with cold water.** Stop out and rebite again, and **so** continue **to do** until the whole work is accomplished.

The darkest parts **of** the etching always **require more** biting-in than the light parts. **Clear** off all the etching ground from the plate, and the work **is** done.

Many ladies **do this work** for amusement, but they give the plate out **to be bitten-in, as the** fumes from the aqua fortis are unhealthy.

The materials for **the art of** etching can be obtained in any village. There are also professed biters-in, **who are** employed by engravers.

Etching **on steel is** done in precisely the same manner, only the biting-in fluid is much weaker.

Etching Fluid for Copper. Mix two ounces aqua fortis with **five** ounces water. Another is verdigris, common salt, and sal ammoniac, each four ounces, alum one ounce, (all in powder), **strong** vinegar, eight ounces, water, one pound; dissolve by boiling **for a** moment; **cool and** decant.

KENSINGTON PAINTING.

ENSINGTON art work probably, at the present time, is attracting more attention than the other methods of painting on silk and velvet. Kensington embroidery had its day, and while it has not altogether passed out of use, it is nevertheless, like many other methods of art needle-work, being improved upon, and for the old method of doing the work with the thread, paint is being substituted, which far exceeds the more ancient work in splendor and simplicity. The great progress lately made in this accomplishment, the amount of mechanical and artistical power, far excels whatever else has formerly been called into use. Notwithstanding all this, however, the art has not reached that wide state of perfection which, from the exquisite effects, it is capable of producing.

Kensington painting, in general appearance, resembles Kensington embroidery, and as the latter seemed to pass away, the former caught up the name, the idea being to produce with paint and brush upon cloth, a *fac simile* of the raised work of embroidery, to answer a demand of artists in oil for something new.

Materials Used. For doing the work procure the following materials: The best probably for the purpose would be a brass pen, one that is very elastic; a goose quill would answer the purpose. Next is a round piece of steel, or needle, such as is used by milliners, and set in a handle if you wish. Three sable brushes, Nos. 3, 5, and 7. Cut from brush No. 3 *all* the bristles, leaving nothing but the abrupt square end of the metal holder; from No. 7 cut away nearly two-thirds of the hair, leaving it with a round end, and you have the required tools.

Now arrange the velvet upon which the painting is to be laid, by stretching it upon pasteboard, and fasten with thumb tacks, so as it may be kept in place for working upon: after this is done, stamp upon it the pattern you wish to have painted. This can better be executed at a place where stamping for embroidery and other work is generally done, and where designs can be found from which you can select just the pattern you wish.

If you have a picture you would like to paint, that is not perforated, you may make a transfer of it to velvet by pricking through with a fine needle, following carefully and completely the full outlines of the copy before you, after this is done, and before the picture is moved, press through the now perforated pattern white powder, with a soft pad, which will show up the outlines of what you seek, on the velvet beneath, or you can use the transfer process given on page 28. It is now ready to receive the painting.

The Colors used are Winsor & Newton's oil colors in tubes, and the opaque mixture for thinning. Flake white, rose madder, cerulean blue, vermilion, chrome green Nos. 1 and 2, burnt sienna, orange chrome, emerald green, mauve lake. For Poppies use Chinese vermilion, a little chrome yellow and green for the centers; for Pansies use mauve lake, with green and yellow for the center; for Daisies (white) with yellow centers, use flake white, with chrome yellow for the center; Forget-me-nots, use light blue, by mixing white with permanent blue, dot the centers with yellow; for leaves, use green, with a little Naples yellow and

Chinese vermilion for autumn leaves; for stems of flowers, use green, and green heightened with white for grasses, and where the leaves require it; for Wild Rose, use rose madder and white, apply same as in poppy.

Applying the Colors. After the piece has been fastened to the board, and the flower is stamped thereon, you may begin the painting. Take first a Forget-me-not. Commence with pencil No. 3. Take upon the brush all it will hold of cerulean blue, mixed with white lake, lay this upon the point which you are to place the flower, and with the brush press it out by rolling the brush from the center to the outline of the petal of the flower, in such quantities as to show a rolled edge, (resembling the embroidery), leaving the center with but little of the paint. With the same brush, or point of the pen, (after cleaning with naptha), touch the center with a small particle of chrome yellow, (about the size of a pin head). Now, with the needle, lay on the stems, using green. In doing this, cover the whole of the needle with the color, and lay on the velvet full length, drawing it over the outline, and rolling in the fingers as you move it. This is also used in making flat grasses and leaves. In painting the daisy a pen is used. Place the paint first upon a palette knife, and then take it off from the knife with the pen, which will be found much more convenient, being particular to get the point full of the color by laying the pen sideways when taking it up, (using flake white), press to the outside of the flower, and by bearing heavy enough you will find it carries the color to the outline of the petal in rolls, leaving the center almost void of color. The instrument used for this should be very elastic, and one not easily broken by bending. After you have gone over each petal, dot the center, by using No. 3 brush, with chrome yellow and burnt sienna, mixed, using enough of the color to fit the space of pistil.

In painting the Poppy, use No. 7 brush for outside petals, and No. 5 for inside, or smaller ones. Press as before directed upon the brush, and turning it at the same time toward the outline, pressing the paint to the margin of the petal, and leaving it there in a roll, with the center of the petal as before mentioned. This being done, take brush No. 3, and with chrome yellow place in the pistil and stamens (commonly called the "heart"). For other flowers, follow instructions as previously laid down.

The outlines of flowers are made with brush No. 3, and the pen. The needle is again employed for drawing in the veins, using for this light green, and apply as heretofore directed, by covering with the color, and draw full length over the outlines endwise.

In making autumn leaves, take No. 5 brush, using for this vermilion, chrome yellow and burnt sienna, and sometimes a little green. For durability, this painting will compare favorably with any other method.

N. B.—When the opaque mixture is used no previous preparation or coating of any kind is necessary. The colors will not spread, run or stain silk or velvet of the most delicate shade or tint, beyond the outline.

Use the opaque mixer, to thin the paint to its proper consistency before applying, using no oils, turpentine, or dryer of any kind with the mixer, as it is of itself a sufficient dryer.

If your silk or material painted shows a dampness beyond the line of color, let it remain until the color dries, and it will all evaporate dry, leaving no stain whatever on the material, placing the paint beautifully in rolls, to imitate what it is intended to, Kensington embroidery.

ARRASENE

AND RIBBON EMBROIDERY,

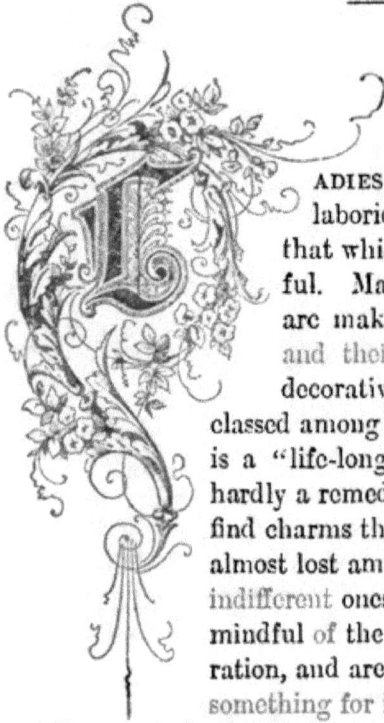

L ADIES are turning away from the more laborious kinds of work, and seeking that which is artistic, useful, and beautiful. Many who have heretofore sat idle, are making their leisure hours pleasant, and their homes resplendent by aid of decorative art. Housekeeping may be classed among those necessities which, to many, is a "life-long torment," for which there is hardly a remedy, although there are those who find charms therein; they at the same time are almost lost amid the vast multitude of ordinary indifferent ones. However, nearly all are kept mindful of the purity of the art of home decoration, and are showing sufficient interest to do something for its elevation.

Arrasene embroidery is comparatively new, yet its beauty has so fascinated the women of taste that teachers of the art are sought after everywhere, and their scarcity has caused the publication of the following instructions.

There is a wool called wool arrasene, and a silk called silk arrasene; the arrasene embroidery is simply the working of these in tufts, to form flowers and other ornaments, such as mottoes, cushions, etc. An owl worked in grey arrasene is beautiful. Inasmuch as the working of flowers seem to better satisfy the taste of arrasene art workers, I will give the instruction.

How to Make a Wild Rose. For this you will need two shades of satin or velvet—either are very pretty. Have the pattern stamped or drawn on whatever you wish to embroider, plush, felt, satin, or other goods; cut the satin in shape of the petal of the flower, and be sure to have them long enough to turn in the edges. Now blindstitch it on the pattern, being careful to leave fullness enough to form folds in the petals, gathering them at the center, using the French knot, or seed stitch, and embroidery silk, yellow and brown for roses. For double rose, cut more pieces for petals, and lay one over the other. For daisies, use narrow white ribbon, plaiting the ribbon in the center, filling in with the French knot stitch, using two shades of yellow and brown.

In making a forget-me-not, use very narrow blue ribbon, for the centers one knot stitch of yellow and one of red. For green leaves and stems, and the green around the rose, (calyx), use arrasene wool or silk, or a part of each. It is much handsomer to use the silk for high lights; for stems of roses use reddish brown.

Many flowers can be very effectively represented by the ribbon embroidery, such as dogwoods, sunflowers, pansies, and other varieties.

PORTRAITURE

IN

BLACK CRAYON.

RAYON PORTRAITURE, to one who knows nothing of the method, seems not only very difficult, but almost unattainable, except after long years of study and practice. Even then many suppose artists are born, not made. The writer of this article has been employed in teaching the art for several years, and could refer to many pupils who, after comparatively few lessons, were able to execute finished portraits of real merit. Any one who can learn to write can learn to draw, but a special method is necessary to enable pupils to work intelligently. Most other branches of art have been elaborately treated by able pens, but crayon drawing as a study, has been hitherto neglected. A careful preparation of written instructions cannot fail to enable one with ordinary ability and taste to master this most beautiful art. One of the first requisites for successful work, is to have proper material, and of the best quality.

PAPER. The best and only paper that should be used is Whatman's imperial, or double elephant. It should never be used by tacking to a drawing board, but must be mounted on a stretcher. All Art Stores have a ready supply of these, but for the sake of economy they can be made in the following manner. Take a pine frame 20x24, or any desired size, lay a sheet of Whatman's paper upon a table, face side down, dampen it with a sponge over the entire surface : lay the frame upon it, and trim the edges of the paper with a knife, about one inch larger than the frame. Cut out the corners, then with a small brush put a little flour paste upon the paper beyond the frame, and also upon the edges of the frame ; turn this paper up on to the edges of the frame, drawing it a little with the fingers to take out the larger wrinkles, and make it adhere firmly. Put away in a cool room, to allow the paper to dry, and a stretcher is ready for use. Do not moisten the paper on the side upon which the drawing is to be made, as this would occasion spots, which would spoil the work.

In selecting materials, buy the small paper stomps, which come in packages of a dozen or more ; one soft rolled chamois stomp, (avoid the hard stiff ones) ; a stick of square Conte crayon No. 3, a piece of Conte rubber, which can be sharpened with a knife when it becomes too blunt, a few sticks of the round glossy Conte crayons, a crayon holder, and a few sticks of soft charcoal. Take a small block of wood, about 3x5 inches, paste a piece of fine sand paper carefully over one or both sides, and let it dry. This block is useful to sharpen and clean the rubber and paper stomps. Upon another block of the same size, or a little larger, paste a piece of Whatman's paper, smoothing it down carefully, allowing this to dry thoroughly. Take the stick of No. 3 square crayon, rub it over this block hard, to make the pulverized crayon to be used with stomps, or use a fine file, and allow the crayon thus pul-

verized to fall upon the block. Keep this free from dust
when not in use. These are all the materials necessary to
execute a crayon portrait.

The next step will be to make the enlargement of the photograph from which a copy is to be made, providing a solar
print is not used. There are several ways of doing this. The
best method is to have a good pentagraph, unless one is able
to draw the outline enlargement free hand. In either or all
cases make the outline upon a piece of manilla wrapping
paper, cut the size of the stretcher intended. When this
enlargement is made, thoroughly blacken the back with a
piece of charcoal by laying the paper upon a smooth drawing
board or table ; turn it over and lay it upon the stretcher,
being careful to place it so the drawing will be in the center
of the stretcher, securing it with tacks or pins at the corners,
in order that it may not slip. With a stylus, or hard lead
pencil, trace over all these outlines again, being careful to
follow them accurately, omitting none. Remove the paper
with care, and a definite outline of the picture will be seen
upon the stretcher. This will rub off with the slightest
touch, therefore take one of the paper stomps, rub it on the
block of pulverized crayon, holding it in the hand as a pencil,
trace lightly over these outlines in order to prevent losing
them while at work upon the picture. Be careful, however,
to do this very lightly, if not, the lines will show when the
picture is finished, and spoil the effect of the work.

The first step to be taken is to put the crayon on the darkest part of the features. Rub the paper stomp on the block
of pulverized crayon very hard, turning it around between
the fingers in order to get the crayon on the whole surface of
the point and tapering end. Apply this lightly but firmly,
and with a broad stroke to the lines or lids above the eyes,
the nostrils, the line through the center of the mouth, the
dark shades in the ears and the eyebrows, following the out-

lines already **upon the** stretcher. **Put in the pupils of** the
eyes very black and heavy. The stomp has now cleaned itself
somewhat. Next darken the iris of the eye, put on **the**
shadows under the eye, the curves of the nose from the eyebrows to the end, and the curves around the nostrils. **Next**
the upper lip, tinting it lightly. Now define the outlines of
the cheeks, working in light strokes inward, and hatching
them, **or** crossing the strokes at an acute angle (never at
right angles). Work for the expression, and hold it.

Having gone thus far the stomp will be quite free of color.
The blending process comes next in order. Work slightly
upward from the **lines** around the eyes, borrowing **from** the
color already there for the shadows desired. The same from
all the features above mentioned, watching the photograph
closely and leaving off such shadows gradually.

Tint all **the** darker shades **on** the **entire** face in the same
manner, not as dark at first as they will **be** required. **Leave
all the strong high** lights perfectly white until the picture is
nearly finished. In putting on these shadows the hatching
process will be found the most effective, not, however, **by**
making **strong lines, but** simply have the strokes **of the**
stomp made **in** such direction, very soft and indistinct. **If**
any large white spots seem **to** remain, **thus** destroying the
evenness of the tone, touch **them** over lightly until the **tone**
resembles in quality a wash with India ink **or** water color,
gradually growing lighter and lighter until lost in the high
lights and half tones. **The** beauty of the finished portrait
will depend very largely **upon** this blending, as there must be
no abrupt ending to **any** shadow. **Leave** the face for the
present, **and** take the chamois stomp, rubbing it on the block
of crayon until the end is thoroughly covered. Lay it very
flat and lightly on the parts of the hair which are the darkest,
commencing at the deepest part of such shades, and ending
toward the high light. Leave these high lights as in the face
perfectly white for the present.

Try and follow the direction in which the hair is combed, but mass it. No attempt should be made to show individual hairs. It is simply light and shade in masses. Next take the clear end of the chamois stomp, borrow from the darker shades to tint the high lights, making broad strokes. If this makes them too dark, lighten with the rubber. All rubber strokes in the hair should also be broad, not fine lines. The drapery comes next in order. A black silk dress or a broad-cloth coat should be worked in the same manner. With the chamois stomp put in the darker places in the drapery first, following the same general rule of hatching only in broad strokes, not lines. Tint the higher lights in the drapery with the clean end of the same stomp, borrowing from the darker places as before. The same rule should be observed in ending the drapery, as in the shadows of the face—let it become lighter and lighter, until lost entirely.

Note carefully the collar and shirt front. Generally there will be seen light shadows upon them. If so, tint lightly with a clean stomp, borrowing the color necessary from the drapery, not from the block.

If the drapery now appears spotty it must be cleaned up in the following manner. Fill up the lighter places with the paper stomp, rubbing lightly in different directions, while the spots that are too dark can be cleaned off with the rubber in light strokes. In this manner the drapery can be worked up very smoothly, and free from spots. The background should be worked up in the same manner as the drapery, only not as dark. Do not put a background around the entire head, only from the shoulders up about half the distance to the forehead. If the subject is a lady, and lace work is desired, make this with the paper stomp. Do not work for details, but in an indistinct manner, following the original design somewhat, but in soft strokes, taking out the high light with the rubber, if necessary. The drapery, background and hair are now supposed to be finished, the above directions having been followed carefully.

The finishing of the features must now be attended to. With a paper stomp, not too black, strengthen all the darkest shades in the face, borrowing color again, working the shades off upon the high lights, preserving the half tones and reflected lights. Unless the high lights are very strong in the original, tint them over slightly with a stomp fairly clean. It is hardly necessary to say the subject, or original photograph, must be studied very carefully. If this is done, and the outlines accurately made, a perfect likeness will be the result.

If the pupils of the eyes, or any very deep shadow, need a little strengthening, it can be done with the round Conte crayon, sharpened to a very fine point, and hatched lightly over such shadows.

The finishing touches must be made by using a clean paper stomp, going over the entire picture, a little beyond all the outlines, to soften them, thus producing a soft and natural effect. Last of all, take out the catch light in the eyes, with a sharp pointed knife, scratching it slightly until it is of the desired shape.

In closing these instructions, the writer wishes to impress upon the pupil or reader the necessity of working at all times, and upon all parts of the picture, *very lightly*, if not, a muddy effect will be the result. The hatching should be tolerably open, but not too much so. This produces the effect of transparency, which is very desirable.

If the above instructions are carefully studied, and patient labor put forth, any one may reasonably expect to obtain excellence in representing life-like and natural portraits.

✴ ANALYSIS OF COLORS. ✴

THEIR NATURE AND QUALITY.

WE will begin with gall-stone, which is one of the finest and brightest in the world, and a very lasting color, although in face painting it should be sparingly used, its wonderful brilliancy being apt to drown all the other colors, and make the work it is used in too warm in its tints.

Of Terra Sienna, it is unburnt, a bright yellow-brown earth, and is used by some miniature painters as a warm yellow; but burnt it is a beautiful color, and partakes of three tints, yellow, red and brown.

Yellow Ochre is a bright yellow earth, and comes from France, is semi-opaque, and works well. Much used by artists, but must be used with caution. It is a lasting color, and of service in the fleshy face tints.

Roman Ochre is a reddish yellow earth of a very great body, and used by some with success in miniature painting. Used with gum water it works well, and being a warm color, it communicates that quality to the tints it is worked on.

Naples Yellow is an earth found near Naples, and is a soft, bright and durable color. A great proportion of that used is composed of lead, alum, sal-ammonia and antimony. This

197

color is not very much used by artists, as it does not stand well. Is a pale, gritty yellow. It absorbs all colors that are worked on it or mixed with it.

Gamboge is the concrete juice of various trees in Ceylon—is a transparent color, and consequently useful as a glazing color.

Yellows have their base in iron, lead, quicksilver and arsenic.

BLUE. Of all blues in use none can equal ultra-marine—its wonderful brilliancy and permanency excelling all others. But it is often adulterated after reaching this country, and the genuine is not common. Put a small quantity on a case knife, and hold it over a candle, keep the smoke from touching it; if adulterated it will appear in grey spots, and if genuine it will remain brilliant as at first. It was formerly made from lazulite, the beatiful variegated blue mineral, worth at one time in Italy twenty-five dollars an ounce. A greater part of that used now is composed of carbonate of soda, sulphur and kaolin, colored with cobalt.

Prussian Blue is a good color, it is a ferrocyanuret of iron, produced in different ways. There is no substitute for Prussian blue for miniature painting on account of its strength of effect and transparency. The best and purest is that which is dark color.

Indigo is beautiful on account of its extreme depth of color, nearly approaching to black; the best is called the rock indigo.

Cobalt is another fine blue, much used in sky grounds, and in the delicate parts of faces and necks.

French Ultra. A beautiful bright blue; it is adapted for ladies' drapery—rather too powerful for pearly tints or flesh.

Permanent Blue, Cerulean. Useful in draperies and backgrounds; also in landscape and flower painting. Not good for flesh tints.

Sap Green is the juice of buckthorn berries, and has proven to be a highly useful color when judiciously mixed with other colors, producing warm fleshy tints which cannot be made without it.

Copper is the base of most blues, though some are formed from iron and cobalt.

REDS. Carmine is a fine bright crimson, inclining to scarlet, and rather an opaque color. From it a variety of fine tints may be made, but it being a very high red, renders it unfit for delicate subjects; in this case use rose madder. There are various kinds of it prepared of other reds, but the deep kind is the best, the lighter being made so by adulteration, commonly made of alum and cream tartar, colored with cochineal, but it fades rapidly by out-door exposure. The genuine is made from kaolin, or China clay, colored with cochineal, prepared with much difficulty, which makes it expensive.

Crimson Lake is a beautiful crimson color, inclining toward the purple, making it useful for the carnation tints in painting delicate subjects.

Chinese Vermilion is a bright red, and useful in miniature pictures, though too freely used, its opacity renders it dangerous to mix much with other colors, but by itself, in touching the lips and other parts that require extreme brightness, it is of good service. It comes from China in small parcels, fourteen ounces each.

The native, or *Mineral Cinnabar*, or vermilion, is very fine in Spain; the French have mines of it in Normandy.

Light Red. Useful in almost all flesh colors, and the ground upon which all the finer tints are made.

Venetian Red. Nearly the same as light red, and used almost for the same purpose. It is an earth, found in many parts of the world.

Rose Madder, indispensable for carnation lips. This, with

cobalt, and almost any **transparent** yellow, **forms all sorts of** pearly and grey tints.

Indian Red is of a deep purple cast, **and** a most excellent color **for** touching the deep red parts, **and** the fleshy **tints.** Also useful in bright backgrounds and draperies.

BROWNS. Umber is a yellowish brown, and mixes well with water colors. Useful in backgrounds. When properly burnt it **is** a charming reddish brown, very useful **in hair. Works extremely** well.

Terra de Cassel, **or** Vandyke brown, so called from the very great estimation **the inimitable** painter of that name held it in, **is the finest rich brown in** the world, in itself producing a **more beautiful** color **than can** be formed by the junction **of any colors** whatever. **It is in general use, and is, in its** natural **state,** rather **coarse and sandy, but** when prepared, it amply **repays** the **artist for his labor ; good glazing** color for hair shadows.

Lampblack is **the smoke of** burning **resin, and is useful for** marking the pupil of the **eye,** and in painting draperies. **It is** a good color when **burnt,** stands and works remarkably well. The smoke of a candle, received on a plate, is found the best, being blacker than the common lampblack. Ivory black is preferred by some.

King's Yellow is a fine **bright** opaque color, and is admirably calculated for painting lace, gilt buttons, etc., but should be **cautiously used, as it is a** rank poison.

Chinese White is permanent, and works remarkably well; it **is** freely **used on** every part of a picture in water colors.

Flake White. This is the only white adapted **for oil colors.** Chinese **white is never** used.

MIXING COMPOUND TINTS FOR THE FACE. Purple is **formed of either ultra-marine, Prussian** blue, smalt or indigo, mixed **with** either carmine **or** lake. Ultra-marine, although the most beautiful and brilliant of colors by itself, loses that perfection in any mixture, but it still retains a sufficient share of brightness to render it a desirable tint in the purpiish-grey tints of the face. Prussian blue, mixed as before mentioned, makes a bright or dark purple, according to the quantity of either color. Indigo makes a still darker purple, owing to its great natural depth of color. French ultra and carmine, or lake, forms nearly the same tint as ultra-marine, and may be used nearly for the same purpose.

Olive Tints. A very fine olive tint is formed of gall-stone, Nottingham ochre and carmine, or lake; and another of sap green and lake only.

TINTS AND THE COLORS WHICH PRODUCE THEM.

Grey is made by combining White and Lampblack.

Buff	"	White and Yellow Ochre, Red.
Pearl	"	White, Black, Blue.
Orange	"	Yellow, Red.
Violet	"	Red, Blue, White.
Purple	"	Violet, Red, White.
Gold	'	White, Stone, Ochre, Red.
Olive	'	Yellow, Blue, Black, White.
Chestnut	"	Red, Black, Yellow.
Flesh	"	White, Yellow Ochre, Vermilion.
Limestone	"	White, Yellow Ochre, Red, Black.
Sandstone	"	White, Yellow Ochre, Red, Black.
Freestone	"	Red, Black, Yellow Ochre, White.
Fawn	"	White, Yellow, Red.
Chocolate	"	Raw Umber, Red, Black.
Drab	"	White, Raw and Burnt Umber.
Pea Green	"	White and Chrome Green.
Rose	"	White, Madder, Lake.
Copper	"	Red, Yellow, Black.
Lemon	"	White, Yellow.
Snuff	"	Yellow, Vandyke Brown.
Claret	"	Red, Umber, Black.

Dove is made by combining White, Vermilion, Blue, Yellow.
Pink   "   White, Vermilion, Lake.
Cream   "   White, Yellow.
Salmon   "   White, Yellow, Raw Umber, Red.
Straw   "   White, Chrome Yellow.
Lilac   "   White, with Violet.
Changeable   "   Red, Green, lightened with White.
Peach Blossom   "   White, Red, Blue, Yellow.
Bronze Green   "   Chrome Green, Black, Yellow, or
    Black and Yellow, or Black and Green.

TRANSPARENT COLORS. Burnt Terre de Sienna, Terre
Verte Asphaltum, Dragon's blood, Carmine, Rose Pink,
Gamboge, Prussian Blue, all the Lakes and all the Gums.

SEMI-TRANSPARENT. Umber, Vandyke Brown, Chrome
Red, Emerald Green, Indigo, Verdigris, Brilliant Ultra-
Marine.

CONTRAST AND HARMONY OF COLORS. One color will
generally harmonize with another when both contain the
same base in different proportions. White contrasts with
Black, Brown, and harmonizes with any other color. Yellow
contrasts with Purple, White, and harmonizes with Orange
and pale colors. Orange contrasts with Blue, and harmonizes
with Red, Pink. Red contrasts with Green, and harmonizes
with Crimson. Green contrasts with Red, and harmonizes
with Yellow. Purple contrasts with Yellow, White, and
harmonizes with Crimson. Black contrasts with pale colors,
and harmonizes with deep colors. Gold contrasts with dark
colors, and harmonizes with light colors.

TAXIDERMY

SKINNING.

WHEN a quadruped is killed, and its skin intended for stuffing, the preparatory steps are to lay the animal on its back and plug up its nostrils, mouth, and any wounds it may have received, with cotton or tow, to prevent the blood from disfiguring the skin. The fox will serve admirably our purpose as an example. Therefore, Reynard being procured, we need not say how, lay him on his back in the same position as before recommended, and having first stuffed the mouth with cotton and tied it up, and measured his neck and body with rule and calipers, and noted them, proceed. Make an incision from the last rib nearly to the vent, but not quite up to it. Having done so, proceed to raise the skin all round the incision as far as the thighs, first skinning one side and then the other, using the flat end of the knife in preference to the blade to raise the skin. Having reached the hind legs, separate the latter at the femur or thigh-bone, close to the back-bone, leaving the legs attached to the skin. Now skin the head quarters close up to the tail, and separate it from the body at the last vertebræ, taking care not to injure the skin. Pull the skin over the heads of the hip-joints, and now the carcase may be suspended by the hind-quarters, while the skin is stripped by pulling it gently and cutting towards the fore-quarters. The fore-legs are separated from the body, as the hind ones had been, close to the shoulder-bone, and the skin fairly pulled over the head and close to the nose, when the head is separated from the body by cutting through the last vertebræ of the neck. Reynard is now skinned, the head, legs, and tail being all attached to the skin, from which the carcase is separated.

The flesh is now cut entirely away from the cheek-bones, the eyes removed, the brains taken out by enlarging the occipital opening behind the cranium, the whole cleaned and supplied with a coating of arsenical paste and stuffed with tow or wool to the natural size.

The legs are now successively skinned by pushing out the bones and inverting the skin over them until the foot-joint is visible; every portion of flesh and tendons must be cut away and the bone cleaned thoroughly, and a coating of arsenical soap laid over it as well as the skin. Wrap tow, or cotton, or any other suitable material, round the bone, bringing it to its natural shape, and draw the skin over it again. Do this to each leg in succession, and the body itself is ready for stuffing and mounting.

The utmost care will not prevent accidents; the fur and plumage will get sullied, and before stuffing it is well to examine the skin, for stains and spots are calculated to deteriorate its appearance. Grease or blood-spots may be removed by brushing over with oil of turpentine, which is afterwards absorbed by dusting plaster of Paris over. Macgillivray recommends that all skins, whether they are to be put away in a cabinet or stuffed, should receive a washing of spirits of turpentine sprinkled on, and gently brushed in the direction of the feathers or fur. Not to trust too much to memory, it is desirable to measure and note the proportions of the animal before skinning, first taking the muzzle to the tail. Afterwards, from the junction of the tail to the tip. Secondly, from the middle of the shoulder-blade, or scapula, to the articulation of the femur, or thigh-bone. Thirdly, the animal being placed on its side, measure from the upper part of the scapula to the middle of the sternum—that is, to the spot where the two sides meet above, and finally from the socket of the scapula to the socket of the articulation of the femur, or thigh-bone. In addition to these, note, by measurement with caliper compasses, the size of the head, the neck, the tail, and other points which affect the shape of the animal. These measurements will serve as a guide in stuffing, and for the size of the case and length of the mounting wires. In the process of skinning, it is important to avoid penetrating to the intestines, or separating any of the abdominal muscles which lead to the intestines; any such accident would be very disagreeable, as well as injurious to the skin.

Stuffing Quadrupeds, etc. Let us suppose the animal which we intend to stuff, to be a cat. Wire of such a thickness is chosen as will support the animal by being introduced under the soles of the feet, and running it through each of the four legs. A piece of smaller dimensions is then taken, measuring about two feet, for the purpose of forming what is termed by stuffers, a tail-bearer. This piece of wire is bent at nearly a third of its length, into an oval of about six inches in length; the two ends are twisted together, so as to leave one of them somewhat longer than the other; the tail is then correctly measured, and the wire is cut to the length of it, besides the oval. The wire is then wrapped round with flax in a spiral form, which must be increased in thickness as it approaches the oval, so as to be nearly equal to the dimensions of the largest vertebræ, or root of the tail. When finished, it should be rubbed thinly over with flour paste, to preserve its smooth form, which must be allowed to dry thoroughly, and then

the surface should receive a coating of the **preservative.**
The sheath of the tail **must** now be rubbed **inside with the**
preservative. This is applied with **a small quantity of lint,**
attached to the end of a wire, **long enough to reach the point**
of the **tail-sheath.** The tail-bearer **is** then inserted into the
sheath, **and the oval part of** the wire placed within **the skin**
of the belly, **and attached to** the longitudinal wire, **which is**
substituted for the vertebræ or back-bone.

Four pieces of **wire, about the** thickness **of a crow-quill,**
are then taken, **which must be** the length of the legs, **and**
another piece a **foot or** fifteen inches longer than the body.
One end of each of these is sharpened with a file, in **a** triangular shape, so **that it may the more** easily penetrate **the**
parts. At the **blunt end of the longest** piece a **ring is**
formed, large enough **to admit of** the point of a finger entering it; **this is done by bending the wire back on** itself a turn
and a-half, by the assistance of **the round pincers. On the**
same wire another ring is formed in a **similar** manner, **con-**
sisting of **one** entire turn, and so situated as to reach just between the animal's shoulders. The remaining part **of this**
wire should be perfectly straight, and triangularly **pointed at**
the extremity.

Another **method of forming the** supporting wires, as practiced by M. Nichols, is to take **a** central wire, which must be
the length of the head, neck, body and tail of the cat; **two**
other pieces are then taken and **twisted round** the **center**
piece, these extremities being left **for the leg wires. After**
the wires are thus twisted together the central one is pulled
out, and **the feet wires of one** side are pushed through **the**
legs of one side from the inside of the skin, and the other two
leg pieces are bent and also forced through the legs, and afterward made straight by a pair of pincers; the center piece,
having been previously sharpened at one end with a file, is
now forced through the forehead and down the neck, till it
enters the center of the twisted leg wires which it formerly

occupied, and pushed forward to the extremity of the tail, leaving a small piece projecting out of the forehead, after which the completion of the stuffing is proceeded with.

This mode is unnecessary for the smaller animals, and it should only be adopted for quadrupeds the size of deer, etc. These wires are, besides, much more difficult to insert by this than by the other method.

All the wires being adjusted, the operation of stuffing is next proceeded with. The skin of the cat is now extended on a table; and the end of the noose seized with the left hand, and again pushed into the skin, till it reaches the neck, when we receive the bones of the head into the right hand. The skull is now well rubbed over with the arsenical soap, and all the cavities which the muscles before occupied are filled with chopped tow, flax, or cotton, well mixed with preserving powder. The long piece of wire is now passed into the middle of the skull, and after it is well rubbed over with the preservative, it is returned into the skin. The inner surface of the neck-skin is now anointed, and stuffed with chopped flax, taking care not to distend it too much. Nothing like pressure should be applied, as the fresh skin is susceptible of much expansion.

Observe that it is always the inner surface which is anointed with the arsenical soap. Take care that the first ring of the wire, which passes into the head is in the direction of the shoulders, and the second corresponding with the pelvis, or somewhat toward the posterior part. One of the fore-leg wires is then inserted along the back of the bone, and the point passed out under the highest ball of the paw. When this is accomplished the bones of the leg are drawn up within the skin of the body, and the wire fastened to the bones of the arm and fore-arm with strong thread or small twine. Brass wire, used for piano forte strings, makes it more secure, and is not liable to rot. These are well anointed, and flax or tow *slivers* wrapped around them so as

to supply the place of the muscles which have been removed.
To give the natural rise to the larger muscles, a piece of silver should be cut off the length of the protuberance required
and placed in the part, and the silver wrapped over it. This
gives it a very natural appearance.

The mode of fixing the legs is by passing one of their pieces
of wire into the small ring of the horizontal or middle supporting wire. Pursue the same plan with the other leg, and
then twist the two ends firmly together by the aid of a pair
of flat pincers. For an animal of the size of a cat, the pieces
left for twisting must be from five to six inches in length.
After being twisted, they are bound on the under side of the
body wire with strong thread; the two legs are then replaced
and put in the form in which we intend to fix them. The
skin of the belly and top of the shoulders is then anointed,
and a thick layer of flax placed under the middle wire. The
shape is now given to the scapulæ on both sides, and all the
muscles of the shoulders imitated. These will be elevated or
depressed, according to the action intended to be expressed.
The anterior part of the opening is now sewed up, to retain
the stuffing, and to enable us to complete the formation of
the shoulders and junction of the neck. This part of the
animal is of great importance, as regards the perfection of its
form, and much of its beauty will depend upon this being
well executed.

If the animal has been recently skinned, the best plan
possible is to imitate, as nearly as possible, the muscles of
the carcase, by which many parts will be noticed which
might otherwise have been neglected. As a rule, COPY NAT-
URE WHENEVER YOU HAVE IT IN YOUR POWER.

It must be observed as a general rule, that the wires for
the hind legs of quadrupeds should always be longer than
those of the fore legs.

The next thing is to form the hind legs and thighs, which
must be done as above described for the fore legs; but with

this difference, that they must be wound round with thread, drawn through the stuffing at intervals, to prevent it slipping up when returned into the skin of the leg. They are then fixed by passing the leg wires into a second ring of the center body wire, which is situated at or near the pelvis; the two ends are then bent, twisting them to the right and left around the ring; and, to make them still more secure, they should be wound round with small brass wire or packthread; the tail-bearer is then attached in the manner formerly described.

Having completed this part of the iron work, the skin of the thighs is coated inside with the preservative, and the stuffing completed with chopped flax or tow. The whole inner parts of the skin which can be reached are again anointed, and the body stuffing completed with chopped flax. Care must be also paid not to stuff the belly too much, as the skin very easily dilates. The incision in the belly is now closed by bringing the skin together, and then sewed within and without, while attention is paid to divide the hairs, and not to take any of them in along with the thread; but should any of them be inadvertently fixed, they can be picked out easily with a point. When this is completed, the hair will resume its natural order and completely conceal the seam.

The seam should now be well primed on both sides with the solution of corrosive sublimate, to prevent the entrance of moths.

The articulations of the legs are then bent, and the animal placed on its feet, and pressure used at the natural flat places, so as to make the other parts rise where the muscles are visible.

A board is now prepared, on which to place the cat. But before fixing it permanently the animal should be set in the attitude in which it is intended to be preserved, and the operator, having satisfied himself, then pierces four holes for

the admission of the feet wires, which must be drawn
through with a pair of pincers till the paws rest firmly on
the board. Small grooves are then made for the reception of
the pieces of wires which have been drawn through, so that
they may be folded back and pressed down in them, and not
be beyond the level of the back of the board; wire nails are
now driven half in, and their heads bent down on the wires
to prevent them from getting loose or becoming movable.

The stuffer next directs his attention to the position and
final stuffing of the head and neck. The muscles of the face
must be imitated as correctly as possible by stuffing in cotton at the opening of the eyes, as also at the mouth, ears and
nostrils. To aid in this also the inner materials may be
drawn forward by the assistance of instruments, and also
small pieces of wood formed like small knitting meshes.

Our next care is the insertion of the eyes, which must be
done while the eyelids are yet fresh. Some dexterity and
skill are required in this operation, and on it will depend
most of the beauty and character of the head. The seats of
the eyes are supplied with a little cement, the eyes put in
their place, and the eyelids properly drawn over the eyeballs;
but if rage or fear are to be expressed, a considerable portion
of the eyeballs must be exposed. The lips are afterwards
disposed in their natural state and fastened with pins. If
the mouth is intended to be open, it will be necessary to support the lips with cotton, which can be removed when they
are dry. Two small balls of cotton, firmly pressed together
and well tinctured with the arsenical soap, must be thrust
into the nostrils so as to completely plug them up to prevent
the air from penetrating, as also the intrusion of moths; and,
besides, it has the effect of preserving the natural shape of
the nose after it has dried. The same precaution should be
adopted with the ears, which, in the cat, require but little attention in setting.

We must again recommend the stuffer to see that he has

sufficiently applied the preservative soap; and the nose, lips, eyes and paws, being very liable to decay, must be well imbued with spirits of turpentine. This is applied with a brush, and must be repeated six or eight times, at intervals of some days, until we are certain of the parts being well primed with it; and, after all, it will be advisable to give it a single coating of the solution of corrosive sublimate.

The methods of stuffing, which we have pointed out in the preceding pages, are applicable to all animals, from a lion down to the smallest mouse. Animals of a large description require a frame-work suited to their dimensions; these we will point out in their order. There are also some animals whose peculiarity of structure requires treatment differing a little from the ordinary course.

Apes and Monkeys. One of the chief difficulties to contend with in setting up monkeys and apes, is the preservation of their hands and hind hands, or what we commonly call their feet; because we must not attempt to deprive these limbs of their flesh, as we never could again supply its place anything like what is in nature. The hands must therefore be dried, and then well imbued with turpentine and the solution of corrosive sublimate, repeated eight or ten times at least, at intervals of four or five days. The other parts of the stuffing should be exactly similar to that recommended for quadrupeds generally. The paws of several will require to be colored with the different varnishes, and, when dry, slightly polished with fine sand paper to remove the gloss. The callosities, on the hinder parts of many of them, will also require to be colored, and treated in the same way as the face.

Bats. The wing-membranes of this varied and numerous tribe do not require either wire or parchment to set them. They are very easily dried by distension. They are laid on a board of soft wood, the wings extended and pinned equally at the articulations, and, when dry, they are removed from the board.

Hedgehogs. When it is wished to preserve hedgehogs, rolled into a ball, which is a very common position with them in a state of nature, there should be much less stuffing put into them than is usual with quadrupeds, so that they may the more easily bend. No wires are required in this case. The head and feet are drawn close together under the belly; then place the animal on its back in the middle of a large cloth, and tie the four ends firmly together; suspend it in the air till thoroughly dry, which finishes the operation.

If hedgehogs are wished with the heads and limbs exposed, the usual method of mounting is adopted. The skins of mice, moles, etc., having a very offensive smell, it will be necessary to add a considerable portion of the tincture of musk to the solution of the corrosive sublimate with which the skins are imbued. The same applies to badgers, wolverenes, polecats and skunks, all of which are strong smelling animals.

Bears. The structure of the wires requires to be different in these larger animals from any we have before described.

Procure a bar one inch thick, two inches broad, and as long as to reach horizontally from the shoulders to the connection of the thighs, or *os pubis*. A hole is bored four inches distant from one of its ends, from which a connecting groove must be formed, extending on both sides to the end of the plank next the hole; this groove must be cut out with a hollow chisel deep enough to receive the wire. The wire is then passed through it, one end of which is just long enough to be twisted with the other at the end of the plank. The wire on both sides is now pressed down into the grooves and twisted firmly together by the aid of a pair of strong pincers. Pierce some holes obliquely into the groove and insert some wire nails into them, which must be firmly driven home, and then bent over the wires to keep them firm. The longest end of the wire should be at least eighteen inches beyond the bar so as to pass through the skull of the animal.

The use of this bar, it will be observed, is a substitute for the central or supporting wires of the body. Two other holes are now bored into it, the one two, and the other three inches from the end which we first pierced; these are for the reception of the wires of the fore legs; and two similar holes must be made at the other extremity of the bar for receiving the wires of the hind legs.

Bears always support themselves on the full expansion of their dilated paws, so that it is necessary to bring the leg-wires out at the claws. The leg-wires are bent at right angles for a length of five inches from the upper end. These are put through the holes in the bar, and when they have passed through they are curved again. Two small gimlet-holes are then made for the reception of smaller wire, by which the leg-wires must be bound together close to the bar. The fore-leg-wires are fixed in the same manner, which completes the framework.

No other means are used for middle-sized animals, such as the lion, tiger, leopard, etc. The stuffing is completed as in other quadrupeds.

The walrus, seals, and other amphibious animals of this order, are treated in the manner of quadrupeds generally, only that leg-wires are unnecessary, except in the fore-feet; the tail, which represents the hind-feet, has merely to be dried and kept properly stretched in during this process, which precaution also applies to the fore-feet. They are the easiest stuffed of all animals, only the skins are very oily; they should be well rubbed with the arsenical soap, and also with the preserving powder.

The stuffing of the walrus, and other large animals of this

family, should consist of well dried hay for the interior parts and tow for the surface next the skin.

Beaver, etc. The beaver, muskrat, common **rat, and** other animals whose skins have a strong smell. These require to be plentifully supplied with the preservative. The tail of the beaver should be cut underneath, and all the flesh removed, then stuffed with tow or chopped flax, and afterwards **thoroughly** dried and well primed with the arsenical soap **to prevent** putrefaction, to **which** it is very liable. It should **also** have repeated washings with oil of turpentine. **The back** should be round and short.

The Porcupine. In **stuffing this animal** considerable and varied expression may be given, both from the attitude and disposition of the quills. Great attention is therefore required in giving these a proper set during the process of drying. They will require to be looked at several times during the first and second day after they have been stuffed, and **any of them** that may have fallen out of the position required, to be adjusted.

Hares and Rabbits. A very pretty attitude **for the hare** or rabbit, is to have it seated in its form in an upright position, as **if alarmed** at the noise of dogs, etc. **An oval is** formed of wire and attached to the interior framework, after having passed one end of it through the anus, which must be passed through a hole in the board on which the animal **is to** be fixed. The wires of the hind legs must be forced through the posterior part of them, and also fixed **into holes formed** for their reception in the board.

Deer, Antelopes, Goats, etc. These animals should be mounted on the same principles as recommended for the bears. A different mode must, however, be adopted in skinning the

animals, which the horns render necessary. It is performed
in the ordinary manner until the operator reaches the neck.
After cutting as near the head as possible, another incision
must be made, commencing under the chin, which is continued to the bottom of the neck, or from eight to ten inches
in length. By this opening, the remainder of the neck is
separated from the head; the tongue is cut out, and the occipital orifice enlarged, and the brain extracted thereby. The
lips are now cut as near as possible to the jaw bones, and the
operator must continue progressively ascending towards the
forehead, and in this manner all the skin will be separated
from the head, except at the nose, or point of the muzzle.
All the muscles are next removed by the scalpel, and the skull
well anointed with arsenical soap. The muscles which have
been cut out are then imitated with chopped flax or cotton,
which may be attached to the bones with cement. When this
is done, the head must be replaced within the skin. The orifice under the neck must now be sewed up with fine stitches,
so that the hair may spread over them to conceal the seam.
The whole other parts of the mounting is completed as
directed for the bear.

The Dolphin, Porpoise, etc. The structure of these animals, as well as of the other species of the first family of this
order, differs but little in general structure.

In skinning these, an incision is made under the chin, and
continued to the extremity of the tail ; the skin is then detached right and left with the scalpel, or a sharp knife.
When the skin has been cut back as far as possible, disengage the vertebræ at the tail, and this will enable the operator to detach the skin from the back ; the vertebræ are now
cut close to the head, and the whole carcase removed.

All this tribe have a thick layer of fat under their skin. In
the operation of skinning it requires considerable dexterity
to leave this fat, or blubber, adherring to the carcase. Prac-

tice alone will **obviate this.** When this has not been properly managed **in the skinning, the** only thing to be **done** afterwards is **to scrape it** thoroughly with a knife. The oil which flows from it during this operation must be soaked up with bran, or plaster of Paris.

There being no muscular **projections in the skin** of the porpoise, there is no use for **wires in** mounting it. A narrow piece of wood the length **of the** body is quite sufficient to keep **the** skin stretched, and stuffed either with tow or **hay.** Some months are **necessary to** render it perfectly **dry and** stiff, **from its** greasy **nature.** The grease almost always leaves some disagreeable looking **spots** on **the** skin. To remove these, and prevent **a recurrence of** them, powdered pumice-stone steeped **in olive oil, is** rubbed thickly **on** the skin with a hand-brush. **It is then gone over a** second time **with** emery and oil. It is rubbéd **in this way** till the skin **has a glossy** appearance, when it may be rubbed dry with a woolen cloth; and to complete **the polish,** a clean woolen cloth may **be** applied with some **force to** complete the gloss, which is natural to the skin **in a living state.**

Where a **very** glossy **appearance** is wished, varnishes become necessary, but **some difficulty has** been experienced in getting these to remain attached **to the** skin in all weathers, because **the** humidity **of rainy seasons** melts gum-arabic when **it is used as a** varnish, and when white varnish **is** applied, both **it and the** gum-arabic **fall** off in pieces. **To** prevent the gum from falling off in this way, by its contracting, the solution should have about an eighth part of ox-gall mixed with it, and the surface of any body to be varnished **should be** washed **with** ox-gall **and water** before the varnish **is applied, which will,** almost to a certainty, prevent it from **cracking and falling off. It must,** however, be thoroughly dried before **the** varnish is applied.

We may here state, **that an animal the size of** a fox **or a** cat, **may** be **skinned, prepared, and finally** set up, in the space of four or five hours, by a person who has had a little practice in the art of taxidermy, and that from ten to fifteen minutes are all that will be required to skin an animal of the size just mentioned.

SKINNING, PRESERVING AND MOUNTING BIRDS.

SKINNING.

IMMEDIATELY after a bird is killed the throat and nostrils should be stuffed with tow, cotton or fine rags, and a small quantity wound round the bill, to prevent the blood from staining the plumage; but should any get on the feathers, notwithstanding this precaution, the sooner it is removed the better, which should be effected by a sponge which has been merely moistened in water. Too much dispatch cannot be used in removing the skin, if the bird is shot in a warm climate; but, in temperate regions, the bird may be allowed to cool.

In proceeding to skin the bird it should be laid on its back and the feathers of the breast separated to the right and left, when a broad interval will be discovered, reaching from the top to the bottom of the breast-bone.

A sharp penknife, or scapel, must be inserted at the point of the bone, and cut the outer skin from thence to the vent, taking care not to penetrate so deep as the flesh, or upon the inner skin which covers the intestines. The skin will then easily be separated from the flesh, in larger specimens by the fingers, or in smaller ones by passing a small blunt instrument betwixt the skin and body, such as the end of the scalpel handle; with this you may reach the back. The thighs should now be pressed inwards, as in the common method of skinning a rabbit, and the skin turned back, so far

as to enable you to separate the legs from the body at the
knee-joint. The skin is then pulled downwards as low as the
rump, which is cut close by the insertion of the tail, but in
such a manner as not to injure its feathers. The skin is now
drawn upwards the length of the wings, the bones of which
must also be cut at the shoulder-joints; it is then pulled up
till all the back part of the skull is laid bare, when the vertebræ of the neck are separated from the head, and the whole
body is now separated from the skin. You next proceed to
remove the brain, through the opening of the skull, for which
purpose it may be enlarged by a hollow chisel, or other iron
instrument. The eyes must then be taken out, by breaking
the slender bones which separate the orbits from the top of
the mouth, in which you may be assisted by pressing the eyes
gently inwards, so as not to break them. In skinning the
neck, great care must be taken not to enlarge the opening of
the ears, and not to injure the eyelids. The whole of the flesh
is next to be removed from the under mandible.

Several species will not admit of the skin being thus pulled
over their heads, from the smallness of their necks; some
woodpeckers, ducks, etc., fall under this description; in which
case a longitudinal incision is made under the throat, so as to
admit of the head being turned out, which must be neatly
sewed up before stuffing. The flesh from the head, wings,
legs and rump, must then be carefully removed with a knife,
and the cavities of the skull filled with cotton or tow. The
whole inside of the skin, head, etc., must be well rubbed with
arsenical soap, or preserving powder, or spirits of turpentine,
or the solution of corrosive sublimate. When it is wished to
stuff the bird, it may now be immediately done, as it will
easily dry if in a warm climate; but in low, damp countries,
it will require artificial heat to do it effectually.

When the skins are merely wished preserved, the bones of
the legs and wings should be wrapped round with cotton or
tow, so as to supply the place of the flesh; the skin is then

inverted and hung up to dry, after using the arsenical soap, as above directed; before doing which, in larger birds, a thread or small string **may be drawn through the rump**, and passed up the inside of the neck and drawn through the bill, to prevent the head **from stretching too much by its own weight.** In larger specimens, where cotton or tow is not easily to be met with, well dried hay may be used.

The incision for removing the skin is frequently made under the wings. This may be done with marine birds to advantage. The penguins and divers may be skinned by making the incision in the back.

The tongue should either be kept in the mouth, or sent home separately with the birds.

The greatest care must be taken to prevent the fat and oily matter, so common to sea-birds, from getting on the feathers: pounded chalk will be found an excellent absorbent for applying to these birds.

In sending home specimens of birds, they should be each wrapped in paper and closely packed in a box; and camphor, preserving powder, and strong aromatics, strewed amongst them, to prevent them from being attacked by insects; and they ought to be kept in a very dry part of the vessel.

It is of the utmost consequence to know the color of the eyes and legs of birds, and these things should be carefully noted the moment they are killed; and it should also be mentioned whether they are male or female; such a memorandum ought to be attached to the birds by a ticket. The season of the year in which the bird is killed, must also be mentioned. It is also of much consequence to have good skeletons, and, for this purpose, the carcases may be sent home in a barrel, either in spirits or a strong solution of salt and water.

Mr. Salt, while in Abyssinia, packed his bird-skins between sheets of paper, in the same manner as a *hortus siccus*, or herbarium, and they reached England in perfect safety, and made excellent specimens when set up. In warm climates, the boxes should be well closed, and the seams filled with warm pitch on the outside, to prevent the intrusion of insects; and the inside should be supplied with camphor, musk, or tobacco-dust, which will prevent the attacks of the smaller insects.

Till practice has given facility to the operator, it will assist in keeping the feathers clean, if, as he opens the skin of the breast, he pins pieces of paper or linen cloth on the outside; but, after a few trials, this will be unnecessary.

Some of the marine fowls are so fat that there is much trouble in separating it from the skin, and, in warm weather, great attention will be required to prevent it from running on the feathers. As much as possible should be scraped off, in the first place, with a blunt table-knife or palate-knife, and a quantity of powdered chalk applied, to absorb what remains, which, when saturated with the oily matter, should be scraped off, and a fresh supply used; after which a much larger proportion of the preserving powder should be applied than in other birds which are not fat.

When shooting on the sea coast, if the ornithologist is not provided with these requisities for absorbing the oil, which flows quickly from any wounds of the skin, he will find dry sand a tolerable substitute.

If, however, after every precaution, the oily matter should get on the feathers, the sooner it is removed the better, as, in birds where the plumage is white, if it is allowed to become hardened it will produce a very disagreeable appearance; and, besides, render that part particularly liable to the attack of insects. There are several effectual methods of removing the greasy stains; the first, safest, and best is, by taking a quantity of diluted ox-gall—or, where it cannot be commanded, sheep's-gall, or that of any other animal—mix it with about double the quantity of water, and apply it with a sponge to the place which the fatty matter has touched, when it will immediately remove it. The next is by using a solution of salts of tartar, or potash, or soda. This must be made very weak, not exceeding half a teaspoonful to a cup of water, which will have the same effect as the gall. Whichever of these are used, the place must be immediately afterwards washed in pure water, so as to leave none of the gall or alkaline substance remaining. The gall has a gummy tendency, and will glue together the fibers of the feathers, and, besides, it has a great attraction for moisture, and, in humid weather, will become damp, and therefore produce mould; the other alkaline substances must also be used with much caution and quickness, because they have the power of changing the colors of the plumage, so that they are most useful in white plumage, and therefore should only be used on colored feathers, where gall cannot be procured.

One general observation applies to the preservation of all animal skins, which is, they must be made perfectly dry, so that the sooner they are exposed to a free current of air the better; and unless they are speedily and thoroughly dried, the skin will become putrid and rotten, and the hair or feathers will consequently fall off. If a skin is properly dried, soon after it is killed, it will keep a considerable time without any preservative whatever, only it will be the more liable to be attacked by insects afterwards.

The following excellent general directions for skinning are given by Mr. Waterton:—" While dissecting, it will be of use to keep in mind, that in taking off the skin from the body, by means of your fingers and little knife, you must try to shove it, in lieu of pulling it, lest you stretch it.

" That you must press as lightly as possible on the bird, and every now and then take a view of it, to see that the feathers, etc., are all right.

" That when you come to the head, you must take care that the body of the skin rest on your knee, for if you allow it to dangle from your hand, its own weight will stretch it too much.

"That, throughout the whole operation, as fast as you detach the skin from the body, you must put cotton immediately betwixt the body and it, and this will effectually prevent any fat, blood, or moisture, from coming in contact with the plumage.

"As you can seldom get a bird without shooting it, a line or two on this head will be necessary. If the bird be still alive, press it hard with your finger and thumb, just behind the wings, and it will soon expire. Carry it by the legs, and then, the body being reversed, the blood cannot escape down the plumage and through the shot-holes. As blood will have often issued out, before you have laid hold of the bird, find out the shot-holes, by dividing the feathers with your fingers, and blowing on them; and then, with your pen-knife, or the leaf of a tree, carefully remove the clotted blood, and put a little cotton on the hole. If, after all, the plumage has not escaped the marks of blood, or if it has imbibed slime from the ground, wash the part in water, without soap, and keep gently agitating the feathers with your fingers, till they are quite dry. Were you to wash them, and leave them dry by themselves, they would have a very mean and shriveled appearance.

"In the act of skinning a bird, you must either have it upon a table, or upon your knee; probably you will prefer your knee, because, when you cross one knee over the other, and have the bird upon the uppermost, you can raise it to your eye, or lower it, at pleasure, by means of the foot on the ground ; and then your knee will always move in unison with your body, by which much stooping will be avoided, and lassitude prevented."

Stuffing Birds. The first thing to be done in stuffing is to replace the skull, after it has been well anointed with the arsenical soap, and washed with the solution of corrosive sublimate inside. The thread, with which the beak is tied, is taken hold of by the left hand, and the head is repassed into the neck with the forefinger of the right hand, while the thread is pulled on the opposite side; and we are careful that the feathers, at the margin of the opening, do not enter with the edges of the skin. The bird is now laid on the table with the head turned towards the left hand, and the legs and wings adjusted to their proper situation. A flat piece of lead, about a pound in weight, is laid on the tail, while the feathers of the margins of the opening are raised by the forefinger and thumb of the left hand, to prevent their being soiled. The inside of the neck is now coated with the arsenical soap; flax is stuffed into it, but not too tightly. The back and rump are anointed, and the body should then be stuffed with tow, to about a third of the thickness required, so that the wire may have a sort of cushion to rest on.

Four pieces of wire are then prepared, of the thickness proportionate to the size of the bird to be stuffed. The center-piece should be somewhat longer than the body of the bird. At about a fourth of its length a small ring is formed, by the assistance of the round pincers or plyers, and the other end is pointed with a file. This wire is oiled and introduced across the skull, and passed into the neck, through the center of the flax or tow with which it is stuffed, the ring being situated toward the anterior part of the skull, for the purpose of receiving the points of each of the wires that are passed through the feet and thighs.

The following is the mode in which this performation is effected: A hole is bored with a bradawl the caliber of the wire which it is intended to use. The wire, which is to continue in the leg, is passed across the knee and brought out interiorly, and, placing it into the ring above mentioned, the same operation is performed on the other side. The extremities of the wires of the legs, and the end of the central wire beyond the ring, are all twisted together with flat pincers, and then bent towards the tail. The tail-bearer is next formed,

which consists of the fourth piece of wire, with which an oval
is formed, by twisting the two ends two or three turns, so
that they may form a kind of fork, with the oval nearly the
length of the body of the bird; the two points of the fork must
be sharpened with a file, and near enough to enable them to
enter the rump, through which they must pass, and their
points will be concealed by the rectrices, or large straight tail
feathers, while the oval is within the body of the bird. If the
bird is large, the tail-bearer must be firmly attached to the
interior wires, by twisting a small wire several times round
both. But unless the bird be very large, it may remain
quite free.

All the parts of the skin at which we can come must be
thoroughly rubbed with preserving soap, the rump in particular, which should besides be soaked with the solution of
corrosive sublimate. The stuffing is now proceeded with, by
inserting chopped flax or tow, till it has attained its proper
dimensions. The skin is brought together and sewed up,
while we take the greatest care to separate the feathers at
every stitch.

The orbits of the eyes are next finished, by inserting, with
small forceps and a short stuffing stick, a small quantity of
chopped cotton, while attention is paid to round the eyelids
properly. The glass eyes are now inserted, taking care to
place them properly under the eyelids. But, before fixing the
eye, a little calcareous cement must be used, to prevent them
from coming out. If any part of the nictitating membrane
is visible below, it must be pushed up with the steel point.

The stuffing of the bird being now completed, the next
thing is to place it either on a branch, or, if a bird which does
not sit on trees, on a piece of plank; whichever of these it is,
two holes are bored for the reception of the wires, which have
been allowed to protrude from the soles of the feet, for fixing
the bird. (See fig. 8.) These, of course, are pierced in such
situations as are necessary for the attitude or position of the

legs. The wires are put through these holes, and twisted so as to secure the bird in its position. The attitude of the bird will, of course, depend upon the fancy and taste of the operator, and ought to be in conformity with the manners of the bird in a living state.

The wire frame-work, above described, is the most simple of any in its construction, and is better adapted for small than large birds. Indeed, it will hardly suit those of the larger species. The following is another method of constructing the framework, which may be used either in large or small birds:

Like the former it is constructed of four pieces of wire. The center piece should be double the length of the bird; it is bent at a third of its length in an oval form, and twisted two turns, the shortest end being passed into the oval, and then raised against the longer end, so as to produce a ring at the end, outside of the oval, large enough to admit the two wires which pass from the feet to the inside of the bird. It is now twisted a second time, and firmly united to the longer end, which ought to be straight, with a sharp point, effected by means of a file. As before directed, it is rubbed with oil, and forced through the stuffing of the neck. It ought to be so constructed, by measurement, that the oval part of the wire shall be in the center of the body inside. The wires of the feet and legs, as before directed, ought to be straight and pointed, and passed through the soles of the feet as before. When the point is penetrated, the other end of the wire may be bent, so that by means of it we may be able to assist in forcing up the remainder of the wire. The two internal ends of the foot-wires are twisted together, and curved within, so as to pass through the small circle or ring of the middle branch above the oval, to each side of which they are now attached with a piece of small string.

The tail-bearer is constructed on the same principles, and attached in the same manner, as before described, and the latter apparatus is introduced after the neck and back are finished in the stuffing.

This practice of introducing the neck-wire, after the neck is stuffed, was first adopted at the Jardin des Plantes at Paris, and is now invariably adopted in that establishment in preference to introducing it before the neck is stuffed. The neck of a swan or other long-necked and large birds, are even done so. It is unquestionably the best plan which has hitherto been discovered, as it preserves the cylindrical shape of the neck.

Mr. Bullock's Method of Stuffing Birds. Mr. Bullock, of the London Museum, Egyptian Hall, had another method of arranging the wires which, after what we have already said, will be easily comprehended by a reference to Fig. 8, where we have given a figure of his mode. After the skin is taken off and prepared, different sized nealed iron wires are procured, according to the size of the bird they are to support. The skin is laid on its back without stretching it; cut two pieces of wire, the one rather longer than the bird, and the other shorter, so as not to reach to the head of the bird, twist them together, sharpen the ends of the longer by means of a file, and pass one end through the rump and the other through the crown of the head, near the base of the bill. Care must be taken not to extend the neck beyond its ordinary length—a very common fault in most preservers. Lay a little tow along the back of the skin for the wire to rest on, then take two other pieces of strong wire and file them to a point at one end; these are passed through the soles of the feet and up the center of the leg-bone, or tarsus. When within the body, they are to be fastened to the first wires by twisting them together, which, when accomplished, may be supposed to represent the back bone. The wire should be left two or three inches out of the soles of the feet, to fasten them in a standing position, as before directed. Two smaller wires are then passed through the wings, as in the legs, and afterwards fastened to the back wires a little higher up than the leg wires, taking care that no part of the skin is to be extended beyond its natural position.

A New and Easier Method of Bird Skinning and Stuffing. A fair specimen being obtained, take common cotton wadding, and with an ordinary paint-brush stick plug the throat, nostrils, and, in large birds, the ears, with it, so that when the skin is turned no juices may flow and spoil the feathers; you must then provide yourself with the following articles: A knife of this kind, which is very common; a pair of cutting plyers, a pair of strong scissors, of a moderate size; a button-hook, a marrow spoon, and a hand-vice. With these, a needle and thread, and a sharpener of some kind, to give your knife an occasional touch, you are prepared, so far as implements go. Then provide yourself with annealed iron wire of various sizes; some you may buy ready for use, some not; but you can anneal it yourself by making it red hot in the fire, and letting it cool in the air. Common hemp is the next article, cotton wadding, pounded whitening, and pounded alum, or chloride of lime; as to the poisons which are used, they will be spoken of by and by. You should also have a common bradawl or two, and some pieces of quarter-inch pine whereon to stand the specimens when preserved, if to be placed as walking on a plane; if not, some small pieces of twigs or small branches of trees should be kept ready for use, of various sizes, according to the size of the bird. Cedar, or common laurel cut in December, will be found to answer best, but this must be regulated by fancy and the requirements of the case; oak boughs are sometimes of good shape.

The best time for preserving specimens is in spring, because then the cock birds are in the best feather, and the weather is not too warm. In mild weather three days is a good time to keep a bird, as then the skin will part from the flesh easily.

If a specimen has bled much over the feathers, so as to damage them, wash them carefully but thoroughly with warm
water and a sponge, and immediately cover them with
pounded whitening, which will adhere to them. Dry it as
it hangs upon them slowly before the fire, and then triturat-
ing the hardened lumps gently between the fingers, the
feathers will come out almost as clean as ever. To test
whether the specimen is too decomposed to skin, try the
feathers about the auriculars, and just above the tail, and if
they do not move you may safely proceed.

Lay the bird on his back, and, parting the feathers from the
insertion of the neck to the tail, you will find in most birds a
spare space. Cut the skin the whole length of this, and,
passing the finger under it on either side, by laying hold of
one leg and bending it forward, you will be able to bring the
bare knee through the opening you have made ; with your
scissors cut it through at the joint; pull the shank still adhering to the leg till the skin is turned back as far as it will go;
denude the bone of flesh and sinew, wrap a piece of hemp
round it, steep in a strong solution of the pounded alum, and
then pull the leg by the claw, by which means the skin will
be brought again to its place.

After having served both legs alike, skin carefully round
the back, cutting off and leaving in the tail with that into
which the feathers grow, that is, the "Pope's nose." Serve
the wing bones the same as the leg, cutting them off close to
the body, and turn the skin inside out down to the head.
The back of the skull will then appear, and you will now find
it of advantage, as soon as you have got the legs and tail free,
to tie a piece of string round the body, and hang it up as a
butcher skins a sheep. Make in the back of the skull a cut
with your knife, which you can turn back like a trap-door,
and with the marrow-spoon entirely clear out the brains;
Having done this, wash the interior of the skull thoroughly
with the alum, and fill it with cotton wadding. The

next operation requires care and practice—namely, to get out the eyes. This is done by cutting cautiously until the lids appear, being careful not to cut the eye itself, and you can then, with a forceps, which you will likewise find useful, pull each from its socket; wipe the orifice carefully, wash it with the alum solution, and fill it with cotton wadding. Cut off the neck close to the skull, wash the stump, and the whole of the interior of the skin with the alum, and the *skinning* is done. Now comes the stuffing. The ordinary mode used by bird-preservers is a simple one, and answers very well; there is a French method, however, which has its advantages, and will be adverted to hereafter. Take a piece of the wire suitable to the size of the bird (Fig. 11)—that is, as large as the legs will carry—and bend it into the following form, *a* representing the neck, *b*, the body, and *c*, the junction of the tail, allowing sufficient length of neck for the wire to pass some distance beyond the head, and being sharpened at each end, which may be done by obliquely cutting it with the plyers. Wind upon this wire hemp to the size of the bird's body, which you should have lying by you to judge from, and it will present something of the appearance of Fig. 12. You can shape it with the hand, but be careful not to make it the least *too large;* and, after you have finished it to your satisfaction, you may singe it, as the poulterer would singe a fowl, which will make all neat; but be particular to wind the hemp very tight. Then take the skin, lay it on the table on its back, and pass the wire at the head into the marrow where the neck is cut off, through above the roof of the mouth, and out at one nostril, and draw it up close to the skull; turn the skin back, and draw it down over the hemp body, and pass the wire spike, protruding at the lower end, through the flesh upon which the tail grows, about the centre, and rather below than above. The skin may now be adjusted to the hemp body, and sewn up, beginning from the top of the breast, and being particularly careful always to take the stitch from *inside*, otherwise you will draw

in the feathers at every pull.   At first sew it very loose, and
then, with the button-hook, draw it together by degrees.

With the plyers cut two lengths of wire, long enough to
pass up the legs and into the neck, and leave something over
to fasten the bird by to the board or spray upon which it is to
be placed.   The next operation requires some address and
great practice, namely, the passing the wire up the legs.   This
is done by forcing it into the center of the foot, and up the
back of the legs, into the hemp body, through it obliquely,
and into the neck, until it is pretty firm.   In doing this, you
must remember the ordinary position of a bird when alive,
and, therefore, instead of passing the wire the whole way
within the skin of the leg, when you get to the part where you
have cut off the bone, that is, the knee-joint, pass it through
the skin to the outside, and in again, through the skin, from
the outside, where the knee would come naturally in the attitude of standing or perching—it makes little difference which.
This is essential, because, if the wire be passed the whole way
inside the skin, it produces a wrong placing of the legs.   Fig.
13 will illustrate this, *a* representing the line in which the wire
should run.   The bird is now stuffed, and you may at once
place it upon a spray or board, as the case may be.   In placing
a bird upon a spray, the first joint should be bent almost on a
level with the foot; and, in placing a bird on a board, one leg
should be placed somewhat behind the other.   If the wings
are intended to be closed, as is usually the case, bring them
into their place, which may be done by putting the fingers
under them, and pressing them together over the back; you
may then pass a needle, or large pin, of which you should
have a good supply by you, through the thick part of the
upper wing into the body, and so by the lower wing, and if
you allow these to protrude, you may fasten to one of them a
piece of thread, and wind it carefully and lightly round the
body, which will keep the feathers in their places, and this
thread should be kept on for a fortnight or three weeks, until

the bird is dry. The tail should be kept in its place, also, for the same time, by a piece of thin wire bent over it.

The only thing now to do is to put in the eyes. The color, of course, depends on the bird, and these you may buy at any fishing-tackle store. If you do not use eyes too large, you will find little difficulty; the juice of the lids will act as a sufficient cement. As to the mounting, I shall say nothing about that now, but shall only advert shortly to a French method of preserving, which is more difficult, but has the advantage of superior firmness. It is this: Measuring from the insertion of the neck to the tail, make a wire frame. Upon this wind hemp for the neck only, and place in the skin in the same way as before directed, only that, instead of one wire being passed through that in which the tail grows, it is a fork that is passed through it. Having formed this frame, fit on to it two legs, and after the frame itself is in the skin, pass these from the *inside* down each leg, instead of from the outside, and fasten them on to the frame with the plyers, by twisting the ends round the frame. This will make all firm, and you can then fill the body with cut hemp, and sew up. One word as to the other preparations used by bird preservers. These are either corrosive sublimate or regulus of arsenic, which is yellow and of a consistence like butter. As I have said before, in cold weather, when there are no flies about, alum will do perfectly well; in warm weather either of the two others may be used. I should prefer the former—corrosive sublimate—as the other is "messy," and the chief object is to dry up anything which can be attacked by flesh-seeking insects. When you have finished your bird, you can lay the feathers with a large needle—it is as well to have one fixed in a handle and kept for this purpose—and, tying the two mandibles of the bill together with a piece of thread until the whole specimen has hardened and dried, the work is done.

THE ART OF MOUNTING BIRDS, DRIED SKINS, FEATHERS, ETC.

MOUNTING IN GENERAL.

WE will suppose that a proficiency, from practice, has been attained in the art of bird-preserving, according to the instructions given. The proficiency in preserving may apply only to the preservation and the form, great and necessary things, no doubt, as preliminaries; but, like matter without manner, of little avail alone. For attitude, I would say, as has been said to many a young artist, go to Nature, and there you will find an original in perfection. Would you make a willow-wren look like a willow-wren, watch him as he there hangs upon the weeping birch, or stands on a bough peering in quest of food? Each bird has its own manner; and if you cannot hit the manner, or make your stuffed skin so far amenable as to assume the attitude, it is either ill-stuffed, or you want the requisite knowledge of that which you should copy.

Bird Pinned Up. Having fixed on the attitude, it now only remains to put the feathers into their natural order as smoothly and regularly as possible; and to keep them in this state they should be bound around with small fillets of muslin fastened with pins. The bird should then be thoroughly dried, by placing it in an airy situation, if in summer; or if in winter, near the fire, but not so close as to affect the natural oil contained in the feathers. The want of proper attention in drying ruins many a fine specimen; if long kept damp putridity ensues despite all preservatives, when the skin will become rotten, and the feathers will soon fall off; besides, the mold and long-continued damp change the chemical properties of the preservatives used.

After the bird has been thoroughly dried, the fillets are removed; the wire which protruded from the head is cut off as close to the skull as possible, with the wire-cutting pincers elsewhere shown. It must then be attached to a circular, or other shaped piece of wood, with the generic and specific name and sex, as well as its country and locality attached to it, on a small ticket, when it may be placed in a museum.

Young hands commonly suppose that a bird should stand bolt upright, with the legs almost perpendicular, or at right angles to the perch. This is a great mistake, and never to be found in nature. Do we stand rigid, like a foot-soldier on drill? Does not a bird, as well as ourselves, accommodate itself to the thing on which it rests? Assuredly it does; for birds do not, as a young bird-stuffer endeavors to do, find always a perch to rest upon in the plane of the horizon. It therefore follows that, as he keeps himself upright, his legs must accommodate themselves to his perch. So in the ground-birds there is a gentle slope backwards from the hind toe, the balance being preserved in both cases by throwing the body forward in proportion. It is not uncommon to see birds preserved with wings and tail spread. Now, ordinarily speaking, this is very objectionable, because very unnatural. A bird preserved is supposed to represent a bird in a state of repose, that is, not in flight; the only modification allowable being with regard to those birds whose manner it may be to have the wings more or less open on occasions; thus the falcon tribe, supposing they are represented as devouring a quarry, or two birds toying with each other. It may be that a bird essentially aërial, like the swift, or perhaps some of the terns or the frigate bird, may be represented as actually on the wing. In this case, of course, the wings must be spread; and this is best done by passing a wire, not too thick, from the base of the quill-feathers on the under side, alongside the bone into the body, where it should be carefully and coaxingly inserted towards the tail until you feel that you have a pretty good hold,

You may then pass it carefully under the longest quill-feather, and through the back of the case, and fasten it by bringing it back again through and clinching it, concealing it so by the oblique position of the bird that it is not detectable. It is obvious that by passing the wire alongside the bone, you may bend the wings to any angle you please. With regard to the case there are two methods: one a bell-glass, which, glass being now so reasonable, is certainly a very pretty and reasonable way of mounting, but inapplicable to birds which are to be placed on a wall, or to be represented flying; although this may be managed by attaching one wire from the point of the wing to a twig sufficiently firm, which it will scarcely appear to touch, if managed adroitly. It is likewise indispensable that a bird for a shade should be stuffed so well as to look nicely in all positions. One thing must always be remembered, *do not have your case a shade too large,* just clear the object so as not to stint it for room; and in flat cases this applies chiefly to depth, for it should have sufficient light, or it will not look well. Wooden cases should be made as slight (in thickness) as is consistent with firmness; well-seasoned white deal is best; and the case should be formed of back, top and bottom, open at the front and sides, and at each corner of the front two slight deal supports, rabbited on their inner edges, and presenting on the whole a good appearance.

Having the case prepared, it should be papered with ordinary demy paper on the top and back within, and, when the paste is dry, washed over carefully with size and whitening, tinted with a little stone-blue; some add some touches of white subsequently to represent clouds, the ground representing the air; some also paste a landscape on the back, but this must be good, or you had better have plain color. The bird to be placed in this case is either perching, standing, or flying. For the latter, directions have been given. As to the two former, the perch must be firmly fixed in the small piece of flat wood upon which it previously stood, and put in upon it, the wood being fastened to the bottom of the case, either by screwing from below, from above, or gluing with stout glue, or by passing wire through two holes in the bottom of the case and the wood, and clinching above. In this case, or in screwing from below, let the wire or the screw into the wood, and putty over, and so if the bird is represented standing. The bird being fixed, the next thing is the decorating or " weeding," as it is technically called, and here we enter upon a subject so entirely of taste and fancy, that no fixed rules as to the disposition can in all cases be given. One rule applies equally to this as to landscape painting, viz., that there should always be a compensation of objects. That is, if you have a tuft of grass on one side which rises towards the top of the case, there should be something in the lower opposite corner to strike the eye, but not to rise above midway up at the furthest, and the ground, or floor, should not be overfurnished with mosses, etc. After the bird is fixed, the whole bottom should be carefully glued over with thin glue, taking care, where the bird's feet are on the bottom, not to touch the toes with the glue. Some fine-sifted sand or gravel should then be sifted over it, and it will adhere wherever the glue has touched; for this purpose a small tin shovel is best, about two inches wide by four long, with a handle in proportion, which can be made to order at any tinman's for a trifle.

Everything used in " weeding" should be baked in a slow oven, otherwise spider's eggs and minute creatures, which are pretty sure to be contained in it, will make their appearance after the case is closed in the disagreeable form of destroying your specimen. Moss, etc., by being slowly dried, will also keep its color better. Yellow moss, found on the roofs of old barns, and dark gray of the same species, are very generally useful; and where yellow moss cannot be had, the white or gray may be colored with chrome, and looks as well. Water plants fade, being more or less succulent, and hence a little common water-color with gum will be used with advantage

and look less artificial than oil plant, which is often used.
Fern looks very pretty as an adjunct for heath-birds, but it
should be dried gradually and carefully, when *quite* full
grown, and a small touch of light green, permanent white
forming a portion of it, will give it a freshness and more
natural appearance. Grass in seed (not in flower) of various
kinds is also a very pretty addition; but bird preservers have
a habit of using dyed grass, and yellow and red *Xeranthy-
mum*, or Everlasting, which is certainly to be avoided, and
indeed anything which is unnatural.   If it is wished to introduce a lump of earth, or an apparent bank, a piece of thick
brown paper, bent to the requisite shape, and glued over and
covered with sifted sand or gravel, has a very good effect; but
insects and butterflies, or artificial flowers, unless they are
extremely natural, should certainly be avoided. Regard
should also be had to the season at which the bird is usually
seen.   For instance, summer birds are, of course, surrounded
by green and living objects, but autumn or winter visitants
by decaying or dead herbage. It has often been made an experiment to represent snow, but it is difficult to obtain anything white enough, and at the same time of a crystalline
character, which, of course, it should be. Potato farina
nicely dried, mixed with Epsom salts pounded very fine, does
not make a bad substitute; but the real difficulty lies behind,
namely, in fixing it, and, more than all, the least damp takes
very much from its appearance, if it does not destroy the
effect, and hence we must have recourse to mineral aid, and
any very white mineral powder mingled with pounded glass
is perhaps best. It is unnecessary to say that the herbage
upon which it is meant to rest should be touched all over with
paste, not glue, and the white mixture shaken over and left
to dry. What will heighten the effect very much, if prettily
executed, is a black landscape with a dark leaden sky and
nearly black earth mingled with moss. To represent water, a
piece of looking-glass, surrounded by moss, etc., answers very

well. The bills and legs of birds should be always varnished, and where the natural color fades after death it should be restored by a thin coat of oil-color of the required shade. The bird being fixed and the case garnished, nothing remains but to put in the glass; this is in three-pieces, one for the front and a piece at each end. This can be pasted in with very strong paper round the edge, advancing sufficiently over the glass to hold it. In doing this it is not necessary to be very particular to avoid pasting the glass, as after it is dried it can be wiped clean with a damp cloth. The last operation is a very simple one, and done in a few minutes. You must procure some black spirit-varnish, which you can make yourself by dissolving the best black sealing-wax in spirits of wine, and should be kept corked; when this is good it acts as paint and varnish at the same time, and dries as fast as it is put on. One or two brass rings screwed on at the top of the back of the case will finish the bird, and if the case be nicely and closely made, there is no limit of time to which the preservation of the specimen may not extend.

Method of Mounting Dried Skins. We must now say something respecting the setting up of skins which have been preserved by travelers, and sent home from distant parts.

The general method is exactly the same as in stuffing recent specimens. There are, however, some preliminary steps, which it is necessary to know.

If the specimen sent home has been partially stuffed, our first business is to undo the stitches, if it has been sewed—which was an unnecessary process. We then remove the whole cotton or tow from the inside, by the assistance of forceps, and from the neck with a small piece of wire, twisted or hooked at the end. Having finished this, small balls of wet cotton are placed in the orbits of the eyes, and the legs and feet are wrapped round with wet cotton or linen rags. A *damp* cloth is then thrown over the bird, and it is allowed to remain in this state till next day. The neck and body are then filled with wet linen or cotton, and it will be ready for commencing setting up in four or five hours.

The eyes are now put in, as directed in the recent subjects, and then stuffed in exactly the same manner. Some difficulty will, however, be experienced with respect to the leg-wires, and it will require more time and care, from the dryness of the legs, to get the wire to penetrate. Having proceeded so far as to get the bird generally formed, the wings are next adjusted; this also is frequently difficult, owing to the stiffness of the tendons, and want of proper attention in skinning and drying them at first. Indeed, with some of the South American birds, a proper adjustment of the wings is found impracticable, owing to the attempts of the native Indians of Guyana, who seldom dispose them properly.

When these skins—frequently exceedingly valuable from their rarity—are undone, to be remounted, it is oftentimes found utterly impossible to get the wings to take a natural set, in which case there is no other remedy but cutting them off close to the body, and fixing them anew. The scapulars are separated, they are softened with damp cloths, and then wrapped up with bands of sheet lead, to give them a proper set. When we have got them in their natural shape, they must be fixed to the sides by cement and cotton, and a long pin through each, with the head concealed amongst the feathers. The scapulars, which we have cut off, must then be cemented on, and they will effectually cover the joining of the wings. The bird being now arranged, and all the feathers adjusted, it is wrapped round with small bands of fine linen or muslin, and set aside till thoroughly dry.

Should any feathers be disengaged during the mounting, they must be kept, and, when the bird is dry, we can replace them in their proper situations with a pair of forceps, after they have been touched on their shafts with the cement; the feathers around the place in which we intend to insert them, must be held up with the probing-needle.

If any of the feathers are deranged in mounting, and have got a wrong set, the only way to remedy the defect is to pull them out with forceps, and re-insert them with cement.

Of Mounting Birds, **Feather by Feather.** Rare birds **are frequently** received from foreign countries, the skins of **which are in** such a state of decay, that it is impossible to mount them by the ordinary processes above described. The only way in which they can be preserved, is to mount them feather by feather, which, **however,** is a very tedious method. It is as follows:

Procure a piece of **soft pliable wire, such as is used by bell-** hangers; or take some of the ordinary wire used, **and make it** red-hot in the fire, and allow it to cool gradually, when it will become quite pliable. Take five pieces of this, of different lengths, and **form them into the skeleton of a** body; namely, **two for the back, one on each** side, and **one to** represent the breast bone. Imitate the shape of the bird's body, as nearly **as possible.** The wires must be roughened with a file, at the place where all the wires meet, **at the** neck and **rump; and** first wrap the place next the neck **round** with **strong thread** or fine brass wire. Two pieces intended for the **back must** bend gently downwards, and be gradually **separated from** each other towards the center, and brought **together again at** the place intended for the rump, **where** they must intersect each other, and be twisted two or three times, to keep **them** in their place; they are then spread out as supports **for the** tail; the side pieces are **next formed, so as to represent the** natural bulge of a bird's body, and attached to the rump; the piece representing the **breast is then formed, joined at the** rump, **and** afterwards continued **as** long as the other tail- pieces, to support the center of the tail; while at the front extremity a piece is **left, for** the purpose of **forming a neck to** which to attach the head. The leg-wires are attached to the side-wires, being rolled round them for several turns, making a framework the shape of the bird.

After this body has been properly formed, it must be wrapped round with tow-sliver, and the neck thickened to its required dimensions. When this is accomplished, the head, legs, wings and tail are softened in the usual manner; the eyes are then fixed in with some cotton introduced into the orbits, with a little of the cement. The wings and tail are now placed on a table, with a flat leaden weight above each, to restore them to their natural shape. The leg-wires are then passed through the legs, commencing at the top, and bringing them out at the soles of the feet, and left with a piece extending beyond the claws.

The tail is now fixed on, by first attaching to it a quantity of cotton with the cement, and, when dry, it is fixed to the part intended as the rump.

The feet of the bird must be fixed into a piece of wood, as a perch, the ends of which must be left some inches beyond the body. The end next the tail is fixed into a table-vice, with the belly upwards, and the head pointing towards the operator. The feathers are now put on, commencing, under the tail, or crissum, with what are termed the under-tail coverts; a coating of cement must be previously laid on, to attach the feathers with. It is proceeded with upwards to the breast, and finally the length of the neck, taking care to put the proper feathers on their respective sides, as the side-feathers have all an inclination to one side. The bird is now turned with the back up, still keeping the head towards the stuffer; and the wings are fixed on with cement, and pins forced through the beards of the feathers to conceal the heads. When this is done, put on the feathers of the rump, and proceed upwards, as has been done with the belly. After reaching the top of the neck, the head is then fixed on with some cotton immersed in the cement, and allowed to dry before attempting to put on the feathers.

In this mode of mounting a bird there are several things which must be attentively adhered to ; these are—first, not to put the feathers too thick, for there is a danger of running short ; secondly, all the shafts of the feathers must have a small bit cut off the tip, so as to admit the cement and to give them a firmer hold ; and thirdly, that the feathers should all occupy their respective parts ; and fourthly, that they should be arranged as they are in nature on these parts, as the disposition of every part of the body is peculiar to itself.

At first, this mode of setting up birds will be found a difficult task, but, by a little practice and experience, it will become familiar and comparatively easy, although it will always be found a tedious process. We have seen some specimens set up in this way, which we could hardly detect from those mounted in the ordinary manner.

Besides what we have already said concerning the stuffing and preparing of birds, there are many details connected with particular species which demand our attention, and which can only be described as regarding that species. It will, however, be impossible for us to enter into all these minutely, but only give a few examples as general guides. We shall take these in systematic succession.

Preservation of Colors. In the preservation of the feathers of birds, little else is required to prevent the dissipation of their colors than to keep them as much as possible from air and light. These two agents, which were indispensible to their beauty and perfection in a living state, now exercise their influence as destroyers, and that influence will sooner or later work its ends according to the quality, texture, or color of the object with which it is contending. The feathers are now deprived of two agents, which in a living state contributed to their vigor and their beauty, namely, the

internal circulating juices which they received from the body
of the animal, and the external application of oil by the bill
of the bird, supplied from a gland which is placed over the
rump of all birds.

The colors of the rapacious tribes are not so evanescent as
those of many others, as they, for the most part, are composed of intense browns and blacks, which are not so easily
absorbed by light or air, so that they continue for a very long
period without any sensible difference.   There are, however,
certain other points which are liable to almost immediate
change of color after the death of the animals, and these are
the cere and skin of the legs and feet, and the naked skin on
the heads and necks of vultures and their congeners.   We
shall treat of these individually.

Now, as all these colors which we have described are liable
to change immediately after death, it is evident that considerable nicety will be required to give the preserved specimen
the appearance of nature.   These must, therefore, be supplied
artificially with the varnish colors, which we have particularly described in their proper place, as also the combinations
for the formation of compound colors.   The reddish-brown
color mentioned, of which the fold is composed, must be
touched by a mixture of the scarlet varnish, with a little powdered burnt umber, and the blue streaks with which it is
traversed, colored above with cobalt blue.   All the varnish
colors have a tendency to shine, which, it will be evident, is
not the character of any part of the skin or earuncle of the
bird described.   As soon, therefore, as it is thoroughly dry,
which will be in about an hour, the whole surface must be
gently rubbed with very fine sand-paper, which will completely remove the gloss and give the appeance of nature.

Some nicety will be required in painting betwixt the hairs,
but it can be easily managed with a little caution.   Sometimes these hairs are liable to become brown, in which case
they can be touched with the black varnish.

As these birds are inhabitants of warm climates, some care is requisite after killing them, to prevent decay ; the tendons of the legs should be extracted to prevent their being attacked by moths, and their place supplied by some cotton and pre-servatives. The tendons are extracted by means of a longi-tudinal incision made behind the tarsus. The edges of this incision can easily be brought together when the bird is under the process of preparation.

COLLECTING AND PRESERVING BIRDS' EGGS AND NESTS.

FEW objects of natural history are more interesting than the nests of birds. To the reflecting naturalist they open up a wide field for inquiry. Speaking of the examination of birds, in the exercise of their me-chanical arts of constructing nests, Professor Rennie says: "This work is the business of their lives—the duty which calls forth that wonderful ingenuity which no experience can teach, and which no human skill can rival. The infinite variety of modes in which the nests of birds are constructed, and the exquisite adaptation of the nest to the peculiar habits of the individual, offer a subject of almost exhaustless inter-est." The number and variety of the eggs of birds are curious subjects of contemplation, and should be carefully noted whenever opportunity offers. They are as essential to the per-sonal history of the species, as any other part of our inquiries.

The eggs are emptied of their contents by making a very small hole at each end with a point. By blowing at one of the ends, the contents will escape by the other, unless the young has been already formed; in which case a larger hole must be made in the side of the egg, and the contents removed with a small hook. The hole should then be stopped up by pasting a little goldbeater's leaf over it. The eggs are then either returned to their nest, in which they ought to be cemented, or should be fixed down by one side to cards, with the name and locality attached.

The best manner of conveying loose eggs to a distance, is to put some cotton at the bottom of the nest, and then another layer above them. The nests should all be put in separate boxes if possible, and so packed that the pressure of the lid may not injure the eggs, or a box with several compartments should be used, taking care that each is carefully marked. It would also be of consequence to have the nests attached to the branches, with those species which build on trees, which will enable us to trace the ingenious means employed by those little animals in constructing their habitations. In sending home specimens from a foreign country, the seams of the box should be covered by pitched cloth to protect them from the influence of moisture.

To preserve the shells of eggs, first take care to clear them of their contents; get a small, fine-pointed common syringe, such as is sold in toy-shops for a penny or twopence, and inject the specimen with water until it comes out quite clean. When an egg has been partly hatched or addled, the removal of the contents generally includes that of the internal membrane or pellicle; this makes the shell weaker. When the specimens are quite clean internally, and have become dry (which will be in a day or two), take the syringe and inject them with a strong solution of isinglass (with a little sugar-candy added to prevent its cracking); blow this out again whilst warm. Let the shell get dry, and then wash the outside with a soft wet cloth to remove saline particles, dirt from the nest, etc. This method varnishes the inside, and the first specimen on which it has been tried was the before-mentioned hedge-accentor's egg, which is to this day as bright in color as a fresh specimen.

Also in a pair of nightjar's eggs, of which species the delicate gray tint is particularly evanescent, one was injected in the manner described, and the other was not; in the first the gray is still perfectly defined, in the other it has entirely disappeared. Eggs which have lost their internal pellicle become strengthened by this process, and those which have not lost their color greatly improved.

SKINNING, PRESERVING, AND SETTING UP REPTILES, AND MOLLUSCOUS ANIMALS, ETC.

TORTOISES AND TURTLES.

SKINNING. The first operation is to separate the back and breast shells with a strong short knife, or chisel. If the force of the hand is inadequate, a mallet may be used, taking care not to strike so hard as to crack the shell.

These two bony plates being covered by the skin, or by scales, the scapula, and all the muscles of the arm and neck, in place of being attached to the ribs and spine, are placed below, from which cause the tortoise has been termed a retroverted animal. The vertebral extremity of the scapula is articulated with the shield, and the opposite extremity of the clavicle with the breast-plate in such a manner that the shoulders form a ring for the passage of the windpipe and gullet.

After the turtle is opened, all the flesh which adheres to the breast-plate, and also to the upper shell, is removed, while attention is paid to the parts as above described. The head, fore-feet, and tail are skinned as in quadrupeds; but none of these must be removed from the upper shell, but left attached.

All the fleshy parts being removed, the shells are washed

out with a sponge, and carefully dried.   They are then slighty rubbed with the arsenical soap.

Stuffing.   Wires are now passed through the middle of the legs, after the skin has been **rubbed** with the preservative. The skull is returned to its place, and the whole of the head, neck, **and** legs stuffed with chopped flax or tow.   The parts of the skin which have been cut are then sewed together.   The back and breast-plates are then united by four small holes, being bored at their edges, **and** united by strings or small wires.   The junction of the bones may then be attached with the cement, colored so as to correspond with the shell.

If the calipash is dirty, it may be cleaned with a slight solution of nitric-acid **and water;** afterwards clean washed, oiled, and then rubbed hard with **a woolen rag,** to give it **a** polish.

CROCODILES AND LIZARDS IN GEN-ERAL.

Skinning.   All this tribe are skinned in the same manner as quadrupeds.   **Care is,** however, required in skinning the tails of **the** smaller species, as they are very liable to break. The skins being of a dry nature, require but little of the preservative.   After they are thoroughly dried **they** will **keep** a **very long time** without decay.

Stuffing.   Stuff them as directed for quadrupeds.   They admit of but little variety of attitude.   The small species are exceedingly apt to change **color** in drying, which must be **imitated** with the colored varnishes, and afterwards dimmed with sand-paper.   To keep them in their natural colors, they should be preserved in spirits.

The skins of such as are **glossy** should be varnished after they **are** perfectly **dry.**

SERPENTS IN GENERAL.

Skinning. In skinning serpents there is some nicety required, to cut them so as not to disfigure the scales; the opening should be made in the side, commencing at the termination of the scales; and they should on no account be divided, as upon their number the species is mostly determined.

It is a very frequent practice to send home serpents without the head, which renders them quite unfit for any scientific purpose. This proceeds from the fear of receiving poison from the fangs. But there is not the slightest danger of being affected, as these can easily be cut out by means of pincers. The head should be cleaned and the brain removed, in the same manner as recommended for birds and quadrupeds, the skull anointed and then returned into the skin.

When the skin is removed, it may be rolled up and packed in small space. Tho simplest way to preserve small species is to put them in spirits, which must not be too strong, as it will destroy the colors.

Mr. Burchell, in his four years' journey through Africa, glued the skins of the smaller serpents perfectly flat on paper, which preserved the size of the animal, and the skin retained all the beauty of life.

Stuffing. The skin, if not recent, must be first softened in the manner recommended for birds. A piece of wire is taken, the length of the animal, which must be wrapped round with tow till it is of a proper thickness, and above the whole a spiral band of sliver should be carefully wrapped. It is then placed inside of tho skin, and sewed up. The eyes are placed in, as directed for quadrupeds and birds. When dry, give the serpent a coat of varnish, and then twist it into any attitude wished. A favorite and striking one is to have it wound round some animal, and in tho act of killing it.

FROGS AND TOADS.

Skinning. The mouth is opened, and the first vertebræ of the neck is cut. The whole inside of the mouth is cut out with scissors. The two jaws are next raised up and the skin is pushed back with the fingers of the right hand, while the body is drawn back in a contrary direction with the other hand, and the whole body is then drawn out at the mouth. The legs are then returned to their proper place.

Stuffing. The simplest method of stuffing these animals, is with sand. A small funnel is placed into the mouth, and pour in well dried sand. When full, a small piece of cotton is pushed into the throat, with some of the cement, to keep the sand from escaping on moving the animal.

The frog is then placed on a board, and in an attitude. When quite dry, give it a coat of varnish. When this has perfectly dried, very small perforations are made under the belly with the point of a needle, and the sand allowed to escape, leaving the body in its natural form.

These animals are liable to change of color from drying, and should, therefore, be painted with the varnish to their natural hues. There is less difficulty with toads in this respect, as they are usually of a brown color, and not liable to much change.

They may be perfectly preserved in spirits.

PRESERVING SPIDERS, GALLY-WORMS, AND INSECTS.

SPIDERS.

THE general directions which we shall give respecting insects, hold good as to spiders, only we must mention there is considerable difficulty in preserving the bodies of spiders, which generally, in a very short time, shrink into a shapeless mass. To prevent this, the body should be pricked with the triangular awl and the contents pressed out; it should then be stuffed with very fine carded cotton or down, which can be pushed in by a pricker, blunted a little at the point. When properly distended, the small aperture should be filled up with a little cement, or a solution of gum-arabic. The legs of the larger species, such as the bird-catching Mygale and the Scorpions, are also liable to shrink, and should be stuffed in the same manner as that of the body.

In those species of spiders which we have thus prepared, and whose colors are rich and likely to be affected by the action of the atmosphere, we must endeavor to arrest its progress by immediately imbuing the animal, after it is set up, with the solution of corrosive sublimate, and in an hour after with a thin coating of a very weak white-spirit varnish; for this purpose, take a teaspoonful of the ordinary white-spirit or elastic varnish, and add to it two teaspoonfuls of spirit of wine; apply this wash with a fine camel hair brush, which will quickly dry, and have a strong tendency to preserve the color. The varnish, being thus reduced in strength, will not leave any gloss on the insect, nor will it be at all perceptible.

Mr. Samouelle, author of "The Entomologist's Useful Compendium," in speaking of preserving spiders, says: "The best preserved specimens that I have seen are those where the contents of the abdomen have been taken out and filled with fine sand. **I have preserved several in this way, and find it** answer the purpose."

Mr. Donovan makes the following observations **on the** preservation of spiders:

"To determine whether some species of spiders could **be** preserved with their natural colors, I put several into spirits of wine; those with gibbous bodies soon after discharged a very considerable quantity of viscid matter, and therewith all their beautiful colors; the smallest retained their form, and only **appeared** rather paler in the other colors than when they were **living.**

"During the course **of** last summer, among other **spiders,** **I met with** a rare species; it was of a bright **yellow color,** elegantly marked with black, red, green, and purple; **by some** accident it was unfortunately crushed **to** pieces in the **chip-** **box wherein it** was confined, and was, therefore, thrown **aside** **as useless; a** month or more after that time I observed that **such parts of the** skin as had dried against **the** inside of **the** **box, retained the** original brightness of color in a **consider-** able degree. **To** further **the** experiment, I **made a similar** attempt, with some caution, on the body of **another** spider, and, though **the colors were** not perfectly preserved, they appeared distinct.

"From further observations I find, that **if** you kill the spider and immediately after extract **the** entrails, then inflate them by means of a blow-pipe, you may preserve them tolerably **well; you** must clean them on the inside no more than is sufficient **to** prevent mouldiness, lest you injure the colors, which certainly, in many kinds, depend on substance that lies beneath the skin."

Scorpions, and all the **spider** tribe, may be sent **home** in spirits, which will preserve **them** perfectly, and when taken out and dried, they will be found **to** have suffered nothing **from** their immersion. **We** have seen some specimens set up, after being **sent** home in spirits, **which** rivaled any which have been preserved in a recent state. The animals of this class are particularly liable to the attacks of insects, particularly in warm countries, on which account the mode of transporting them and keeping them in spirits is, perhaps, superior to all others. If, however, they are set up in a warm climate, they should be well soaked with the solution of corrosive sublimate, made according to the recipe of Mr. Waterton.

For the setting up of this class, see the directions for preserving insects.

INSECTS.

Every country of the world is replete with this extensive and interesting class of beings, whose forms are infinitely diversified, and whose species are the most numerous of any class in the animal kingdom.

Before any attempt is made to collect insects, certain apparatus must be provided, not only to enable us to secure them, but also to preserve them after they are caught.

First, then, we must be provided with a quantity of wooden boxes, from 18 to 20 inches long, 15 to 17 inches wide, and two inches deep. These should have well-filled lids, with hinges, and fastened by a wire catch, or small bolt. The bottom should have a layer of cork, about the sixth of an inch in thickness, which should be fixed down with very strong paste, made according to our recipe; and also some wire nails, to prevent it from springing. Over the cork should be pasted white paper. The box should be anointed inside with oil of petroleum. If that cannot be procured, make an infusion of strong aromatic plants, such as cinnamon, aloes, thyme, laurel, sage, rosemary, or cloves, and wash the inside with it. A small packet of camphor should be wrapped in a piece of rag, and deposited in a corner of the box.

We must also be provided with a quantity of *insect pins* of different sizes, corresponding with the size of the insect.

The pins used for setting should be longer than those which are taken to the field.

Bottles, with mouths from an inch and a quarter to two inches in diameter, must also be procured, and these must be three-fourths full of spirits, such as weak brandy, rum, gin, or whisky.

Hunting-Box. We must, besides, have what is termed a hunting-box, for carrying in our pocket, when seeking after insects. This should be made of strong paste-board or chip, for lightness, or, if this is no consideration, of tin. It must be of an oblong-oval shape, rounded at the ends, for the convenience of the pocket. It should be from eight to ten inches long, four to five inches wide, and two-and-a-half to three inches deep. It must have a layer of cork both in the bottom and top of the lid, inside for attaching insects to, when caught during the day. The larger insects are placed at the bottom, and the smaller ones on the lid.

The Entomological. We next procure a net, as in figure 26, constructed similar to a bat-fowling net. This is either made of fine gauze or coarse muslin; it may either be green or white—the latter is the best for observing small insects which may be caught; the green, however, is better adapted for catching moths. The net-rods should be made of hickory, beech, hazel, or holly; they ought to be five feet in length, quite round, smooth, and tapering to an obtuse point, as at figure 24; the oblique cross-piece at the point should be of cane, and fitted into the angular ferrule; the rod must be divided into three or four pieces, so that it may be taken asunder and carried in the pocket; the upper part of each joint must have a ferrule affixed to it, for the purpose of articulating the other pieces. Each joint should have a notch or check to prevent the rod from twisting.

The net itself, figure 31, must have a welting all around it, doubled so as to form a groove for the reception of the rods. In the center of the upper part or point it must have a small piece of chamois leather, so as to form a kind of hinge; this must be bound round the welting and divided in the middle, so as to prevent the cross pieces from slipping over each other; it shows about four inches of the gauze turned up, so as to form a bag; there are strings for the purpose of passing through the staple, to which the net is firmly drawn on each side. When the net is used a handle is to be held in each hand.

If it is intended to take insects on the wing, by means of this net, for which it is admirably adapted, it may be folded together in an instant. If the gauze is fine enough, and preserved whole, even the smallest insect cannot escape. It may be also applied in catching coleopterous insects, which are never on the wing, as well as caterpillars. When used for this purpose the entomologist must hold it expanded under trees, while another must beat the branches with a stick. Great numbers of both insects and larvæ will fall in the gauze, and by this means many hundreds may be captured in a day.

Another method is to spread a large table-cloth under trees and bushes, and then beat them with a stick. An umbrella reversed has frequently been used for the same purpose. Bose, the celebrated naturalist, used this last method—he held the umbrella in the left hand, while he beat the bushes with the other.

The Hoop or Aquatic Net, Figure 26. This net is used for capturing aquatic insects, which are either lurking at the bottom, swimming through the liquid element, or adhering to plants. It may also be successfully used in sweeping amongst grass and low herbage for coleopterous insects and others which are generally to be found in such situations. The socket, for the handle, may be made of such dimensions as will answer the second joint of the entomological net-rod, which will save carrying another handle; or a walking-stick may be made to fit it.

A Phial, Figure 33. This may either be made of tin or crystal, and used for collecting coleopterous and other creeping insects. The mouth should be nearly an inch wide, and a cork exactly fitted to it, in the center of which must be inserted a small quill, to afford air, and inserted about an inch beyond the cork, to prevent the insects from escaping. If the bottle is made of tin, and of a larger size, a tin tube must be introduced into its side, and terminating externally at the surface.

A Digger, Figure 28. The instrument is either made of iron or steel, and is about six or seven inches in length, fixed into a turned wooden handle. It is used for collecting the pupæ of lepidopterous insects, at the roots and in the clefts of the bark of trees; and also for pulling off the bark, particularly from decayed trees, under which many curious and rare insects are frequently found. It is most useful with an arrow-headed point.

Setting Needles, Figure 29. Fitted into a small wooden handle, the needle itself should be about three inches long, and about the thickness of a small darning-needle, slightly bent from about the middle. Figure 30 is a straight needle which is used for extending the parts of insects; at one end of the handle is the needle, and at the other a camel-hair pencil, which is used for removing any dirt or dust which may be on the insects. The pencil may be occasionally drawn through the lips, brought to a fine point, and used for disposing the antennæ and palpi of insects of the minute kinds.

Brass Pliers, Figure 25. These are used for picking up small insects from the roots of grass, etc. They may also be used for laying hold of small insects, while they are yet free and not set up.

Fan Forceps. This very useful instrument to the entomologist, must be made of steel or iron, and about eight or ten inches in length; its general construction is like that of a pair of scissors, and it is held and used in the same manner. Towards the points are formed a pair of fans, which may either be square, oval, hexagonal, or octagonal in the edges, and the centers covered with fine gauze. The general size of the fans is from four to six inches. These are used for capturing bees, wasps, and muscæ. They are also used for catching butterflies, moths, and sphinges. If an insect is on a leaf, both leaf and insect may be inclosed within the fans; or if they are on a wall or the trunk of a tree, they may be very easily secured by them.

If a butterfly, sphinx, or moth, are captured by the forceps, while yet between the fans, they should be pressed pretty smoothly with the thumb-nail, on the thorax or body, taking care, however, not to crush it. It may then be taken into the hand, and a pin passed through the thorax, and then stuck into the bottom of your hunting-box.

Quills. These are of great use in carrying minute insects. They should be neatly stopped with cork and cement at one end, the other end should be provided with a small movable cork for a stopper. Each end should be wrapped carefully round with a silk thread waxed, to prevent them from splitting.

Pocket Larvæ-Box. For collecting caterpillars, this box is very essential: it consists merely of a chip-box, with a hole pierced in the center of the top and bottom, and covered with gauze, for the admission of air. It will be necessary to put into the box some of the leaves on which the larvæ feed, as they are very voracious, and cannot long exist without food.

Pill-Boxes. No entomologist should be **without five or six dozen** of these useful articles. **They are of great value in** collecting the smaller species of lepidopterous insects, such as the tinea, etc., and only one specimen should be put in each box, as, if more than one, **they** are apt to injure each **other's** wings by beating against each other.

Setting Boards. These must be made **of** deal board, from a foot to fifteen inches long, and eight or ten inches broad, with a piece of **wood** run across the ends, to prevent them from warping. **They are** covered with cork, which must **be** perfectly smooth **on** the surface, with **white** paper pasted over it. Several boards will be required, by persons who are making collections, as some of the insects take a con-siderable **time to dry, so** that they may be fit **for introducing into a** cabinet.

The boards should be kept in a **frame made** for the purpose. **It** should consist of a top, bottom, and two sides; the back and front should have **the** frames of doors attached by small hinges, and their centers covered with fine gauze, for the free passage of air; the sides should have small pieces of wood pro-jecting from them, for the boards to rest on; which should be at such a distance from each other that the pins may not **be** displaced in pushing the boards in or drawing them out. The frame should be placed in **a** dry, airy situation.

Braces. These are merely small pieces of card, **cut in** the form exhibited, Fig. 36, attached to the butterfly and other insects; and also at Fig. 39. They are pinned down on the insects, to keep their wings, etc., in a proper state, till they acquire a set.

SETTING AND PRESERVING INSECTS.

Of the orders Coleoptera, Orthoptera, and Hemiptera. These are easily preserved.

They are killed by immersing in scalding water, and then laid upon blossom or blotting paper, for the purpose of absorbing as much of the moisture as possible; or they may be placed in a tin box, with a little camphor in it, near the fire, which soon kills them. This is, besides, of considerable effect in their preservation.

Insects of the genera *Gryllus* (Cricket), *Locusta* (Locusts), etc., have tender bodies, and are sure to shrivel in drying. The intestines should therefore be extracted, while they are yet moist, and skin filled with cotton, as directed with some of the spiders.

When Coleopterous insects are set with the wings displayed, the elytra should be separated, and the pin passed through their body near the middle of the thorax, as in Fig. 35. The wings are exhibited as in the act of flying, and are retained in this situation until they are quite dry, by the cord braces. The insects of this order should always have the pin passed through the right elytra on the right side, as shown at Fig. 37, that is, it should pass underneath, between the first pair of feet and the intermediate ones.

The legs, palpi and antennæ should be displayed in a natural order on the setting board, and retained in the position by means of pins and braces, as shown in Figs. 35, 37. These must be kept in that state, either longer or shorter, according to the insect and the state of the weather, as, if placed in a cabinet before they are quite dry, they are sure to get mouldy, and will ultimately rot.

Minute insects should be attached to cards with gum, as shown, Figs. 34 and 39, with the legs and other organs displayed. Entomologists generally adapt triangular cards as at Fig. 38, as less liable to hide the parts of the insects.

Order Lepidoptera. Mr. Haworth, in mentioning the tenacity of life in the Goat Moth, states that " the usual way of compressing the *thorax* is not sufficient to kill this insect. They will live several days after the most severe pressure has been given there, to the great uneasiness of any humane entomologists. The methods of suffocation by tobacco or sulphur are equally inefficacious, unless continued for a greater number of hours, than is proper for the preservation of the specimens. Another method now in practice is better, and however fraught with cruelty it may appear to the inexperienced collector, is the greatest piece of *comparative mercy* that can, in this case, be administered. When the larger Moths must be killed, destroy them at once by the *insertion of a strong, red-hot needle* into their thickest part, beginning at the front of *the thorax*. If this be properly *done,* instead of *lingering through several days, they are dead in a moment.* It appears to me, however, that insects being animals of *cold* and *sluggish juices,* are not so susceptible of the sensations we call pain, as those which enjoy a warmer temperature of body, and a swifter circulation of the fluids. To the philosophic mind it is self-evident that they have not such acute organs of feeling pain as other animals of a *similar size,* whose juices are endowed with a quicker motion, and possess a constant, regular and genial warmth.

Butterflies are soon killed by passing a pin through the thorax. The pin passed through the thorax of small moths generally proves almost instantly fatal to them.

The best manner of preserving the minute species of moths is by pill-boxes, as above stated, each moth being kept in a separate box. We have found the following the best mode of destroying them:

A piece of flat hard-wood is taken, and a circular groove cut in it, sufficiently deep to admit the mouth of a tumbler being placed within it. In the center of the wood, pierce a hole about a third of an inch in diameter in its center: place the pill box under this tumbler, with the lid off, and the insect will soon creep out; but whether it does so or not, a match well primed with sulphur is lighted and placed into the hole under the center of the tumbler, which will suffocate the insect in a few seconds. I have also found this an effectual method of killing the larger species of butterflies, and moths. In piercing them, the pin should be quite perpendicular, that no part of their minute frame should be hidden by its oblique position.

The larger insects of this order are set by braces chiefly. A single one should in the first place be introduced under the wing, near the thorax, as shown in Fig. 36, and a longer brace extending over the wings. These should not bear upon the wings, but be ready to rest gently on them, when required. The wings are now elevated to their proper position by the setting needle, and other braces are used as necessity dictates. The feet and antennæ are extended and kept in their places by means of pins, in which operation small braces are also occasionally used.

The French entomologists set butterflies, moths, and sphinges, on a piece of soft wood, in which they have excavated a groove for the reception of the body, as deep as the insertion of the wings. They are otherwise preserved as above directed.

In the larger butterflies, moths, and sphinges, the abdomen should be perforated, its contents extracted, and then stuffed with fine cotton, after having been washed internally with the solution of corrosive sublimate. Indeed, the cotton should also be rubbed with arsenical soap before being introduced, as these insects are particularly liable to the attack of smaller insects, such as the mite.

Several of the moth tribe are extremely liable to change their color some time after they have been placed in a cabinet. This change is frequently occasioned by an oily matter which is common to many of them. This first makes its appearance in small spots on the body, but soon spreads itself over the abdomen, thorax, and wings; and ends in a total obliteration of all the beautiful markings. A method which has been sometimes successfully adopted is to sprinkle all the wings with powdered chalk, and holding a heated iron over it; the chalk absorbs the grease, and may then be blown off by means of a pair of small bellows. Another way of applying the chalk, and perhaps the better of the two, is to throw some powdered chalk on the face of a heated iron, and then put it into a piece of linen cloth, and apply it to the body of the insect; the heat of the iron will soften the grease, and the chalk will absorb it.

Another method is to hold a heated iron over the insects for a few minutes, and then to wash the spotted or greasy places with ox-gall and water, applied with a camel-hair pencil, and afterwards wash it with pure water, and dry it by an application of blotting paper, and when perfectly dry imbue it with the solution of corrosive sublimate. But grease seldom appears where the contents of the abdomen have been removed.

Orders Neuroptera, Hymenoptera and Diptera. The Dragon Flies (*Libellulæ*) are frequently very difficult to kill, being powerful and nervous animals. When caught they should be transfixed through the sides, and it sometimes becomes necessary to put braces on their wings to prevent them from fluttering while in the hunting box. They may also be killed sometimes by placing them under a tumbler and suffocating them. Some entomologists put them in scalding water for an instant.

The contents of the abdomen should always be removed from Dragon Flies, otherwise it will become black and shining through the skin, and destroy the beautiful bands with which they are ornamented. They can be stuffed with cotton or a small roll of paper introduced. If these precautions are attended to, the insect will preserve the perfect beauty of its living state.

The other species of these orders soon die after being transfixed. They may be set by braces and pins, as represented in Figs. 35 and 37.

Some of the *Dipterous* insects are very perishable in point of color after death, particularly in the abdomen, the skin of which is very thin. The only way of remedying this is to pierce the abdomen, and after taking out the contents the cavity should be filled with a powdered paint the same color as the living subjects, which will shine through and give it all the appearance of nature.

METHOD OF RELAXING DRIED INSECTS.

Insects frequently get stiffened before the entomologist has leisure to get them set; and it usually happens that those sent home from foreign countries have been ill set, and require to be placed in more appropriate attitudes after they have fallen into the hands of the scientific collector. They may be relaxed and made as flexible as recently killed specimens by the following simple process, from which they can receive no injury: Pin them on a piece of cork, and place the cork in a large basin or pan of tepid water, and cover the top tight with a damp cloth, taking care that it is sufficiently high not to injure the insects. In most cases a few hours is sufficient to restore them to their original flexibility, so that they may be easily put in their proper positions. In some instances, three or four days are necessary to relax them thoroughly, so as to set the wings without the risk of breaking them; no force whatever must be used with any of the members. When set up, after being relaxed, they must be treated in exactly the same manner as recent specimens.

We must again caution the entomologist to be careful that he applies the solution of corrosive sublimate to all his species, otherwise there is little chance of their continuing long without being attacked by the mite; they ought to be frequently imbued.

Mr. Waterton, who has studied deeply the subject of preserving animal substances, and applied them not only in our own country, but also under the influence of a tropical climate, makes the following observations on the preservation of Insects: "I only know of two methods," says he, "to guard preserved insects from the depredations of living ones. The first is, by poisoning the atmosphere—the second is, by poisoning the prepared specimens themselves, so effectually that they are no longer food for the depredators. But there are some objections to both these modes; a poisoned atmosphere will evaporate in time if not attended to, or if neglected to be renewed; and there is great difficulty in poisoning some specimens on account of their delicacy and minuteness. If you keep spirits of turpentine in the boxes which contain your preserved specimens, I am of opinion that those specimens will be safe as long as the odor of the turpentine remains in the box, for it is said to be the most pernicious of all scents to insects. But it requires attention to keep up an atmosphere of spirits of turpentine; if it be allowed to evaporate entirely, then there is a clear and undisputed path open to the inroads of the enemy; he will take advantage of your absence or neglect, and when you return to view your treasure you will find it in ruins. Spirits of turpentine poured into a common glass inkstand, in which there is a piece of sponge, and placed in a corner of your box, will create a poisoned atmosphere and kill every insect there. The poisoning of your specimens by means of corrosive sublimate in alcohol, is a most effective method. As soon as the operation is properly performed, the depredating insect perceives that the prepared specimen is no longer food for it, and will forever cease to attack it; but then every part must have received the poison, otherwise those parts where the poison has not reached will still be exposed to the enemy, and he will pass unhurt over the poisoned parts till he arrives at that part of your specimen which is still wholesome food for him. Now, the difficulty lies in applying the solution to very minute specimens without injuring their appearance; and all that can be said is, to recommend unwearied exertion, which is sure to be attended with great skill, and great skill will insure surprising success."

I am convinced that there is no absolute and lasting safety for prepared specimens in zoölogy from the depredations of insects, except by poisoning every part of them with a solution of corrosive sublimate in alcohol.

Mr. Waterton is of opinion that tight boxes with aromatic atmospheres are not to be depended upon in the preservation of insects. He says: "The tight boxes and aromatic atmospheres will certainly do a great deal, but they are liable to fail, for this obvious reason, viz.: That they do not render forever absolutely baneful and abhorrent to the depredator that which in itself is nutritious and grateful to him. In an evil hour, through neglect in keeping up a poisoned atmosphere, the specimens collected by industry and prepared by art, and which ought to live, as it were, for the admiration of future ages, may fall a prey to an intruding and almost invisible enemy, so that, unless the solution of corrosive sublimate in alcohol is applied, you are never perfectly safe from surprise. I have tried a decoction of aloes, wormwood and walnut leaves, thinking they would be of service on account of their bitterness. The trial completely failed."

Many entomologists are satisfied with possessing the insect in its perfect or image condition. But it is exceedingly interesting to be able to trace these through their different states of existence from the egg to the perfect insect. Besides, we are certain to produce the insects in the highest state of preservation when we breed them ourselves, and it is besides very interesting to have the eggs of the different species as well as the caterpillar and pupa.

The Eggs of Insects. The eggs of insects preserve their form and color in a cabinet, in general, without much trouble. Swammerdam had a method of preserving them when they appeared to be giving way. He made a perforation within them with a fine needle, pressed out their contents, afterwards inflated them with a glass blow-pipe, and filled them with a mixture of resin and oil of spike.

The Larvæ, or Caterpillars. The easiest way of destroying the Caterpillar is by immersion in spirits of wine. They may be retained for a long time in this spirit without destroying their color.

Mr. William Weatherhead had an ingenious mode of preserving larvæ. He killed the caterpillar, as above directed, and having made a small puncture in the tail, gently pressed out the contents of the abdomen, and then filled the skin with fine dry sand, and brought the animal to its natural circumference. It is then exposed to the air to dry, and it will have become quite hard in the course of a few hours, after which the sand may be shaken out at the small aperture and the caterpillar then gummed to a piece of card.

Another method is, after the entrails are squeezed out, to insert into the aperture a glass tube which has been drawn to a very fine point. The operator must blow through this pipe while he keeps turning the skin slowly round over a charcoal fire; the skin soon becomes hardened, and, after being anointed with oil of spike and resin, it may be placed in a cabinet when dry. A small straw or pipe of grass may be substituted for the glass pipe. Some persons inject them with colored wax after they are dry.

The Pupa. When the insects have escaped from their pupa skin, the skin usually retains the shape and general appearance it did while it contained the insect. It is therefore ready for the cabinet, without any preparation whatever. But if the animal has not quitted its envelope, it will be necessary either to drop the pupa into warm water, or to heat it in a tin case before the fire; the former mode, however, is the best, and least liable to change the colors of the pupa.

METHOD OF BREEDING INSECTS.

Breeding Cages. These must be made of oak, or other hard wood, as pine is apt to kill the caterpillars from its strong smell of turpentine. The best form for these is represented in Fig. 32. The sides and front are covered with gauze; a is a small square box, for the reception of a phial of water, for placing the stalks of plants in, on which it is intended the caterpillars are to feed. The most convenient size for a breeding cage is eight inches in breadth, four deep, and one foot in height. It is not proper to place within a cage more than one species of caterpillar, as many of them prey upon each other. Indeed, animals of the same species will devour each other if left without food. The caterpillars of insects, for the most part, will only eat one particular kind of food, so that it is better to have no more than one sort in a cage.

There must be at the bottom of the cage earth to the depth of two inches; this should be mixed with some fine sand and vegetable earth, if possible, to prevent it from drying. The cages should be kept in a cool cellar or damp place, because many insects change into the pupa condition under the earth; so that it would require to be somewhat moist, to prevent the destruction of the animal. The shell or case of the pupa also becomes hard, if the earth is not kept moist; and, in that event, the animal will not have sufficient strength to break its case at the time it ought to emerge from its confinement, and must consequently die, which but too frequently happens from mismanagement.

Some seasons are more favorable than others for the production of caterpillars, and to keep each kind by themselves would require an immense number of cages, as well as occupy much time in changing the food, and paying due attention to them. To obviate this, some persons have large breeding cages, with a variety of food in them, which must be cleaned out every two days, and fresh leaves given to the caterpillars; as, on due attention to feeding, the beauty and vigor of the coming insects will much depend.

The larvæ of insects, which feed beneath the surface of the earth, may be bred in the following manner: Let any box that is about three or four feet square, and two or three feet deep, be lined internally with tin, and a number of very minute holes be bored through the sides and bottom. Put into this box a quantity of earth, replete with such vegetables as the caterpillars subsist on, and sink it into a bed of earth, so that the surface may be exposed to the different changes of the weather. The lid should be covered with brass or iron network, to prevent their escape, and for the free admission of air.

The young entomologist should obtain a cabinet of about thirty drawers, arranged in two tiers, and covered in with folding doors. There is a great convenience in this size, as the cabinet is rendered more portable, and at the same time admits of having another of the same size, being placed above the top of it, as the collection increases, without injuring the uniformity, and thus the drawers may be augmented to any extent. It is immaterial whether the cabinet is made of mahogany or oak; sometimes they are constructed of cedar, but seldom of pine, or any other soft wood. Small cells must be made in the inside of the fronts for camphor.

Corking of Drawers. The simplest way to get the cork is to purchase it of a cork-cutter, ready prepared, but it will

be much cheaper for the entomologist to prepare it himself.
In this case, it should be cut into strips of about three inches
wide, with a cork-cutter's knife, to smooth the surface and to
divide it. The strips should be fixed in a vice, and cut to the
thickness required with a fine saw; but grease must not be
used in the operation, as it will not only prevent the cork
from adhering to the bottom of the drawer, but will also
grease the paper which should be pasted on its surface. The
black surface of the cork should be rasped down to a smooth
surface. After having reduced the slips to about three quarters of an inch in thickness, the darkest, or worst side of the
slip should be glued down to a sheet of brown, or cartridge
paper; this should be laid on a deal board, about three feet in
length, and the width required for a drawer or box; a few fine
nails, or brads, must be driven through each piece of cork to
keep it firm and in its place until the glue is dried; by this
means, sheets of cork may be formed the size of the drawer.
All the irregularities are filed or rasped down quite to a level
surface, and then polished smooth with pumice-stone. The
sheet, thus formed and finished, is glued into the drawers.
To prevent its warping, some weights must be equally distributed over the cork, that it may adhere firmly to the bottom
of the drawer. When quite dry, the weights are removed,
and the cork covered with fine white paper, but not very
thick. The paper is allowed to be quite damp with the paste
before it is placed on the cork, and when dry it will become
perfectly tight.

Insect cabinets should be kept in a very dry situation, otherwise the antennæ, legs, etc., will become quite mouldy. The
same evil will ensue if the insect is not perfectly dry before it
is placed in the cabinet. Should an insect be covered with
mold it can be washed off with a camel's hair pencil, dipped
in camphorated spirits of wine; in which case, the insect
must be dried in a warm airy situation, before being placed
in the cabinet.

There should always be plenty of camphor kept in the drawers, otherwise there is great danger to be apprehended from mites; where these exist, they are easily discovered by the dust which is under the insects by which they are infested. In which case, they must be immediately taken out, and rubbed clean with a fine camel's hair pencil, and well imbued with the solution of corrosive sublimate, and then placed near a fire, taking care, however, that too great a heat is not applied, as it will utterly destroy the specimen. The butterfly, sphinx and moth tribes are extremely liable to the attack of mites, and should, therefore, be frequently examined.

SHELL FISH, TO PRESERVE—AND THE ART OF POLISHING SHELLS.

CUTTLE FISH, and all other molluscous animals, can only be preserved in spirits. The same observation applies to the animals which inhabit that numerous tribe called Testaceous Shells. They must be detached from the shells, and put into spirits, while the shells themselves must be preserved, independent of the animal.

Shells naturally arrange themselves under three distinct heads: Marine, Land, and Fluviatile, or Fresh Water.

Marine shells are only to be expected perfect, when procured in a living state. The way to extract the animal is to pour some warm water on it; but, if too hot, it is liable to crack the shells. When the animals are dead, they can easily be pulled out with any hooked instrument, or fork, or if the animal is small, by a common pin. This applies to all marine shells; whether univalve, bivalve or tubular. It is of great consequence to preserve the ligament of bivalve shells entire, so that the valves may not be separated. The animals of land and fresh water shells are killed by the same means, only that the water requires to be very hot.

Unless the shells are covered with extraneous matter, it is not necessary to clean them. Marine shells are, however, very liable to be incrusted with other marine bodies, particularly with serpula and balani, etc. These must be started off by means of a sharp instrument; an engraving tool is well adapted for this purpose. This must be done with great caution, in species which have spines, and other excrescences, as they are very liable to be broken. Should any of the calcareous matter still adhere, this must be removed, by applying to it a *very weak* mixture of muriatic acid and water, applied with the point of a quill, and then plunged into water, and allowed to remain till the acid is quite extracted. But on no account whatever attempt to eradicate these parasitic bodies by means of acid, or acid and water alone, as the chances are that the shell will be completely destroyed by their application. We have seen many fine and valuable shells destroyed by an injudicious application of acids—they should never be used when it can possibly be avoided. We have, on the other hand, seen shells which were so completely enveloped in calcareous crust, that it was impossible to trace their external surface, most thoroughly cleared of all this, without being touched at all by acids, the whole being removed by a small knife or other sharp instrument; and these, in many cases, having long and tender spines externally.

Nothing can be more monstrous than the application of pumice-stone, which some recommend, for polishing shells; as is also the use of tripoli, rotten-stone, and emery. Neither do we approve the application of varnishes, as such shells never have their natural luster.

If a shell is found dead upon the beach it is probable that it will have undergone a certain degree of decomposition, that is, it will have parted with part of its animal matter, and consequently the colors will have faded and the surface present a chalky appearance.   To remove this take a small **proportion of Florence oil and** apply it to the surface, when **the** colors which were invisible will **appear.   When** completely saturated with oil let the **shell be rubbed** dry and placed in a cabinet. Oil may also be **applied after** acid has been used, and it will be found extremely useful **when** applied to dry the epidermis, which it **will** prevent **from** cracking **or** quitting the shell **entirely, which it frequently does.**

Whether marine **shells are** procured in a living **or dead** state, a very necessary precaution is to immerse them in pure **tepid** water after **the animal** has been extracted, **and** allow them to continue in it for an hour or two so as completely to extract any salt **or acid which may** be in them.

Fresh water shells **are liable to a** calcareous or **earthy incrustation,** which must **be removed by** immersing them in **warm water, and** afterwards **scraping and** brushing them with a nail or toothbrush.   **Much nicety is** necessary in cleaning these, as **their great thinness** renders **them,** in general, liable **to be broken.**   A little **Florence oil** will improve the appearance **of the** epidermis and **render it less** liable to crack.

Land shells **seldom require any** cleaning except washing in water, **as they are not liable to** incrustations of any kind.

When **shells** are perforated by marine animals, or otherwise broken, if the specimen is rare, it is desirable to remedy these defects as far **as possible; they may** therefore be filled up, or pieces added to them **with the cement, which** may be **colored** when dry to its original state.

Of Polishing Shells.   Many species **of** marine and fresh water shells are composed **of** mother-of-pearl, generally **covered** with a strong **epidermis.**   When it **is wished** to exhibit the external structure **of shells, the** epidermis is removed and **the** outer testaceous **coatings polished down** till the pearlaceous structure **becomes visible.   It has been** a common practice to remove **the strong** epidermis of shells by means of strong acids, but this is a hazardous and tedious mode of operating. The best method is to put the shells into a pan of cold water with a quantity of quicklime and boil it for two to four hours, according to the thickness of the epidermis. The shells afterwards must be gradually cooled, and some strong acid applied to the epidermis, when it will easily peel off. Two hours are sufficient for the common muscle being boiled. The shells are afterwards polished with rotten-stone and oil, put on a piece of chamois leather.

The epidermis of the uno margaritifera is so thick that it requires from four to five hours boiling. After the epidermis has been removed, there is beneath it a thick layer of dull, calcareous matter, which must be started off with a knife or other sharp instrument; this requires great labor, but, when accomplished, a fine mother-of-pearl is exhibited which adds an agreeable variety as a specimen.

Various turbos and trochuses are also deprived of their epidermis and polished with files, sand-paper, pumice-stone, etc., till the pearly appearance is obtained; but all these modes are invented for disfiguring rather than improving the shells in the eye of the naturalist, and should never be resorted to except where the species is very common, in which case it is well enough to do so with one or two specimens to show the structure of the shells.

After the operation of polishing and washing with acids, a little Florence oil should be rubbed over to bring out the colors and destroy the influence of the acid.

THE CHASE AND MANNER OF COLLECTING ANIMALS.

QUADRUPEDS AND BIRDS.

IT is hardly necessary to recommend a double-barrelled gun. One of the barrels should be loaded with small shot or dross of lead for small birds and the other with large shot. These should have much less powder than an ordinary charge, so as not to tear and injure the animals. Paper, cotton or flax and powdered dry earthen ashes should form part of the naturalist's stores.

When a bird is killed, a small quantity of dry dust is to be put on the wound. For this purpose the feathers must be raised with a pin, or a gun-picker, close to the wound. The bill of the bird should have a small quantity of cotton or flax introduced into it to prevent the blood from flowing and spoiling the plumage. The feathers must be all adjusted, and the bird then placed on the ground to allow the blood to coagulate. Every specimen should be placed in a piece of paper of the form of a hollow cone, like the thumb bags used by grocers. The head should be introduced into this, the paper should then be closed around the bird, and packed in a box filled with moss, dried grass or leaves.

Birds taken alive in nets and traps are to be preferred to others for stuffing, and also those caught by birdlime, which must be removed by spirits of wine.

Birds should always be skinned the same day they are killed, or next day at farthest, particularly in summer; as there is a danger of putrefaction ensuing, by which the feathers will fall off. However, in winter there is no danger for some days; but in tropical climates they must be prepared soon

QUADRUPEDS AND BIRDS. 273

after they are killed. The same observations apply generally to quadrupeds.

Bats and owls are caught during the day, in the hollows of aged trees, in the crevices of walls, and ruins of buildings. These are animals which, it may be presumed, are still little known in consequence of their nocturnal habits.

Those who prepare for the chase, with the intention of preserving animals, should take care to provide themselves with implements necessary for fulfilling the objects advantageously. The articles most needed are one or two pairs of large pincers, scissors, forceps, scalpels, knives, needles, thread and a small hatchet, as well as one or more canisters of preserving powder, some pots of arsenical soap, or arsenical composition, and some bottles of spirits of turpentine. Cotton may be employed in stuffing the skins, and therefore a considerable quantity should always be taken along with the naturalist. In parts of Asia and Africa, where this cannot be procured, tow must be employed, or old ropes teazed down; and where even this cannot be found, dried grass and moss may be used. M. Le Vaillant used a species of dog-grass while in Africa, which is very abundant in that country; and it answered the purpose remarkably well.

It being supposed that a traveler has an ample caravan, provided with all the necessaries which we have pointed out, and having killed a quadruped, he will skin it immediately, according to the method which we have pointed out. He will then sew up the skin after receiving a partial stuffing, and having been anointed with the arsenical soap or composition. All the extremities must then be imbued with spirits of turpentine, and the skin should be placed in some convenient place to dry, so that it may have the advantage of complete exposure to the air. The turpentine must be again applied at the end of three or four days, more especially around the mouth of the quadruped.

It will be of the utmost advantage to remain a week or ten

days at one place; by which means the naturalist will have had
time to render himself somewhat acquainted with the animals
which localize in that neighborhood. And as some species
frequently confine themselves to a very limited spot, by leaving the place too hurriedly he is apt to overlook them.

After the traveler has determined on leaving his canton-
ment, he must see that all the objects he has collected are in
a condition to be removed. He must examine carefully each
specimen, and see that they have not been attacked by the
destructive insects, so abundant in warm climates. Should
flies have deposited their eggs in the lips of the quadrupeds
or birds, these must be destroyed by spirits of turpentine.
When a set of animals or birds are thoroughly dry, they should
be packed in a box or case, which has been well joined.

A journal ought to be kept detailing all the circumstances
connected with the animals, the places in which they were
killed, and the color of their eyes, together with any information that can be procured of their habits from the
natives. People are too apt to forget particulars when
engaged in such varied pursuits, and the sooner they are
committed to paper the better.

When the traveler arrives in Africa, he will meet with
animals of the largest size, such as the elephant, the rhino-
ceros, hippopotamus, giraffe, quagga, urus, bubulus, con-
doma, as well as large antelope and deer. He will unquestionably find some difficulty in his endeavors to bring with
him the skins of these animals, as in that country it is even
troublesome, in many cases, to transport the necessaries of
life. But the ardor of the zealous naturalist will here be
increased by beholding such splendid specimens as he can
never meet with elsewhere. All his energies will be strengthened and every sacrifice made to enable him to transport the
fruits of his toils.

We need only to recur to the zeal manifested by Le Vaillant in his travels, and the rapturous delight experienced by

him when he first beheld and killed the giraffe. He brought this large skin from Caffraria, where he killed the animal, a distance of two.hundred leagues from the Cape of Good Hope.

Should the traveler, accidentally, or in pursuit of natural objects, find himself possessed of the carcase of one of these large and fine animals, he would deeply regret not being able to fetch away the skin from want of a knowledge how to separate it from the body. We shall, therefore, suppose that he has killed an animal the size of a bull. He must first make an incision under the belly, in the form of a double cross. The central line must reach from the chin to the anus; the two other transverse cuts must reach from one foot to the other. These are always made inside, so that the seams may be less conspicuous when the animal is mounted. When the skin is stuffed, the hoofs are detached by laying them on a stone, and striking them with a hatchet or mallet. The nails or hoofs must be left attached to the skin. After this, the skin is removed from the feet, legs, and thighs, and treated in other respects as pointed out in skinning other large animals. The bones of the head must be preserved if possible, leaving it attached at the muzzle only. All the muscles must be removed from the head, and the bones rendered as clean as possible.

As it is probable that an animal of this magnitude has been killed at a great distance from any habitation, there will not be an opportunity of macerating the hide in alum and water. The skin will also be too thick for the arsenical soap to penetrate with effect. Under these circumstances, the next best thing to preserve it is to take the ashes of a wood fire, and rub it well inside. The skin should then be stretched along the boughs of a tree, and allowed to dry. The skull, after it has been dried, must be returned into the skin, and the lips, ears, and feet imbued plentifully with turpentine, which operation must be several times repeated at intervals. Nothing is more effectual in preventing the attacks of insects than this spirit, and no larvæ will exist in places which it has touched.

The skin will be sufficiently dried within two or three days, so that the hair may be turned inwards. If some common salt can be procured, a solution of it should be made, and the hair rubbed with it. Both sides of the skin must be rubbed with this two or three times, at intervals of a day.

When sufficiently dry, the skin may be rolled up and packed. The hair ought to be inwards, with a layer of dried grass intervening, to prevent friction during conveyance. The operation of rolling up the skin must be begun at the head.

If the journey is long, the skin should be unrolled, and placed in the sun for a few hours, and the places liable to the attack of moths should be again rubbed with turpentine.

When a skin thus prepared has reached the place where it is to be put up, it must undergo a preparation previous to its being mounted. In the first place, it must be extended along the ground with the hair undermost, so that it may acquire fresh pliability, and those parts which remain stiff must be moistened with tepid water. The skin must then be placed in a large vessel of water saturated with alum, there to remain eight or ten days; after which, it must be extended on half rounded pieces of wood, and thinned with a sharp knife, which is facilitated by the projections of the wood, enabling the operator the more easily to cut it, while it is gradually shifted, till the whole has been pretty equally thinned. When this operation is completed, it is allowed to soak in water with an equal quantity of that saturated with the alum. Twenty-four hours will be sufficient.

In hunting for snakes, great caution must be exercised, as it is well known that the bite of some of these proves fatal within a quarter of an hour, particularly that of the rattle-snake and some others. Indeed, it would be more prudent to allow the natives to hunt for these poisonous reptiles, as they are better acquainted with their haunts, and the means of defense to be employed in this dangerous pursuit. They are also better acquainted with those which are poisonous. We may, however, remark, that the poisonous snakes have, in general, much larger heads than those which are harmless, and their necks are also narrow.

Shells. Shells, on account of the elegance and variety of their forms, and beauty of their colors, are objects much sought after, not only by naturalists but also by most persons who are unacquainted with science. There is no species, particularly in remote climes, which does not deserve to be brought home, the things most common in those countries being frequently the most rare in ours. Shells are found on every part of the surface of the globe. Some are inhabitants of the land, while others only frequent rivers, lakes, ponds, and ditches; and another and more numerous class live in the ocean. Land-shells are spread over the whole surface of the earth, and although more accessible, are perhaps less known than those which inhabit the "mighty deep."

Land-Shells, for the most part, are to be found creeping abroad either in the evening or after a gentle shower of rain. During the heat of the day they retire to shaded retreats, under thick bushes, the crevices of rocks, the hollows of decayed trees, or under their bark; beneath stones, amongst moss, or in holes in the ground. A little experience will teach the naturalist readily to find their retreats.

Fresh Water Shells must be sought for, if in deep lakes, with a dredge, or if in shallow places, with a tin spoon fixed on the end of a stick. This is made of a circular piece of tin four inches and a half in diameter, beat concave, and then perforated with numerous small holes, not exceeding the sixteenth part of an inch in diameter; around this must be soldered a perpendicular rim three-quarters of an inch broad, and also perforated with holes. To this must be attached a hollow tubular handle three inches long, for the insertion of

a walking-stick. It must have a few holes towards its outer
end for passing a string through to tie it firmly and prevent
it being lost. With this spoon the collector must rake along
the mud at the bottom of ditches or ponds, and after bringing a quantity to the surface, he must wash the mud entirely
away by shaking the spoon on the top of the water, and it
will pass through the holes and leave the shells. The sharp
edge of the spoon is also useful for detaching aquatic shells
from the under surface of the leaves of water-plants.

The large swan-muscle (*Anadonta Cygnea*), and other ana-
dons, generally lie deep in the mud, so that they cannot be
procured by dredging. I found it necessary to invent a net
to fish for these. This consisted of an iron triangle of twelve
inches, with a hollow handle fixed on its base, and in this is
inserted a pole of sufficient length to reach the bottom. It is
firmly screwed to the handle. A net is attached to the triangle either of twine or hair-cloth. The point of the triangle
should be sharp so that it may the more easily penetrate the
mud, and it is drawn through it in situations where shells
are supposed to exist.

Marine Shells. These are to be found in all seas; some
of them inhabit rocks on the shore within high-water mark;
others reside in deep water, and can only be taken by dredging, or by the use of a kind of net called in France the gan-
gui, and an instrument called the rake has also been successfully used.

Different species of sea-weed are frequently covered by
minute shells—weeds should always be carefully examined.
Many of the smaller and microscopic shells are found at
high-water mark among the fine dross and drifted fragments
of shells; this sand should be brought home and examined
at leisure. To facilitate the process a small wire-cloth sieve
should be made of about six or seven inches square and all
the sand sifted through it and the shells left,

Molluscous Animals. Many species of worms and other soft invertebrate animals are to be caught also by the dredge. There is no way of preserving these animals except by putting them in spirits. Animals of this kind are still very imperfectly known, notwithstanding the researches of Lamarck, Poli, and other celebrated naturalists. Every opportunity should, therefore, be embraced of bringing them home; indeed, we are still little acquainted with those which inhabit our own seas.

When animals of this kind are procured in foreign parts a careful noting of the latitude should be taken; and it should be stated whether they live singly or are congregated, if they are phosphorescent, and if they were taken in deep water. And as these animals are very liable to lose their colors by being put in spirits, a careful noting of these should be taken whenever they are caught, as the colors are very evanescent; or, what would be still better, a drawing of the animal should be made.

Intestinal Worms. Whenever we have killed either a quadruped, bird, or fish, we should carefully examine the stomach and intestinal canal of the animal to see if there are any worms; indeed, there are few animals without them; they must also be preserved in spirits. Besides the stomach and intestines, worms are also found in the livers and other parts of the body; also in the back of Skates and various fishes.

INSECTS.

This class is subject to infinite variety, according to climate and soil. The entomologist, or the mere collector, must not confine himself to those whose beauty of coloring renders them attractive, but collect all that come in the way. Those species which have wings, and fly around plants, we take by means of gauze nets, and also those which swim in the water.

Those which live on putrid substances, and such as are disagreeable to the touch, are seized with pincers; they are first put into camphorated spirits to render them clean. Trees are the habitations of innumerable insects; many of them skulk under the old rotten bark, and others attach themselves to the foliage. A cloth should be spread under the trees, or an umbrella, and the branches shaken with considerable force, when they will fall down, and may then be caught.

Insects are killed by making a crow-quill into a long point and dipping it into prussic acid; an incision with it may be made immediately below the head of the insect betwixt the shoulders, which usually produces instant death. But this acid must be used with much caution, because its effects are almost as instantaneous and fatal in the human subject as in the lower animals. When cork cannot be had for lining the bottoms of the boxes, a layer of beeswax may be used in its stead. The pin should be deeply sunk in this substance, as it is more liable to loosen than when in cork.

It is of much importance to procure the caterpillar as well as the insect, and, in this case, some of the leaves on which it feeds should be placed in a box beside it, so that it may reach maturity. A small perforation should be made in the box for the admission of air.

Every kind of insect, except butterflies, sphinges, and moths, may be preserved in bottles of spirits, which will not injure them; when they are taken out they are immediately placed in the position in which it is wished to preserve them, and they are then allowed to dry. Another mode of preserving coleopterous insects, such as beetles, etc., is to put them in a dry box amongst fine sand. A row of insects is placed in a layer of sand, and then a new layer of about an inch in depth laid on the top, and so on till the box is filled. This mode of packing will not, however, do with soft insects and those having fine wings.

It is extremely desirable that all the different kinds of

Spiders should be caught, particularly those said to be venomous; also termites, or white ants, the different scolopendra, and gally worms, etc. The nests of spiders and other insects should also be sent home; in short, every insect which is remarkable, in any way, either for its history or properties.

It is also of much importance to bring specimens of the plants on which they feed; these should be dried, and their localities marked, the kind of soil on which they grow, and the situations, whether moist or dry, should be noted.

BRITISH INSECTS.

Woods, Hedges, and Lanes. By far the greatest portion of insects are found in these situations. In woods, the entomologist must beat the branches of the trees into his folding net, and must select for this purpose the open paths, skirts, etc. The trunks of trees, gates, and timber which is cut down, should be carefully examined, and a great many lepidopterous and coleopterous insects are found in these situations, and in no other. In hedges and lanes, many of the most valuable and beautiful insects are found, as also in nettles and other plants which grow under them; these should be well beat, but more especially when the white thorn blossoms in the months of May and June. Hedges where the roads are dusty are very seldom productive.

Heaths and Commons. Many insects are peculiar to these situations from the plants which grow on them, as well as from the dung of cattle, by which many of them are frequented, in the latter of which many thousands of insects may be found in a single day, in the months of April and May. These are principally of the Order Coleoptera.

Sand Pits. These are favorable for the propagation of *Capris lunarius, Notoxus monoceros, Lixus sulcirostris* and

other rare insects. Minute species **are found** abundantly at
the roots of grass.

Meadows, Marshes and Ponds. In meadows, when
the ranunculi or buttercups are in blossom, many *Muscæ* and
and dipterous insects generally abound. The flag-rushes are
the habitations of *Cassida, Donacina* and others. Drills in
marshes should be examined, as many species of insects are
found on long grass. The larvæ of various lepidoptera and
neuroptera are confined to these situations, more especially
if hedges and trees are near the spot. Ponds are rich in
microscopic insects. These are obtained by means of the land-
ing net, which, for this purpose, need not be so long as
represented in Fig. 26, and should be made of pretty thick cotton cloth, but sufficiently thin to allow the water to escape.
The mud, which is brought up from the bottom of ponds and
ditches, should be examined, and what small insects are
found may be put in a small phial filled with water, which
will not only clean them but keep them alive; and in many
instances the naturalist will be surprised, upon the examination of these, the most wonderful productions of nature.

Moss, Decayed Trees, Roots of Grass, Etc. Many
insects will be found in moss and under it; the roots and
wood of decayed trees afford nourishment and a habitation to
a number of insects; many of the larvæ of *Lepidoptera* penetrate the trunks of trees in all directions; most of the ceram-
byces feed on wood, as well as some species of *Carabidæ Ela-
teridæ*, etc. In seeking for these it is necessary to use the
digger. It is sometimes requisite to dig six or seven inches
into the wood before they are found.

Banks of Ponds and Roots of Grass. These are a
never-failing source of collecting, which may be followed at
all seasons of the year, and in general with great success;

those banks are to be preferred which have the morning or noon-day sun.

Banks of Rivers, **Sandy Sea** Shore, Etc. These situations afford a great variety of *Coleoptera*, *Crustacæ*, etc. The dead carcases of animals thrown on the shore should be examined, as they are the receptacles and food of *Silphiodæ*, *Staphilinidæ*, etc. May and June are the best seasons for collecting these insects.

Dead Animals and Dried Bones should be constantly examined, for these are the natural habitats of several insects. It is not uncommon for country people to hang dead moles on bushes; under these the entomologist should place his net, and shake the boughs on which they are hung, as many of the coleoptera generally inhabit these.

Fungi and Flowers. These are the constant abode of insects, and many curious species will be found on them.

It is a mistaken idea that insects are only to be found in summer, as they are to be met with, either in a living or pupa state, at all seasons. Dried moss, beneath the bark of trees and under stones are extremely likely places to find insects in winter; and even then the entomologist is more likely to procure some of the rare species than in summer, as these are ranging in search of food and in situations hidden from view.

At this season, if the weather is mild, the pupæ of *Lepidoptera* will be found at the roots of trees, more especially those of the elm, oak, lime, etc., or beneath the underwood, close to the trees, and these frequently at the depth of some inches under the ground.

In the months of June, July and August the woods are the best places to search for insects. Most of the butterflies are taken in those months, flying about in the day-time only. Moths are either found at break of day or at twilight in the evening. The following method of taking moths is pointed out by Haworth, in speaking of the Oak Moth (*Bombyx Quercus*). "It is a frequent practice with the London Aurelians," says he, "when they breed a female of this and some other day-flying species, to take her, whilst yet a virgin, into the vicinity of woods, where, if the weather is favorable, she never fails to attract a numerous train of males, whose only business seems to be an incessant, rapid and undulating flight in search of their unimpregnated females, one of which is no sooner perceived than they become so much enamored of their fair and chaste relation as absolutely to lose all kinds of fear for their own personal safety, which, at other times, is effectually secured by the reiterated evolutions of their strong and rapid wings. So fearless, indeed, have I beheld them on these occasions as to climb up and down the sides of a cage which contained the dear object of their eager pursuit in exactly the same hurrying manner as honeybees, which have lost themselves, climb up and down the glasses of a window."

RECIPES

FOR VARIOUS ARTICLES USED IN THE PRESERVATION AND SETTING UP OF ANIMALS.

SOLUTION OF **CORROSIVE SUBLI-MATE.**

Mr. Waterton's Method.

PUT a good large teaspoonful of well-pounded corrosive sublimate into a wine bottle full of alcohol (spirits of wine). Let it stand over night, and the next morning draw it off into a clean bottle. When the solution is applied to black substances, and little white particles are perceived on them, it will be necessary to make it weaker, by the addition of some alcohol.

A black feather dipped in the solution, and then dried, will be a good test of the state of the solution; if it be too strong it will leave a whiteness upon the feather.

ARSENICAL SOAP.

Invented by Bécœur, Apothecary, Metz.

Arsenic, in powder,	-	-	-	2 pounds.
Camphor,	-	-	-	-	5 ounces.
White Soap,	-	-	-	-	2 pounds.
Salt of Tartar,	-	-	-	12 ounces.
Powdered Lime,	-	-	-	-	4 ounces.

The soap must be cut in small and very thin slices, put into a crucible with a small quantity of water, held over a gentle fire, and frequently stirred with a wooden spatula, or a piece of wood of any kind. When it is properly melted, the powdered lime and salt of tartar must then be added and thoroughly mixed. It must now be taken off the fire, the arsenic added gently, and stirred. The camphor must be reduced into a powder by beating it in a mortar, with the addition of a little spirits of wine. The camphor must then be added and the composition well mixed with a spatula while off the fire. It may be again placed on the fire to assist in making the ingredients incorporate properly, but not much heated, as the camphor will very rapidly escape. It may now be poured into glazed earthen pots and allowed to cool, after which a piece of paper should be placed over the top, and afterward some sheep leather, and then set aside for use. The composition is about the thickness of ordinary flour paste.

When it is necessary to use the soap, put as much as will answer the purpose into a preserve pot and add to it about an equal proportion of water. This is applied to the skin or feathers with a bristle brush.

N. B. It should be kept as close as possible and used with caution, as it is a deadly poison.

The above is the recipe made use of at he Jardin des Plantes, Paris.

Mr. Laurent's Recipe.

A distinguished French naturalist, Laurent, recommends the following composition, after ten years' experience, for preserving the skins of stuffed animals. He observes at the same time that it penetrates them with greater readiness, and preserves them much better than any preparation which has hitherto been in use.

Arseniate of Potash, -   -   - 2 drachms.
Sulphate of Alumine,   -   - 2 drachms.

```
Powdered Camphor,    -    -    -   2 drachms.
White Soap, powdered,   -    -   ½ ounce.
Spirits of Wine,   -    -    -    -   6 ounces.
Essence of Thyme,   -    -    -   3 drops.
```

The arseniate of potash, sulphate of alumine, and soap, are to be placed in a phial with a large mouth, and the spirits of wine to be poured on them at a heat of *twenty-five* degrees, and they will be perfectly combined in twenty-four hours. The essence of thyme is then added, when the phial must be carefully corked. This composition is to be shaken together before it is made use of, and it must be spread over the skin of the animal or bird with a brush.

SOLUTION OF PEARL-ASHES.

Two ounces of pearl-ash to one gallon of water.

ANNEALED IRON WIRE.

Take common iron wire, make it red hot, and suffer it to cool gradually; this renders it soft and pliable, so that it may be easily bent in any direction.

CEMENT.

```
Fine Whitening,    -    -    -    -   2 ounces.
Gum-Arabic,    -    -    -    -   2 ounces.
Finest Flour,    -    -    -    -   ½ ounce.
Ox-Gall, a teaspoonful.
```

The whole to be dissolved, and mixed well with water into thick paste.

This is well adapted for attaching different objects, and especially for fixing shells to pasteboard, etc.

GUM PASTE.

```
White Sugar Candy,    -    -    -   2 ounces.
Common Gum-Arabic,    -    -   4 ounces.
```

Let these be melted in a pot of hot water, and then strained through a linen or horse-hair sieve. When properly dissolved, add to it two tablespoonsfuls of starch, or hair-powder, and mix the whole well together. This paste may be used for many purposes, and it never spoils. It may be dried, and by pouring a little warm water on it, it will soon be ready for use. If it is wished to be all melted, and hurriedly, the pot containing it should be placed in warm water, or sand.

<h3 style="text-align:center">FLOUR PASTE.</h3>

Make flour paste in the ordinary way, and add to it a small portion of the solution of corrosive sublimate, or powdered corrosive sublimate. This will prevent the attack of mites, to which paste is very liable when dried. This paste may be dried into a cake, and moistened when required.

<h3 style="text-align:center">SOLUTION OF GUM-ARABIC.</h3>

The solution of gum-arabic is made by simply adding water to it. When used as a varnish, or for attaching objects, it is extremely apt to get too brittle, in very warm weather, and to crack, or split off in scales; to prevent this, a quarter of an ounce of white or brown sugar-candy must be added to two ounces of gum-arabic.

<h3 style="text-align:center">PAPER PASTE, GUMMED.</h3>

Take a coffe-pot, filled with water, and add to it a quantity of paper, which has been slightly sized, like that used for printing engravings. Let it boil three hours, and, when the water has evaporated, boil it again for a similar length of time. Take out the paper, and squeeze it well in a colander, and then pound it in a mortar, until it is reduced to a very fine paste. It must then be dried. When it is required for use, add to it some of the solution of gum-arabic, and keep it in a pot for use.

<h3 style="text-align:center">POLLEN POWDER.</h3>

The paper made as above directed, when well dried, is pounded in a mortar till it becomes a very fine powder; it is then put into a tin pepper-box, and when any of the parts of parrot's bills, etc., are wished to have this powdered appearance, a little of the solution of gum-arabic is washed over the part with a camel-hair pencil, and the powder dusted on it and allowed to dry.

RED VARNISH.

Take a stick of red sealing wax, beat it down with a hammer, and then put it into a phial, with an ounce of strong spirits of wine, which will dissolve it within four or five hours. It may be applied to any part with a camel-hair pencil, and it will dry in less than five minutes.

Black, yellow, and green, or indeed any color of varnish, may be made from sealing-wax of these various colors.

To those unacquainted with the combination of colors, we may mention, that a mixture of blue and yellow produces green; pink and blue makes purple; red and yellow, orange; black, red, and yellow, brown; black and blue, gray. These may be varied, in an infinity of shades, by either color predominating, and by the addition of other colors.

LUTING FOR RENDERING BOTTLES AIR-TIGHT.

Common Resin.
Red Ochre reduced into a fine powder.
Yellow Wax.
Oil of Turpentine.

These must be melted over a fire in the following manner, and the vessel in which it is made should be capable of holding three times the quantity required, to allow room for boiling up. An earthenware pipkin with a handle is the best thing for the purpose, and a lid must be made of tin to fit it. The luting will be rendered more or less brittle, or elastic, as the red ochre prevails:

The wax is first melted, and then the resin; the ochre is then added in small quantities, and stirred quickly with a spatula each time. When all the ochre has been added, it must be allowed to **boil** six or eight minutes; the turpentine is then added, and briskly stirred with the spatula, and continue **to** boil it. There **is** considerable risk of the mixture taking fire, and should **it** do so, the lid must immediately be put on the vessel to extinguish it.

To ascertain the consistence of the luting, a little must be, **from** time **to time,** dropped on a cool plate, or flat piece of iron. If it is too soft, more of the ochre must be added to it; and if too hard, additional wax and turpentine.

TOW AND FLAX SLIVERS.

These **are** fillets **of prepared** tow and flax, of from one **to** three inches in breadth. They are extremely uniform in their thickness, being made to weight, and can easily be procured from any flax-spinning mill, at **a** moderate price per pound weight.

METHOD OF MAKING ENAMEL-EYES FOR ANIMALS.

Much of the character and expression of animals depends upon their **eyes;** it will, therefore, be evident that great attention is necessary in the artificial imitation of these.

In this operation, a **pipe of** baked **earth** is used, or a tube **of** glass six or seven inches in length, at the end of which a little white enamel is placed. This is placed to the flame, so **that it may** be blown. This enamel forms a globe, whose dimensions depend upon the quantity of air introduced. When this globe is of the size wished, we place in the middle, and prependicularly to the point of the pipe, the quantity of enamel necessary to form the enamel. The second enamel is then incorporated **with** the first by presenting it to the flame, while attention is paid to turn the pipe gradually round, so that the enamel may diffuse itself equally, and the iris be exactly circular. If it **is** required that this iris should be of **various** colors, **like** that of **man,** for example, small filaments of enamel are distributed **in** diverging rays of the suitable color; the eye is then placed in the flame, until these have incorporated with the iris, after which the pupil is placed as before directed, and the glass applied as before directed.

During this operation, the globe is almost certain of sinking down, partly from the air escaping, partly from the heat, and from the pressure which is used in applying the different substances; air must again be supplied from time to time to prevent it from losing its form. This becomes particularly necessary when glass is applied, and when it is extended over the whole surface of the iris.

The eye having got its form and size, the pipe is taken away. To effect this, after the air has been introduced, the entrance of the pipe is stopped with the finger, and the back part of the eye exposed to the flame; when the air contained in the globe, and rarefied by the pipe, comes through at the place where the flame has most action. This opening is prolonged by turning the point of the flat pincers, or an iron-wire, all round the pipe; one point only is left by which the eye remains fixed. It is then warmed equally all over, after which it is exposed to a gentle heat, and when it again cools, it is separated from the pipe.

ARTICLES REQUIRED FOR SKINNING AND MOUNTING QUADRUPEDS, BIRDS, REPTILES, AND FISHES.

1. A box containing scalpels of different shapes; a pair of scissors with pointed blades, and two or three pointed forceps of different sizes, the extremities of one of which ought to be indented.
2. Two flat pincers, or pliers, large and small.
3. A round pincer for turning wire.
4. A cutting pincer for wire.
5. A hammer.
6. Two files.
7. A triangular.
8. Points for perforating holes.

9. A saddler's awl for drilling holes; also various shoemakers' awls, which will be found useful.
10. Brushes of different sizes for putting the preservative on the animals' and birds' skins, and **for** smoothing **and** dusting the feathers.
11. An assortment of iron-wire of all **sizes**.
12. **Flax and** tow, coarse cotton. When these cannot be had, untwisted ropes or cords. A quantity of tow and flax slivers **for** twisting round the leg-bones of small quadrupeds and birds.
13. **Some small hardwood** meshes for assisting in stuffing.

Instructions to Travelers. **The best** means of procuring living animals, is by applying to the natives of the different countries, who are accustomed to their habits, and the situation in which they are likely to be found, and to take them in traps and snares. They are also more likely to be able to find their retreats, so that they may take these animals in a young state, and also birds in their nests.

By thus securing animals while young, they are much more likely to reach home in a living state. Every exertion should be used to render them familiar, when, being habituated to the appearance of man, they will be more able to resist the effects of a tedious sea voyage than those which have been taken when wild, and are under a continued degree of excitement. Every care should be taken to soothe and caress them; and there is no animal whose manners cannot be softened by gentle treatment. During fine weather, they should be allowed to take exercise on the deck, as nothing is so injurious to their health and growth as being long pent up in a small cage. While thus confined, it will be obvious that they require a much smaller portion of food then when they can have sufficient room to exercise themselves. Many of these animals are lost from over-feeding. Their diet should be given with great regularity, but always in such quantity as they can easily digest.

Next to food, cleanliness is of the utmost importance, and if this requires too much of the attention of those who are bringing them home, it will be easy to procure the assistance of some of the crew. And unless this is strictly attended to, there is little chance of preserving their health.

When animals' skins are imported, it is also necessary to bring the head and feet. Those of the mammalia, which can be put into a barrel or bottle, should be preserved entire in spirits.

In the event of not being able to transport the carcase, the next best thing is to bring the skeleton along with the skin. It will not be necessary to mount these. All that is required is to boil the bones, take off the flesh, and dry them. Afterwards all the bones belonging to the same skeleton should be put in a bag by themselves, taking care to fill up the bag with dried moss, or any other substance which will prevent friction. The more effectually to secure this, the small and tender bones ought to be wrapped in paper. It is of the utmost consequence that not a bone should be lost.

In shooting birds, it is of much importance not to use the shot too large; indeed, it ought to be proportioned, as nearly as possible, to the size of the bird to be shot at. When the bird is killed, the blood must be carefully wiped away, and a little cotton must be put into the bill to prevent the blood flowing from it to injure the feathers. The wound should also be stuffed with cotton.

Birds should be skinned as soon as possible, as the feathers are apt to fall off if kept too long. The os coccygis must be kept attached to the skin. If several individuals of the same species be killed, one should, if possible, be preserved entire in spirits, with the whole muscles of the body. If the bird has a fleshy crest, it ought to be preserved in spirits.

It is of the utmost consequence to procure the male, female

and young, and these at different ages besides, as many
species are subject to great variety, in their progress from the
young to the adult state. This is more particularly the case
with Eagles and Hawks, many of which have been described
as different species in their immature state. The eggs and
nest should also be procured.

Reptiles. The chief thing to be attended to in skinning
reptiles is not to injure the scales; and in the lizard kind,
care must be taken not to break the tail. But for all the
smaller and middle sized species, the best mode is to preserve
them in spirits; and of the larger kind which are skinned,
the skeletons ought to be kept. The flesh should be taken
away with knives and scalpels as well as possible, and the
bones thoroughly dried, and packed in a box with cotton or
grass, and they can be articulated after they are brought
home. When the skeletons are too large, they may be separated into convenient parts for packing.

www.ingramcontent.com/pod-product-compliance
Lightning Source LLC
Chambersburg PA
CBHW031410270326
41929CB00010BA/1392